AMERICA'S MELTDOWN

The Lowest-Common-Denominator Society

John Boghosian Arden

Westport, Connecticut
London

Library of Congress Cataloging-in-Publication Data

Arden, John Boghosian.
    America's meltdown: the lowest-common-denominator society / John
Boghosian Arden.
        p. cm.
    Includes bibliographical references and index.
    ISBN 0–275–97639–4 (alk. paper)
        1. United States—Civilization—1970-   2. Popular culture—United
States. 3. United States—Social conditions—1980- 4. Mass media—
Social aspects—United States. 5. Social psychology—United States.
    I.   Title.
    E169.12 .A724 2003
    306′.0973—dc 21   2002030727

British Library Cataloguing in Publication Data is available.

Library of Congress Catalog Card Number: 2002030727
ISBN: 0–275–97639–4

First published in 2003

Praeger Publishers, 88 Post Road West, Westport, CT 06881
An imprint of Greenwood Publishing Group, Inc.
www.praeger.com

Printed in the United States of America

∞™

The paper used in this book complies with the
Permanent Paper Standard issued by the National
Information Standards Organization (Z39.48–1984).

10 9 8 7 6 5 4 3 2

Contents

vi   Contents

1
The Meltdown

In America you watch TV and think it is totally unreal, then you
go outside and it's true.

Joan Armatrading

Not long ago, a perplexing commercial appeared on television in
which a man in a white coat stated, "I'm not a doctor, but I play one
on TV." As if he is now worthy of our respect, he goes on to recommend that the viewer buy a certain over-the-counter pain-relieving
medication. What has caused many in our society to accept an actor
as a medical authority?

There are, in fact, many signs that our society is gravitating to an
overly simplistic and often absurd view of reality. We might be melt-
ing down to the lowest common denominator (LCD). We can see the
LCD syndrome emerging in what we consider newsworthy, what we
regard as entertaining, how we dispense medical care, and how we
educate our children. We hear about children going on rampages at
their schools with assault weapons. In the emerging LCD society,
sensationalism, gossip, and a constitutional crisis erupted over a sex
scandal.

Consistent with the LCD society, George W. Bush accused Al Gore
and others like him of being "thinkers." After assuming the role of
President, Bush joked that he was a "C" student and that other C
students could hope to become President too.

Despite the September 11, 2001, terrorist attacks, the LCD syndrome has deepened. That same proud C student used terms such
as "Axis of Evil" and "crusade" in the political campaign against
terrorism. Yet his popularity soared.

Sales of gas-guzzling, environment-ravaging, and collision-
mangling SUVs have not dampened. In fact, the LCD cruisers
proudly fly the American flag as an expression of patriotism. Few

have asked if our manic hunger for cheap oil has driven American foreign policy to continue to prop up dictatorships called "kingdoms" on the Saudi Arabian peninsula. These dictatorships have wiped out all moderate dissent, leaving only terrorists masquerading as pious Muslims to express their dissent.

The forces contributing to this meltdown in consciousness are pervasive. Never before have we witnessed such dramatic synergy between mass media, demographic change, and corporate domination of the economy. The combination of these factors has restructured every aspect of society. For example, individuals with controlling interests in the multinational corporations know that the way to ensure profits is to use the media to sell their products to the largest number of customers. To reach that audience, they appeal to the LCD by using overly simple formatting in ads and programs.

Advertising consultants pay attention to the 250,000 Americans who wrote to Marcus Welby for medical advice. These consultants also know that several studies have shown that information delivered by a familiar person is more easily accepted than the same information from an unfamiliar person. Thus we see actors who play doctors selling medicine. This type of persuasion occurs even when the presenter is contradicted by the facts. We seem far more touched by our vicarious experiences with a character on television than we are by facts.

In the new LCD society, political candidates operate with this dynamic in mind. For example, during the Reagan years polls indicated that many voters who did not agree with his political positions or his version of the "facts" about our society voted for him anyway. To borrow a phrase uttered as a Freudian slip by the great communicator himself, "Facts are stupid things."

UNCONSCIOUSLY INTO QUICKSAND

As we sleepwalk into the twenty-first century, we might be stepping into quicksand. Many of the societal changes now swaying our consciousness are self-perpetuating. Consider that since the advent of television, there has been a steady decline in social participation and civic engagement.

With the exception of a brief resurgence of a sense of community post September 11, 2001, Americans volunteer less, participate in fewer political discussions, and attend fewer dinner parties. We spend less time at meetings or bowling leagues and simply converse less with one another. In short, we spend approximately a quarter of the time socializing today than we did 35 years ago.[1]

We have replaced social ties with dependence on the electronic media. It has been estimated that the television is turned on in the average American family home from two and a half to five hours daily, and Americans spend on average 40 percent of their leisure time watching it.[2]

In a survey of Americans between the ages of 15 and 25 conducted in 2002, it was found that despite the brief sense of trust in government institutions, actual involvement in the community continued to go down.[3] The percentage of these people who volunteer even occasionally has dropped 7 percent in just one year. Since 1998 there has been a 14-point drop in people who made a charitable donation, an 11-point drop in those who have joined an organization, and a 10-point drop in the percentage of those who volunteer at community organizations.

According to a Gallup Poll, the number of people admitting to having read no books the previous year shot up from 8 percent in 1978 to 16 percent in 1998.[4] John Robertson of the University of Maryland showed that between 1948 and 1985, the percentage of people who read magazines on a given day dropped from 38 to 28 percent.[5]

The reliance on the electronic media as a replacement for socialization has contributed to mutations in our consciousness. Social disengagement has also long been associated with impairments in physical and mental health.[6] Researchers have shown that people with decreased levels of social support experience a corresponding increase in illnesses, depression, and difficulties in intimate relationships. For example, in a recent study, 54 percent of children ages 4 to 6 indicated that they like television better than they like their fathers.[7]

On the other hand, technological and media advances have enabled people to communicate with one another over geographical distances once thought unfathomable. Cell phones now make it possible for a dying climber on Mt. Everest to have contact with family members in New Zealand. With a few strokes on a keyboard, an e-mail letter can be transmitted in a matter of seconds from Cairo to Hong Kong. The latest news can be viewed on television or heard on the radio from Antarctica to Greenland. Styles and modes of communication can be modeled on television and in motion pictures for

viewers anywhere in the world, thanks to satellite dishes, cable, an-
tennas, and videotape machines.

But as New York University Professor of Media and Journalism
Michael Stephens has argued, the advances in film have led to less
reliance on the written word because of a greater ability to communicate ideas through images. Though he applauds this development, he acknowledges that the reliance on visual imagery has led
to a superficial orientation to the world. He writes:

Indeed, the increasing reliance upon images, which began with photography
and accelerated with film, certainly seems to have contributed to an increasing concern with image—with style, possessions and public relations, with
surfaces and appearances, with what Coke commercials are selling.[8]

Simultaneous with the shift from the written word to visual imagery, the number of people with deficits in attention span, short-
term memory, and intellectual curiosity has increased. Also, the
number of people seeking immediate gratification through material
possessions and entertainment has surged. We have come to crave
gossip over substance, acrimony over harmony, and sensationalism
over deep meaning.

What we consider hard news has essentially disintegrated into
gossip. We discuss in great detail a President who has affairs and
congressmen with secret lovers who disappear. A generation ago
these subjects were not considered worthy of mainstream news coverage. The mainstream press followed a code of ethics. The press
did not cover the speculation about alleged extramarital affairs of
Presidents Roosevelt, Eisenhower, Kennedy, or Johnson. Today
these stories are omnipresent despite the fact that the viewing audience claims to be disinterested. A media think tank in Washington
reported that television coverage of the Clinton/Lewinsky sex scandal was more extensive than coverage of the other seven big stories
in 1998 combined.[9]

During the summer of 2001, Congressman Gary Condit was all
over the media despite the fact that there was no breaking news
about this story. Only after the September 11th terrorist attacks did
Condit drift out of the news. Then actor Robert Blake was charged
with the murder of his wife, and Condit was supplanted by a new
personality.

The tabloids have always attracted a readership interested in gossip about celebrities. There was a time when stories about a Presi-

dent's affairs did not grace the front page of *The New York Times* or *Washington Post*. Now they do. The House of Representatives participated in the news tabloidization by releasing graphic details of former Independent Council Kenneth Starr's report to the Internet. Anyone with a computer was able to read about President Clinton's sexual encounters with Monica Lewinsky, including their use of a cigar, oral sex, and phone sex.[10]

Meanwhile, violence in the workplace, massacres in schools, and international terrorism get little in-depth debate or analysis. The response to one of these stories amounts to flash headlines almost as if it were a commercial for a television show titled "America Strikes Back."

Many observers of gun violence in our schools have blamed it on television, the movies, computer games, guns, and increased feelings of alienation. The massacres cannot be tied to any of these factors alone but to all of them combined. They represent an episodic nightmare in our emerging LCD society.

The potential for more terrorism hangs over us like an invisible cloud. The Office of Homeland Security issued reports of daily risk for terrorism the way television meteorologists forecast the weather. They have developed a color-coded forecasting system. Will it be a red or yellow day tomorrow? Or is anyone paying attention anymore?

TWO WORLDS INTO ONE NOT-SO-BRAVE NEW WORLD

Half a century ago, two popular views of the future of civilization were described in literature. One view was put forth by George Orwell in his novel *1984*. He envisioned a totalitarian state in which "Big Brother" policed the thought and behavior of its fearful citizens.

Orwell described the Ministry of Truth as an organization responsible for controlling the minds of citizens. The Ministry used Newspeak and the following mind-bending slogan of the Party: WAR IS PEACE; FREEDOM IS SLAVERY; IGNORANCE IS STRENGTH.[11]

The rigid control of the press in the former Soviet Union, its satellites, and the People's Republic of China are but contemporary examples of societies where the ignorance of the masses has been factored into the stability of the State. The brutal repression of freedom of speech in Tiananmen Square in 1989 and the incarceration of dissidents in Soviet gulags showed the autocratic hand of Big Brother.

The other view of the future of civilization was put forth by Aldous Huxley and illustrated best in his novel *Brave New World*. He suggested that the meltdown in human consciousness would occur as the result of a public narcotized by titillating imagery in the multimedia and a drug called "soma." Citizens would have little desire to ask questions about the world they inhabit because they would be pacified by a feel-good society.

Huxley wrote tongue in cheek that the citizens in the new society could sing the following song while dancing in a circular procession:

Orgy-porgy, Ford and Fun,
Kiss the girls and make them one,
Boys at one with girls at peace;
Orgy-porgy gives release.[12]

The Huxleyan world may be best represented by contemporary American society through its "orgy" of media stimulation, cornucopia of drugs, and consumerism. Television, motion pictures, the Internet, and material opulence, narcotize and make passive those that rely on them for sustenance.

This feel-good world appears to be far more desirable to most of our world's inhabitants than does the Orwellian world. Indeed, the world of Orwell seems less of a threat since the demise of the Soviet Union. Mikhail Gorbachev led the dismantling of the core of the Orwellian world. Through his glasnost (openness) and perestroika (reconstruction), he set the stage for his successors Boris Yeltsin and Vladimir Putin to attempt to transform Russian society. But the demise of the Orwellian world has not necessarily resulted in feeling good. Though Russians have yet to see the horror of children opening fire in schools with assault weapons, they have experienced a surge in crime, economic turmoil, and social disarray.

Meanwhile in the United States, violence in schools has become commonplace, and easy access to anesthetizing entertainment and material possessions has not brought us health and joy. Neil Postman asks whether we are amusing ourselves to death.[13] James Twitchell argues that we have created a "carnival culture."[14] Are we, in fact, entering the Huxleyan world in which the LCD is an orgy of entertainment, consumerism, and intellectual atrophy?

Before examining this question, we must first explore those factors that are contributing to the meltdown. If we are truly to reap benefits from the end of the cold war and before we get too far into the surreal war against terrorism, we must understand what the Huxleyan world might bring.

MONEY, MOBILITY, AND MEDIA

The United States has been pervasively influenced by a recent and rapid accumulation of wealth. Just as mining boomtowns in the late nineteenth-century American West experienced uncontrollable social transformation, much of the country experienced a massive social transformation after World War II. And as in those boomtowns, late-twentieth-century American society is vulnerable to uncontrollable social ills.

During the 1950s and 1960s, millions of people moved from the East to the West and from the cities to the suburbs. When they moved to their new homes, they left behind family and social ties—a social support system—and entered a world of loose social ties.

The same era saw a proliferation of electronic media sources. In 1950 fewer than one out of ten American households had a television set. By the mid 1990s, 98 percent of American households owned one.[15] These suburban pioneers unknowingly looked to television for a sense of community. The reliance on television for socialization promoted superficial ties and a lack of cohesion.

To compound the sense of impermanence, new waves of immigrants come to this country from Asia and Latin America wanting to assimilate into American society. They also turn to the television and motion pictures for acculturation. The United States, therefore, is in an odd predicament. Television and motion pictures have propagated American culture, increasingly neutralizing our desire to be enriched by the diverse perspectives of our immigrants. The commercial media empire has become the great acculturator of the LCD.

Further, the Americans who are having more children are those who are less educated and more likely to spend their leisure time watching television. More educated members of our society defer having children to pursue education and career goals. When they do have children, they have fewer than those who did not pursue education and career goals. The bottom line is that the less educated people in our society are less likely to limit their children's access to mass media. Thus, lower educated and more media-prone people now outnumber those who are not so media-prone.

Large corporations have paid close attention to these societal changes and have poured millions of dollars into the media. Consequently, corporate-sponsored television is the most powerful and omnipresent form of media in history. It "programs" consciousness. People sitting hour after hour, day after day, in passive positions in front of a television set are manipulated by commercial interests.

But it is far too simplistic to assume that television and motion pictures are inherently evil. On many occasions television has served a socially constructive function. The media coverage of the famine in sub-Saharan Africa and the devastation of Central America from a hurricane resulted in massive relief efforts. The war in Vietnam lost public support largely because of the nightly news coverage.

The fact is that people still have a choice to consume what they please, despite the power of corporations. But the venders of the multimedia, as we shall see in later chapters, are consolidating through corporate mergers, and fewer choices might be the result. Commercial interests and viewing "choice" are intertwined and have narrowed together. As television, radio, and motion picture companies compete with one another for the highest profit margin from sponsors, they have found that gratuitous violence, base humor, and simple plots are the LCD ingredients necessary to sell to the largest possible audience.

Any attempt to attract large numbers of customers by using thought-provoking motifs falls short of ensuring significant profits; consequently, corporate television, motion pictures, and advertising have dumbed down to the LCD. The programming trend is to gravitate toward the most basic levels of human consciousness, where large numbers of people find ideas, styles, and beliefs in common. For example, though we do not often admit it, we all share a craving for gossip, respond easily to anger and outrage, and find it easier to accept stereotypic beliefs than to think for ourselves or test our own assumptions. Consequently, during the past quarter century we have been witnessing a rekindling of these most primitive aspects of our consciousness.

A motion picture thirty-five years ago did not need graphic violence to grab the attention of the viewer. In dramatic contrast, today's big blockbuster movies often require a standard formula of graphically portrayed violence, driving suspense (usually the threat of more violence), car crashes, and other high-cost special effects spread throughout the movie. It is as if we, the viewing public, are asleep and these elements are embedded within the movies to keep us awake.

So obvious is the regression that there has been a tempered outcry to curtail media violence. It is ironic and symptomatic of our LCD society that some of the advocates of less violence are themselves perpetrators. For example, during the 1996 Presidential campaign, violence in the media became an issue. Republican Presidential candidate Bob Dole brought out his Hollywood supporters to endorse his criticisms of Hollywood. Bruce Willis, Sylvester Stallone, and Arnold Schwarzenegger, three actors commonly seen in movies of this violent genre, joined Dole to condemn movies of this very type before they went on to star in several subsequent bloody blockbusters. Four years later, Academy Award winners such as Nicolas Cage and Dustin Hoffman joined them to milk the cash cow of action movies.

There has also emerged a public perception that television offers few benefits to its viewers. Indeed, because some people believe that television offers emptiness, the major broadcast channels have tried to change the subject by using paradoxical humor. During the late 1990s, an ABC television ad campaign pled with us: "Six hours a day, that's all we ask." Or, "You can afford just a few brain cells."

In the spring of 2000, ABC News dispatched actor Leonardo DiCaprio to interview President Clinton. ABC producers reasoned that DiCaprio would draw young viewers to its network. Only after news of the story broke and their own seasoned reporters became angry did ABC try to blame the planned interview on President Clinton.

Meanwhile, at the supermarket today it is rare to see newspapers and newsmagazines at the checkout stands. Instead we are offered *The National Enquirer, Globe,* and *People* magazine. We can see the same trend in television news programs. Serious news programs are out, and TV magazines are in. Many of these TV magazine programs feature gossip about the rich and famous. Occasionally, they help make sensational news stories into pure entertainment. In spring of 2000 the television program *Entertainment Tonight* featured a detective once involved in the JonBenet Ramsey murder investigation.

The most popular television programs in mid 2001 were *Who Wants to Be a Millionaire* and *The Weakest Link*. Programs of this type tap into the increasing craving for wealth and flash over substance. Even the questions asked the contestants reflected a strong drift toward embracing "knowledge" of entertainment. Many of the questions yielding the highest monetary returns asked about movie actors and television shows.

The popularity of these shows matched the trend toward a hollow materialism. This trend can best be illustrated by a series of studies that surveyed the goals of incoming college students. When asked if they are more concerned with being materially wealthy or with developing a meaningful philosophy of life, the craving for wealth has steadily grown while the interest in a meaningful philosophy of life has dropped (see Figure 1.1).[16]

Several studies have shown that material wealth does not necessarily increase one's sense of happiness. Lottery winners, for example, have been noted to feel worse about their lives. Although few of us are lottery winners, most of us have been affected by an increase in the average monthly income over the past 40 years. Yet

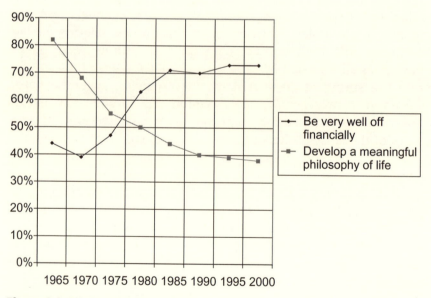

Figure 1.1 What Is More Important?

Source: David G. Meyers (2000). The Funds, Friends, and Faith of Happy People. *American Psychologist*, vol. 55, no. 1.

that increase has not factored into an increase in the number of people reporting to be happy. According to a survey conducted by The National Opinion Research Center at the University of Chicago, the number of people reporting to be happy has actually dropped since 1956.[17] As shown in Figure 1.2, this trend lies in marked contrast to the steady rise in monthly income.

Thus, despite the fact that we are achieving our goal of becoming a more wealthy society, we are not reaping the emotional lift we had assumed would accompany that wealth. Instead of asking ourselves why we do not feel better about our lives, we bathe in the trash of media gossip and violence.

Not long after the sensational coverage of the Tonya Harding and Michael Jackson scandals, almost every television set in public places ran coverage of the O.J. Simpson trial. Nightly news reports covered the intricate details of the day's events in the courtroom. We were told how O.J. had allegedly yanked his wife's head back and slashed her throat. When Marcia Clark changed her hairstyle, that was the top story. Even before the trial, the famed "white Bronco chase" was aired on nearly every channel. Fourteen channels in the San Francisco Bay Area, including ESPN, covered the event with live footage. People lined up along the Los Angeles freeways to watch the massive caravan of police cars following O.J.'s Bronco.

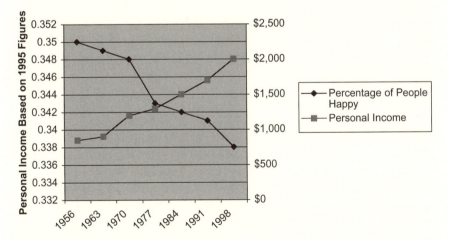

Figure 1.2 Economic Growth and Morale

Source: David G. Meyers (2000). The Funds, Friends, and Faith of Happy People. *American Psychologist*, vol. 55, no. 1.

For several weeks during the spring of 2000, the lead story on the television news programs was the sad story of a 6-year-old boy who lost his mother in a failed escape from Cuba. A media circus grew around the home of his distant, fervently anti-Castro Cuban relatives.

Spectacles such as the Elian Gonzales tragedy, the O.J. Simpson saga, and the Clinton/Lewinsky affair are symptomatic of the emerging LCD society. Though thousands, if not millions of people have expressed the disgust with these spectacles in public opinion polls, how have we come to crave them? The first clue can be found in the degree to which our consciousnesses have become numb and in need of sensationalistic stimulation.

FRAGMENTED AND NUMBED

Within American society, two contradictory trends are occurring today. Although the general population is gravitating toward an LCD society, we are also witnessing a trend toward fragmentation. The trend of fragmentation does not result in actually separate cultures but in interest groups and marketing niches. Corporations have targeted and exploited these marketing niches. Magazine publishers have cultivated these niches with a proliferation of magazines targeting gun hobbyists, hot rod enthusiasts, runners, bicyclists and numerous other groups.

Political candidates have appealed to one-issue interest groups such as the antiabortionists, making them allies with National Rifle Association (NRA) members. Though people in these groups rarely hold political beliefs that go beyond their focus on abortions or guns, political candidates have been able to galvanize the groups into common voting patterns.

Societal fragmentation and the collective gravitation to our LCD occur simultaneously. Each trend increases the intensity of the other. The overall tendency of fragmentation requires people to share a common bond on a societal level. For example, "Christian" antiabortionists and gun advocates might unite with the LCD belief that "it is a God-given right to own a gun."

The surreal justification for gun ownership has gravitated to a new LCD. Following the September 11, 2001, terrorist attacks, the gun manufacturer Beretta put out a new .9 mm pistol called "United We Stand." Now patriotism, piety, and gun ownership have found common footing in the emerging LCD society. We tell ourselves we have come together when in fact we are drifting apart.

Many people in our fragmented and fast-paced society complain that there is little time to spend cultivating depth in their beliefs or relationships. Americans rush from one empty experience to another like rocks skipping on water. In 1984 the average annual number of meals eaten on a take-out basis was 43 and the average number of meals at a sit-down restaurant was 69. By 1996, the number of take-out meals exceeded those of sit-down by 65 to 63. There were 90,000 fast food restaurants in 1973. By 1993 that number jumped to 180,000, four times the rate of the population increase.[18] We now rush to drop off film at drive-thru photomats, bring our clothes to one-hour cleaners, pull up to 20-minute oil-change stations, and perform our banking at ATMs.

With the highly mobile nature of our society and the media saturation, we have become disconnected from one another. Each brief social interaction is followed by yet another. It is as if we are dreaming and the people we encounter are but temporary dream characters.

For an increasing number of people, even the practice of mourning for the deceased has transformed into a brief, surreal experience. Drive-in funeral homes now exist in California, Florida, and Texas. A funeral parlor in Lancaster, Texas, allows relatives and friends to view the deceased more easily because the casket is laid on a tilting device.[19] And now mourners of the deceased can attend a funeral in cyberspace. Through the technical expertise of a company revealingly called "Simplex Knowledge Company," mourners can go to a funeral website to see the coffin. If they feel so inclined, they can click on icons to send flowers or sympathy cards.[20]

Stanley Milgram was one of the first researchers to point out the degree to which we can become numb to one another. He performed a landmark study on how people in large cities survive psychologically.[21] Milgram showed that as people in cities are bombarded with exposure to other people, they find themselves needing to screen out the stimulus overload and, as a result, become numb. A popular example of the overstimulated urban dweller is the resident of New York City. It is a rare event to encounter a pedestrian in New York who makes eye contact or smiles and says hello. If you unknowingly try to initiate such contact with someone on the street, the other person's response is one of suspicion.

People don't just suddenly become numb. Milgram argues that people's response to overstimulation is to construct "filters" to protect themselves from being overwhelmed. These filters contribute to the numbing of consciousness until we are less sensitive to the subtle nuances of our lives and to the people around us.

During the past 50 years, the bombardment of stimuli has grown exponentially. At no other time in history have we seen such a proliferation in the mediums in which information is available. David Shenk has referred to the bombardment of media saturation as "data smog."[22] The omnipresent data smog hangs over and numbs consciousness.

The speed at which data smog is created has increased, in part because of the wide variety of distributors. Many of these distributors, such as network news programs, dispense fragmented information without explaining the context in which the story emerged. Because the information is fragmented, our hunger for information is not satiated. This dilemma of being hungry but overloaded speeds up our quest for information.

Certainly an abundant number of resources are available in libraries, on the Internet, and even on television for researching contemporary developments in science, technology, and the arts. However, libraries are visited less often than 50 years ago, the most popular Internet sites are chat rooms and pornography sites, and situation comedies and glitzy game shows yield the highest ratings on television.

Though the sources of information have multiplied, the bulk of available information is often of little substance. Stimulus from the media is intense and abundant, but the quality of that information is diluted. More is not necessarily better.

Our ability to assimilate information lags dramatically behind our ability to produce it. Indeed, David Lewis has argued that multiple psychological problems have emerged as a result of information glut. Not only does the glut contribute to an increase in irritability and concentration difficulties, but people also find their sleep interrupted and immune systems less vital.[23] Lewis refers to this spectrum of symptoms as "information fatigue syndrome."

Unlike computers, people experience "technostress"—the title of a book co-authored by Larry Rosen and Michelle Weil. Rosen and Weil note that our brains did not evolve to deal with the multiple inputs of information glut.[24] We have endured self-imposed stimulus

overload, resulting in increased irritability, low frustration tolerance, difficulty concentrating, a feeling of disconnection from oneself and others, and free-floating anxiety.

For most people, stimulus overload is the result of what we can
call mind candy. Just as eating candy provides a sugar rush and a
subsequent feeling of anxiety and emptiness, consumption of mind
candy results in scattered thoughts and emotions.

Because many people choose to be exposed to so much mind
candy, their short-term memory is clouded with irrelevant trivia.
When they try to retrieve memories, they are less able to access a
full spectrum of complex associations because of the clutter in their
minds. Therefore, when communicating to others they might use
broad generalities and clichés instead of attempting to thoroughly
understand the context of their understanding and the other person's thoughts.

Because exposure to stimulus overload is chronic, a symptom of
this fatigue is a numbed consciousness. It is my contention that
numbing leads to a simplified mode of consciousness with a tendency to form unsophisticated concepts and an increased suscepti-
bility to the LCD developments in our society. As a result, people
form shallow connections with one another. Many people are not
psychologically ready to reach out to others and search for more
elevated common denominators.

In the rest of this book we will explore how the gravitation to the
LCD has affected the consciousness of most Americans in a variety
of domains. Accordingly, we will look at the dramatic changes occurring in entertainment, news media, cyberspace, politics, work,
medicine, mental health treatment, romantic relationships, education, and spirituality.

2
Cyberspaced

Cloquet hated reality but realized it was still the only place to get a good steak.

Woody Allen

An amazing new form of entertainment is referred to as "virtual reality." This technological wonder offers a computer simulation of an imaginary world. By wearing a navigating glove and a headset that covers the eyes and ears, one can leave a mundane life and enter a "virtual world."

Many people spend hours each day immersed in the virtual world of their computers, playing games or chatting on the Internet. Computer games are increasingly enhanced by sophisticated graphics and video capability. Some games are appropriately named "H.E.D.Z." (for Head Extreme Destruction Zone), "Unreal," and "Half Life." Other games provide "virtual" companionship, such as the game called "Virtual Friend" that features high-tech graphics of an extraterrestrial alien that crinkles its eyes to illustrate emotion as it talks. This virtual friend offers advice, learns, and repeats the language of the game player to more effectively create the illusion of a personalized interaction.

Virtual reality is an appropriate metaphor for the entertainment in postmodern society at the dawning of the twenty-first century. In this virtual society, some people have found it easier to develop friendships over the Internet rather than with people "in person." Internet relationships are often anonymous interactions that take place in chat rooms out in cyberspace. Chat-room pals can play out fantasies with one another. Some foolishly believe in their authenticity.

Virtual reality programs and computer games play an increasing part in the transformation of our LCD society. Computers and the access they provide to the Internet have contributed both positive and negative effects on the individuals who use them. Later in the book we will explore how computers and the Internet function as valuable tools. In this chapter we will discuss the negative consequences on the consciousness of a growing number of individuals who use computers as a substitute for real-life experience.

SIMULATING THE KILL

After the revelation that a significant number of the teenage assassins who terrorized their high schools had been obsessed with playing violent video games, attention finally shifted to how these games are affecting our children. Sissela Bok of Harvard argued in her book *Mayhem* that the new video games are more violent and gruesome than ever before. She states:

The vast assortment of slasher and gore films on video contribute to a climate of violence different from that standard over the past four decades. . . . So does the proliferation of video games offering players the chance to engage in vicarious carnage of every sort. These sources bring into homes depictions of graphic violence, often sexual in nature, never available to children and young people in the past.[1]

In the spring of 2002, Robert Steinhauser shot 12 teachers. He was an avid user of violent computer games. Similarly the teenage assassins who killed 13 people at Columbine High School in Littleton, Colorado, were frequent players of violent video games such as "Doom." This game features a marine who walks around a maze blasting away beasts with a high-tech cannon. The player can look down the digitized gun barrel, blast away fire-spitting beasts, and watch blood splatter on the walls.

The computer game called "Duke Nukem" features a foul-mouthed vigilante who rampages through Los Angeles in alleys and strip clubs with guns and pipe bombs. When he makes a kill, he celebrates by punting the victim's head through a goal post.

According to Dave Grossman, who wrote the now classic book *On Killing*, these video/computer games serve as training instruments. As a former psychology professor at West Point and a Lieutenant Colonel, Grossman specialized in the psychology of killing. He noted this about the new computer games:

[They] are not games of fun. These are mass murder simulators. Nine year olds are practicing killing people in their homes and at a local arcade for hours every day. Everyone knows, computer flight teach you how to fly. These mass murder simulators teach you how to kill. So when a few kids go out and execute what they've been practicing, we should not be surprised.[2]

Grossman has pointed out that in healthy play, the play stops as soon as someone gets hurt. Children learn to understand when to limit their aggression in healthy play. In computer-simulated aggression, the player learns that killing is rewarded and fun. Just as Harris and Klebold were avid players of "Doom," so was Kentucky killer Michael Adam Carneal. He had never fired a pistol before, but he knew just what to do when he shot eight of his classmates, five in the head. Steinhauser did the same.

According to a study published in 2000 and performed by psychologists from the University of Iowa, violent video games influence the expression of violence more than do violent movies or television. Unlike viewers of television and the movies, players of violent video games identify with the aggressor and actively participate in violence.[3]

These games have exploded in sales. Since the release of "Doom" in 1993, more than 15 million copies have been downloaded, purchased, and passed from player to player. Games such as these present a new dilemma for our society. Not only do they provide training for killing, but they also illustrate how thin the line has become between fantasy and reality.

SURROGATE FRIENDSHIP

The computer has transformed technology and the lives of many Americans. By late 1998 roughly 40 percent of American households had a personal computer, and 20 percent of these households have access to the Internet.[4] Since the advent of television, no other invention but the computer has so dramatically changed the way we communicate and entertain ourselves.

Computers were initially computational or "number crunching" machines, linear and logical. They were the domain of highly skilled technicians. Computer consultants and enthusiasts were referred to as "hackers" or "hobbyists." When I was a graduate student, I hired a computer consultant to produce the statistics necessary to "crunch" my data for my Ph.D. dissertation.

By the mid 1980s, with the advent of user-friendly computers such as the Macintosh, we entered a world in which computers were no longer the domain of a select few. "Users" became you and me, people looking for a tool to expand our skills. We became interested in using computers for word processing and personal financing.

Many adolescents and young adults entertained themselves with computer games. Computers were produced with color and detailed graphics. "Pac Man," "Asteroids," and "Space Invaders" ushered in a new generation of computer games.

The development of Nintendo and Atari provided a means for thousands of children to get lost in the interactive graphics. Soon, sophisticated computer games such as the Sim Series, including "SimLife," "SimLit," "SimAnt," and "SimHealth" allowed players to build an ecosystem. Players have to pay attention to pollution control, economic development, and a wide spectrum of environmental issues.

Computers have become increasingly part of postmodern society during the past 15 years. MIT computer sociologist Sherry Turkle has described this transformation in historical terms: "The meaning of the computer presence in peoples' lives is very different from what most expected in the late 1970s. One way to describe what has happened is to say that we are moving from a modernist culture of calculation toward a postmodernist culture of simulation."[5]

Turkle has noted that computers give the illusion of a surrogate or simulated friendship. "Interactive and reactive, the computer offers the illusion of companionship without the demands of friendship. One can be a loner yet never be alone."[6]

We are entering an era in which increasing numbers of children are using computers for entertainment and homework. For children who rely on computers to do much of their homework and play games, many intellectual skills and emotional skills may be delayed. Also, because psychological development depends on how children interact with and understand their environment, the use of the computer has contributed to confusion regarding the relationship of cause and effect.

The Swiss developmental psychologist Jean Piaget drew attention to how children need to develop the ability to categorize and understand the process of cause and effect. Almost a century later Turkle has noted that computers do not provide the "transparency" necessary for a child to understand how they work. In other words, we cannot "see" what makes a computer work. Computers don't have exposed gears or wind-up engines like toys, yet they respond to input from users. Consequently, children rely on psychological terms to understand what the computer does and does not do.

There are psychological consequences for children who excessively use computers. The most obvious consequence is social isolation. Because of that isolation, children have less experience with the natural world.

Piaget taught that a major developmental task children must wrestle with is understanding what is alive and what is not alive. The lack of transparency of computers and the tendency to assign psychological explanations to the computer led Turkle in her book *The Second Self* to argue that children see a computer as a psychological entity. She notes that many of the children she interviewed assigned "psychological states of mind to the computer while playing games, saying it cheated, or it knew."[7]

She went on to state:

For today's children the boundary between people and machines is intact. But what they see across that boundary has changed dramatically. Now children are comfortable with the idea that inanimate objects can both think and have personality. . . . They endow the category of artificial objects with properties, such as having intentions and ideas, previously reserved for living beings.[8]

In the fall of 2000, The Alliance for Childhood, a group of educators and psychologists, noted in a report that computers stunt childhood development. Too early exposure to computers impedes a child's socialization skills and retards emotional responsiveness.

Children run the risk of health problems if they sit at a computer for extended periods of time. Not only are they vulnerable to eyestrain and obesity but also to repetitive stress injuries.

The role of play in a child's life cannot be underestimated. Play is critical for a child's emotional, intellectual, physical, and social development. Excessive computer use puts a straightjacket on a child's imagination. Computer games dictate the imagery and range of experiences possible.

Play is an open-ended activity that cultivates creativity and helps children acquire social skills and construct knowledge. Excessive computer use dampens creativity, limits social contact, and provides no knowledge outside the domain of the computer game.

The dampened creativity results from the lack of any need for imagination. The computer game generates all the imagery through visual stimulation—sometimes gruesome graphics—that manipulates the child's reactions and thoughts.

The social isolation of excessive computer game-playing not only limits acquisition of social skills but programs maladaptive skills, especially if the games are violent in nature. Excessive use of computer games by the shooters at Columbine and Erfurt, Germany, exemplify how frustrated rage can be programmed to spill out on society at large.

The knowledge gained from computer games is certainly based on the type of game played; many games reinforce the idea that violence is an acceptable expression of anger.

Interaction with computers becomes more complex when a child uses the Internet. Millions of websites are but a click away. The Internet is a dramatic new tool with a wealth of information scattered across the globe. Yet Aristotle's maxim "Nothing in excess, everything in moderation" needs to be our motto as we become immersed in our computers and the Internet.

NETTED IN DEPRESSION

The information superhighway we know as the Internet was originally developed and used by academics and researchers. By the mid 1990s, commercial forces moved in to sell Internet access to customers outside academic circles. A wide variety of chat lines and bulletin boards spread across the Internet like wildfire.

Robert Kraut and his associates at Carnegie Mellon University found that interpersonal communication is the dominant use of the Internet in the United States.[9] Despite the fact that many Internet users are "communicating" with people throughout the world, they grow isolated from actual social contact in their lives at home and in their communities.

Indeed, a study performed by Kraut and his associates found that greater use of the Internet leads to shrinking of social contact and support, increased loneliness, depression, and decreased feelings of happiness.[10]

A national survey of Internet users revealed that only 22 percent of the respondents who had used the Internet for over two years actually ever made a new friend.[11] In fact, even these relationships were likely to be of poor quality. The Internet promotes weak social ties. Strong social ties are associated with frequent contact, physical proximity, deep feelings of affection, and obligation to broaden areas of one's life; weak ties are associated with infrequent contact and lack of physical proximity. The weak relationships developed on the Internet are usually oriented to a specific context and can be broken abruptly without consequences. For example, one might develop a relationship with an on-line friend around a common interest such as the television show *Star Trek*.

Kraut and his colleagues noted:

On-line friendships are likely to be more limited than friendships suggested by physical proximity. On-line friendships are less likely than friendships developed at school, work, church, or in the neighborhood to be available for help with tangible favors, such as offering small loans, rides, or baby-sitting. Because on-line friends are not embedded in the same day-to-day environment, they will be less likely to understand the context for conversation, making the discussion more difficult and rendering support less applicable.[12]

Over the past several years, my colleagues and I have seen people in psychotherapy sessions who complain that their husband or wife has been having an "on-line affair." The grieved spouses often say they do not know what to believe or feel about the affair. Is the affair really an affair?

Sometimes these affairs result in the two parties sending pictures to one another over the Internet. Some people, albeit very few, actually do meet and find that the person they thought they were "intimate" with is not the person they had believed him or her to be. These affairs essentially take place in the imagination of the participants.

Kraut and his colleagues found that, as the level of Internet use increases, the majority of users report a corresponding decrease in the level of social support they feel. Not surprisingly, they are more depressed and lonely than people who are not engaged on the Internet. Also, people who use the Internet report a greater number of daily stresses.

Do people gravitate to the Internet because they are depressed? Or does the Internet lead to depression, stress, and loneliness? Is the use of the Internet a symptom of depression? It appears that the use of the Internet is the causal factor. To this point, Kraut notes:

Because initial involvement and psychological well-being were generally not associated with subsequent use of the Internet, the findings imply that the direction of causation is more likely to run from use of the Internet to declines in social involvement and psychological well-being, rather than the reverse.[13]

So pervasive has use of the Internet become that by the mid 1990s *Newsweek* ran an article highlighting the attempt by many people to withdraw from Internet chat lines. "One method is to change your password by banging your head against the keyboard, making it impossible to log back on."[14]

People who do not overtly appear to be addicted to the Internet, nevertheless suffer detriments in social involvement and psychological well-being. Because these people are spending the majority of their time on the Internet in a wide variety of chat lines, we must examine what, in fact, occurs psychologically to people stuck on these lines.

STUCK IN THE MUD

In the 1970s, thousands of high school students engaged in a role-playing game called "Dungeons and Dragons" that included fantasy characters such as wizards, dragons, and knights. By the time the Internet went through its massive expansion, some of the Dungeons and Dragons players fled into the chat rooms. One of the initial formats was referred to as MUDs for "multi-user dungeons." Eventually, the MUDs became referred to as "multi-user domains" to emphasize the increasing diversity of its users.

Participation in MUDs allows users to enter a fantasy world of cyber socialization. Rider University Professor John Suler has studied the MUD titled the "Palace." This highly visual chat environment features popular sites such as the "Mansion" where participants can move from room to room, kitchen to bedroom. Participants represent themselves with icons known as avatars. When avatars talk, balloons with typed dialog pop out of their heads, much like in cartoons. Suler has acted as a consultant or "wizard" to help the "Palace" deal

with participants who introduce pornographic avatars and use pro-
fane language.[15]

In the MUD referred to as "TrekMUSE," participants share an interest in the outer-space-inspired television show *Star Trek: The
Next Generation*. A young man suffering from low self-esteem and
social impotency can become a Klingon Warrior on "TrekMUSE"
and strike terror in the human characters on the starship Enterprise.

In a MUD, one can re-create oneself. A fat and homely man can
transform into a buffed-out, dashing man. One can even create an
environment on one popular MUD referred to as "LambaMoo,"
transforming rooms or creating an entire apartment.

Turkle describes the wide diversity of roles possible in the MUDs:

As these characters or set of characters, a player evolves relationships with
other players, also in character. For most players these relationships quickly
become central to the MUDing experience. As one player on an adventure
type MUD put it, "I began with an interest in hack and slay but then I just
stayed to chat."[16]

There are hundreds of MUDs and millions of people participating
in them. According to Turkle, most participants are middle-class
men in their teens and early twenties. These young males come of
age while stuck in the MUDs.

MUD participants engage in anonymous communication with one
another. They can pretend to be someone they are really not while
they interact with others in the MUD. Like most Internet users, they
do not benefit from any of the social perks or consequences of real-
life ("RL") relationships in which context and proximity are crucial.
MUD participants do not have to see or answer to a person they
might have offended.

A surreal illustration of MUD communication is represented by
the construction of robots or "bots." Participants can choose to leave
a representation of themselves in the form of a bot in the MUD before logging off to enter RL. These bots serve as alter egos and make
small talk with participants still in the MUD. Thus, not only do participants "communicate" with other people shrouded by their own
imagination, but they also "socialize" with robots.

Another measure of the shallowness of MUD communication is
illustrated by the all-too-common practice of simultaneously socializing in the MUDs while engaging in other activities. This type of
scattered interaction is made possible by boxed-off areas of the

screen called "windows." Sherry Turkle has described how some college students do their homework sitting in front of a computer screen that displays a few windows, "socializing" in a different MUD within each window.

In an MIT computer cluster at 2 AM, an eighteen-year-old freshman sits at a network and points to four boxed-off areas on his vibrantly colored computer screen. 'On this MUD I'm relaxing, shooting the breeze. On the other MUD I'm in a flame war. On this last one I'm into heavy sexual things. I'm traveling between the MUDs and a physics homework assignment due at 10 tomorrow.[17]

MUDing contributes to social fragmentation and superficiality and fuels the emerging LCD society. Some have argued that the fragmentation MUDing represents drives home the point that we have "many selves." Many authors have noted that the postmodern world has ushered in an appreciation for psychological fragmentation, the reality of the de-centered self, or that we have many selves. The postmodern world lies in contrast to the modernist view of the self whereby humans are seen as "solid" selves, reducible to a finite solid core.[18] But more fragmentation does not augment psychological development. More fragmentation and distortion in roles played in the MUDs undermines society and leads to confused and superficial relationships between individuals.

Most people would argue that sex is an aspect of intimacy. Sex is also a significant aspect of Internet use. Participants engaging in virtual sex in the MUDs undress, fondle, and have intercourse with other participants. Often it is difficult to determine the RL gender of the participants behind their virtual character masks.

Gender-swapping is a significant phenomenon in the MUDs. Though men outnumber women in the MUDs—by some estimates as much as four to one—the ratio of participants playing roles of women in the MUDs are perhaps two to one.[19] In other words, there is a significant number of "virtual transvestites."

Some suggest that there is an all-too-prevalent "fake lesbian" syndrome played out in the MUDs. Men impersonate women to have sex with another woman on-line. Many of these sex scenes can actually be two men having sex with one another while pretending to be women.

Given that sexual identity is a critical developmental challenge of adolescence and that a significant number of MUD participants are in their late teens and early twenties, MUDing can lead to gender confusion. Gender confusion can delay the next developmental challenge: learning to have an intimate relationship with a lover.

The issue of rape and violence in the MUDs highlights the distortion and confusion of Internet socializing. A debate has been waged over whether virtual rape is "safe" because it is simulated in the imaginary dialog of the participants. Should rape be taken lightly because it takes place only in the minds of the participants? Further, because people watch movies and television with rape acted out on the screen, isn't it just part of entertainment? Violence viewed in the media and played out in computer games leads to more violence acted out in real life. Though parallel studies involving Internet violence have yet to be performed, it is reasonable to assume that the effect on society is not benign.

VIRTUAL THERAPY

In 1966 the first efforts were made to develop a computer program that could function like a psychotherapist. The "ELIZA" program has been modified over the years by its developers Joseph Weizenbaum, an MIT professor of engineering, and Kenneth Colby, a psychiatrist at Stanford University. Weizenbaum has spoken out against ELIZA's psychotherapeutic utility. In contrast, Colby argues that human therapists operate as information processors and decision-makers and therefore function like ELIZA.

Since the development of ELIZA, other "psychotherapy" programs have been constructed. Programs such as "Depression 2.0" operate by definition from a strict set of rules that spit back canned responses to its users. These programs turn around a version of what the user states and respond with suggestions to rethink the problem. The responses are generally based on the cognitive-behavioral perspective that stresses that people get depressed because of unrealistic expectations of themselves and illogical self-criticism. The treatment of depression, therefore, should include a change in personal expectations and more logical thinking.

There is no question that cognitive-behavioral therapy has been shown to be quite effective in the treatment of many types of depression. It is also conceivable that some people might benefit from computer programs that try to replicate cognitive-behavioral treatment. Yet, just as human experience is not canned or codified, canned therapy without some monitoring can be inappropriate.

Similarly, a wide-eyed endorsement of the therapeutic value of "expressing oneself" on the Internet is also inappropriate. Many outdated psychotherapy theorists have argued that simple catharsis—simply venting one's feelings—is therapeutic. Expressing oneself or acting out imaginary roles in chat rooms might provide an outlet for venting one's feelings, but this experience fragments and distorts human experience. Even if these virtual experiences were not superficial and fragmenting, chat rooms provide little opportunity for coherent feedback. It is the opinion of most psychotherapists that cathartic venting without objective feedback is counter-therapeutic. A therapist's job is to contain and respond to the emotional expression of a client, a capacity not inherent to a computer program.

Because chatting on any of the chat lines leads to increased fragmentation of psychological experience, a chatter's sense of selfhood becomes confused as the chatter shifts roles from one character to another. If someone engages in a relationship with a bot, the defining line between what is "I" and what is not "I" becomes increasingly confused.

One of the major challenges of adolescence is to develop a sense of identity. Psychoanalytic theorist Eric Erickson maintained that an adolescent who does not develop an adequate sense of identity feels like a failure. It is through complex, multifaceted, "real" relationships that adolescents learn to cope with living in the world with other people. As we have seen, relationships developed on the Internet are of low quality and often are a substitute for RL relationships.

In early adulthood, the major psychological challenge is to develop the ability to have intimate relationships. For young adults who spend a great deal of time on the Internet in chat rooms, intimacy becomes complicated, delayed, and distorted.

We are, therefore, drifting into an era in which relationships are becoming confused and redefined. Turkle has charted the course of relationships on the Internet for years. She and others now call into attention the drift into more distorted relationships. She writes:

In the past fifteen years, I have noticed a distinct shift in people's way of talking about the case of the electronic lover. In the early 1980s close to the time when the events took place, people were most disturbed by the idea that a man had posed as a woman. By 1990, I began to hear more complaints about Joan's on-line lesbian sex. The shock value of gender-bending has faded. Today what disturbs us is when the shifting norms of the virtual world bleed into real life.[20]

Indeed, because millions of young people are coming to age within the newly emerging cyber society, all the social consequences of poor psychological development and superficial relationships bleed out into the already deepening LCD society.

3
Vicarious Living

I hate television and I hate peanuts. But I can't stop eating peanuts.

Orson Welles

A Detroit newspaper offered $500 each to 120 families if they would turn off their televisions for one month. Few took them up on the offer, and 95 families turned them down.[1]

Television has taken center stage in the lives of the average American family. Millions of people live vicariously, losing themselves while watching television. This type of vicarious living is becoming increasingly addictive. Consider the soap-opera addict who organizes the day around her favorite "soaps," living vicariously through the characters in the programs. She craves the next episode and supplants some of the life she could have lived.

The similarity between expenditures on entertainment and on health care is more than a coincidence. Many people think of entertainment as a way of taking care of themselves. It is not uncommon to hear someone say, "God, it has been a hell of a day. I need to just sit in front of the tube and zone out!" Implicit in that statement is the concept that the best treatment for a bad day is to lose oneself in the world of entertainment.

I have seen numerous patients who have experienced job stress only to try to soothe themselves with massive doses of television viewing. If these patients stay off work and do nothing but watch television for two weeks, their symptoms of stress remain unchanged. No expert in stress reduction has advocated extensive television viewing as a means of coping with stress. The most successful stress reduction techniques include investing oneself in hobbies, meditation, and exercise, unless of course one brings a wristwatch television on the walk.

LOST IN THE TUBE

Television is one of the major decimators of the LCD society. Few people have escaped its influence. It is not by accident that the Baby Boomer generation has been dubbed the TV generation. In 1950 only 10 percent of households had television sets. By 1970 the number had shot up to 95 percent and by 1998 to 99 percent. According to the Nielsen Ratings Company, by 1971 the average American household had the television set on six hours a day. By the 1995–96 viewing season, the average number of hours went up to seven and one half-hours per day.[2]

A study performed by the Kaiser Family Foundation found that the average American child spends about 40 hours per week consuming electronic media—the equivalent of a full-time job.[3] More than half of this time is spent watching television and videos. By the time students graduate from high school, they have spent considerably more time watching television than they spent in the classroom. Thus television has become an inseparable part of a child's development.

According to the National Television Violence Study, about 60 percent of programs contain violence.[4] By the time the average American child graduates from high school, he has vicariously witnessed 100,000 acts of violence, including rapes and assaults. Approximately 8,000 of these are murders.

Television sets usually are placed in a central position in the main living space of the home. They now come in all sizes and shapes. Not only are portable TVs placed sometimes in kitchens and bathrooms, but some people even use wristwatch-size televisions to keep themselves plugged into their vicarious lifelines.

Millions of households now have cable hookups or satellite dishes. The number of cable television subscriptions is rising by 1.5 million households per year.[5] By 1998, 66 percent of American households subscribed to basic cable.[6] With the movie channels and satellite services growing in popularity, a sizable majority of American households have from 30 to 200 television channels to choose from.

Despite the choice of channels, watching television is purely a passive event. Once viewers manage to find a program that holds their attention, they sit passively mesmerized and receive vicarious socialization. Television viewing has filled our time and psyches to such a degree that some people need a withdrawal period to adjust to life without TV's narcotizing influence.

Continual TV viewing intensifies our hunger for escapism and simultaneously dulls perception due to the constant bombardment of visual stimulation dragged out over an extended period of viewing. Television, therefore, has become a drug as it provides empty and addictive stimulation.

It is not uncommon for people to tell me during a psychotherapy session that they keep the TV on all night in their bedrooms. They say, "I like having it in the background—it gives me a sense of security." Many of the same people complain that they have trouble staying asleep. When I point out that the television might be waking them up when the noise level goes up (such as when an actor screams), they are astonished by the insight but often rebut that if they do wake up, "at least I have something to look at."

The world of television is imbued in the consciousness of many people. People come in to their workplace and ask, "Oh, did you see ER last night?" At home, family members might ask one another, "Is there anything on tonight?" Though the answer often might be "Not really," they often spend the evening watching television anyway.

The dividing line between imagery and actual reality has become thin. Because we are so deluged with empty stimulation from television, we have increasing difficulty differentiating the forest from the trees, or what is worthy of our attention and what is not.

In his book *Intimate Strangers,* Richard Schickel stressed the growing phenomenon of celebrity worship.[7] Though celebrities are actually strangers and characters displayed in the media, they are revered by much of the public as intimate parts of their "personal lives."

Because as television viewers we are spending more time in the vicarious world of television and less time with one another, we conform to its language, values, and aesthetics. The socialization provided through the social modeling witnessed on the screen breeds similar behavior.

Neal Gabler argues in his book *Life: The Movie* that we have become a society so saturated and immersed in entertainment that individuals play out "parts" as if they are characters in their favorite movies.[8]

Since the advent of social psychology, researchers have demonstrated that social learning has a profound influence on how we behave and think about the world around us. We view our lives through the lenses that are dictated by the cultures we inhabit and behave in ways in which we believe are socially acceptable.

The social modeling provided by television has served to promote an unreasonable image of what people ought to look like. Despite the fact that ideal women are portrayed as thin and rich, most women are not. And despite attempts to adapt, many women who do not meet this narrowed standard body image often feel depressed and inadequate.

Some young women try to adjust to the "ideal body image" and develop pathological symptoms. It has been demonstrated throughout the world that television viewing exacerbates the incidence of eating disorders in adolescence. For example, according to a study published in an Italian journal in 1997, researchers reported a correlation between television viewing and the preference for a tall and thin body image among adolescent girls in Italy.[9] Those who most strongly preferred this body image were those afflicted with eating disorders.

The same phenomena can be seen on the opposite side of the world. In Australia it was demonstrated that the time women spent watching soap operas, movies, and music videos correlated highly with the drive for thinness.[10] In other words, the more television they watched, the more intense their compulsion to be thin.

Thus television now promotes a distorted view of the acceptable range of human experience. Despite the numerous television programs and many channels available, the diversity of choices is an illusion. It is true that you can choose between a nature program and a crime program, but the LCD formatting, language, and imagery have a distorted and homogenizing effect.

THE THREE "Vs" = PROFIT

The LCD elements of violence, voyeurism, and vulgarity are rapidly becoming part of the standard formula for entertainment in our society. Massive profits are reaped in the television and motion picture industries by using these three ingredients.

To exacerbate this problem, the number of actual entertainment companies is shrinking. Only a handful of studios control 90 percent of the film market. Universal, Fox, Disney, Orion, MGM/UA, and Warner have geared their production teams into making blockbuster films. They have been inclined to take fewer chances and have stooped to rehash what has made big money in the past. The studios have read the LCD tastes of moviegoers and have offered five *Rockys*, three *Rambos*, four *Lethal Weapons*, five *Halloweens*, and a host of other violent and special-effects "bloodbusters."

Rehashed 1950s and 1960s remakes are also a safe bet. We have endured movie versions of *Dennis the Menace*, *Leave it to Beaver*, *The Adams Family*, *The Beverly Hillbillies*, *My Favorite Martian*, and *The Fugitive*. Many people in the movie industry refer to blockbusters as "tent poles" because they provide the support for the entire "big top." They are considered a must-have because the revenue they produce supports the rest of the productions.[11]

However, even making sequels has not been enough to generate the revenues sought by the movie moguls. The cost of making movies has shot up dramatically, partly because sensational special effects draw the largest crowds. In 1989 the average cost of making a movie was $18.1 million dollars. By 1996 the cost more than doubled to $39.8 million. The additional cost of promotion doubled during the same period. In 1989 studios spent an average of $9.2 million in promotion, and by 1996 the cost shot up to an average of $19.8 million.[12] Touchstone Pictures reportedly spent $200 million to produce and promote the 1998 special-effects thriller *Armageddon* and earned over $500 million worldwide. Harry Potter cost $125 million and made $137 million.

The motion picture industry has looked for new ways to generate profit. Apparently there has been not enough profit in simply spawning a new generation of low-brow sequels and bloodbusters to yield the millions producers want to earn at the box office and through video rentals. Now they are learning from their counterparts in television that profit margin increases when the movie includes promos for corporations. They have raked in thousands of dollars for having minor subliminal commercials embedded within a movie. For example, the producers of the James Bond movie *Licensed to Kill* earned $350,000 from Philip Morris to have 007 smoke Lark cigarettes.[13]

The same trend of commercialization and frenzy to rake in high profits is rampant in the television industry. Ben Bagdikian reports that 90 percent of the 11,000 local cable systems are essentially monopolies in their communities.[14] To compound this problem, TCI and AOL Time Warner control two-thirds of these cable channels. Not to be outdone, Viacom made a move in late 1999 to acquire CBS. During the fall of 2000, the Murdoch Company moved to buy Chris-Craft industries and its 10 TV stations, leading to the demise of the UPN network. Murdoch also moved to purchase Direct-TV. Murdoch's group already owned Fox Family, Fox, Regional Fox Sports Network, and local stations in 23 cities. These mega-companies are geared to maximize the profit margin at the expense of aesthetics.

These monopolies have flattened the range of programming to LCD tastes. We have seen an increase in voyeurism and programming based on fear. For example, the addiction to viewing crime, injury, and rescue has resulted in a rash of TV docudramas such as *Real Cops* and *Tales of the Highway Patrol.* These programs offer a vicarious cheap thrill of seeming to be on the front line when cops fight criminals. On one level the program offers viewers cathartic relief when the bad guys are put away. At another level, viewers stir themselves up through the tension and strife depicted in the show.

A new type of voyeurism began in 2000 with "Real TV," which stretches the boundaries between imagination and reality. Real TV viewers are offered the opportunity to see people who are not acting but playing "real parts"—themselves. These real (or unreal) actors compete with one another in provocative and sensationalistic situations.

The early pioneer of Real TV was the NBC hit *Survivor.* This program was essentially a raunchy soap opera that featured the same cast of characters, less one, each episode. The others would vote out or "kill" one of their peers at the end of show. The *Survivor* cast tried not only to avoid being voted out but to do their best to run obstacle courses constructed by the Green Berets, eat snakes, or scavenge for food in the jungle of a deserted tropical island, the Australian Outback, or the African Savannah where everything takes place "on location."

The 2000 season finale of *Survivor* reaped 51 million viewers, the highest ratings of any summer series ever. Only the Superbowl brought in more viewers on a single day in 2000. By 2002, *Survivor* had become a staple on television.

The *Survivor* series ushered in a whole slew of blurred reality programs. ABC developed *The Mole,* a program in which contestants undertake a series of cross-country tasks while trying to root out the imposter in their midst. ABC also bought *Jailbreak* from Britain's Channel 5. *Jailbreak* features contestants who are incarcerated in a specially designed prison and must bravely try to deal with physical and psychological challenges as they simultaneously break out. NBC went for the Dutch production of *Chains of Love* in which a man (or woman) is handcuffed to several persons of the opposite sex day and night. He or she lets go of them one by one in an effort to find Mr./Ms. Right. Fox has produced a sexually enticing program without the chains called *Love Cruise* in which 16 single men and women actually date. According to Fox, the "cameras will capture every tantalizing moment." MTV got into the act with their *Mall Confessions* in which a candid camera sits in a mobile confession booth for shoppers to visit and confess their shopping secrets. Not to be outdone, Court TV developed a new reality show called *Confessions* in which convicted felons tell the camera about their gruesome murders.

The *Survivor* creator even wanted to take Real TV out of this world with the plan to have contestants train at Star City in Russia. Just as in the show *Survivor*, the contestants are followed through the challenge of major obstacles—in this case, space boot camp. One contestant survives to actually travel to space station Mir.

A show that has particularly grabbed the attention of adolescents is called *The Real World*. In this show contestants get jobs, share a household, and compete with one another for attention and romance.

Another expression of Real TV is exemplified by the *Jerry Springer Show*. Guests on this show confront their husbands and wives with deep, dark secrets and sometimes go on to brawl. Barry Diller, chairman of USA Network, toned down this highly rated show to adjust to the news coverage of violence on television and the movies. But he said, "The shock was how many local stations called us to complain about what we did. They didn't feel any responsibilities."[15]

The hunger for salacious voyeurism has taken many forms. People throughout the country purchase radio scanners and sit on Saturday and Sunday afternoons "relaxing" and waiting for the next alarming situation. They use the scanners as an intravenous dose of sensationalism to voyeuristically stay in contact with the police on the beat. Later in the evening they might tune into the evening news and see the caper played out on *Real Cops*, in which cameras follow the police as they take down and cuff violent bad guys.

Violence and fear sell. Horror films have been and continue to be targeted toward an adolescent audience. Violence and vulgarity are a sure way of grabbing the adolescent's attention. But if we examine how the entertainment industry targets teenagers, we find a frightening trend. There is a dramatic difference between the films of Bela Lagosi in the 1930s and 1940s and the *Halloween* series in the 1980s and 1990s. The most obvious difference is that the special effects are far more sophisticated. The horror is no longer based on being caught by a monster. Now movies show in gory detail what happens when a victim is caught. The special effects depict graphic scenes in which heads are torn off, eyeballs plucked out, and blood almost gushes off the screen.

Plots that involve crimes against women and children are likewise exhaustively graphic in depiction of violence. When monsters or bad guys rip the clothes off screaming women, it suggests rape, and when children are captured, it suggests child abuse.

Even cartoons are not immune to the increased violence. In May of 2000, a Harvard study confirmed that over a 40-year period, violence depicted in cartoons has steadily increased. Yet all viewers are "entertrained" by the vicarious experience of these scenes.

Mindlessness has also come to represent an acceptable theme in movies coming out of Hollywood. From *Pulp Fiction* to *Dumb and Dumber*, moviegoers are offered portrayals of the mindless activities of characters who have few traits to admire but much to mock.

With the *Lethal Weapon* series and *Pulp Fiction*, we were treated to mindlessness embedded within a barrage of gruesome and gratuitous violence. The main message seems to have been that, even in a sea of violence, those committing the violence can go on and have a "normal" life. This trite and mindless message seems to win the respect of many moviegoers and critics.

There also seems to be a growing disdain for intelligence. Philip Lopate wrote in an article titled "The Last Taboo" that one is asked to "check one's brain at the door" before entering a movie theater.[16] He points out that in movies such as *IQ*, even the archetypal icon of intelligence Albert Einstein is depicted as recommending to his niece, "Forget your intellectual ambitions and follow your heart."

In *Dumb and Dumber*, the name of the movie tells the entire script. This trend is far more vulgar than the Three Stooges and Abbot and Costello movies of decades ago. Now laughs are generated through the mockery of people with disabilities.

The movie *Beavis and Butthead Do America* grossed $62 million at the domestic box office. In August of 1999, MTV aired a "moron-a-thon" of the *Most Dangerous Episodes of Beavis and Butthead.*

Screenplays are written in an increasingly standardized homogenous form. Scripts are written on a seventh-grade reading level. Seventy-two percent of scripts have simple sentences or sentence fragments. Scenes are shortened and dialogs are abbreviated. Producers are asked to cut out the "talking heads" because there might be too much slack in a script's lengthy dialogs. Lopate points out that the "shorter the scene, the less chance there is for the tension between characters to reach the danger point where true communication can break out between them."[17]

With scenes getting shorter, there is more pressure to produce short one-liners to promote the movie. Clint Eastwood's Dirty Harry says, "Make my day." Arnold Schwarzenegger quips, "Hasta la vista, baby." Later we heard the first President Bush uttering Schwarzenegger's now infamous one-liner, "Read my lips," and the second President Bush talked about an "Axis of Evil" as if he had taken a line from the *Star War* series.

Moviegoers have grown accustomed to non-stop action and suspense. The rapid-fire one-liners provide brief comic relief but leave no room for reflection. Graphically depicted violence keeps viewers distracted from the poverty of content in many films and taps into the wide appeal of the three Vs.

For the past 20 years the Sundance Film Festival has been a chance for low-budget independent filmmakers to show "out of the norm films." However, as alternative news producer Danny Schechter has noted, even at Sundance, diversity is down and glitz is up.[18]

It has been estimated that 90 percent of the feature films shown throughout the world are made in the United States. These films rarely require rigorous thought and are usually the most stylized and sensationalistic that Hollywood has to offer. The French objected to the GATT Treaty because they were concerned about the spread of these elements of American culture. Some Americans wrote off the French concern as another expression of their cultural chauvinism, but such an easy dismissal misses the point. American LCD culture is sweeping the world.

As we export our media to the world, the trend is in the direction of action- and violence-packed movies. The subtle nuances of comedies and even romance are often difficult to translate and understand outside of cultural context. Thus there is an accelerating drift to action-packed movies as they achieve the LCD.

But this cultural exchange is not reciprocal. Fifteen years ago, 7 percent of the films that reached the American market were of foreign origin. That percentage has shrunk to .7 percent.[19] This trend is not hard to explain. Most foreign films have less violence and fewer one-liners and often require viewers to read subtitles.

The omission of foreign films and the monopolization of the American film industry have contributed to shrinkage in the variety of motion pictures available in the United States. Many movies in the past served to elevate. Now we are offered a menu more dominated by movies that sink to the LCD—the celebration of trash culture.

MEDIA TOXICITY

With the dominance of the three Vs—violence, voyeurism, and vulgarity—rashes of social problems have emerged. This has been demonstrated throughout the world. For example, pupils from schools in Wuttenburg, Germany, were interviewed about their television and video viewing habits. A high percentage of male students who excessively viewed horror and violence were assessed to have restrictive imagination, less productive behavior, and higher scores on measures of both death anxiety and guilt anxiety. Not surprisingly, there were the elevations in scores measuring hostility.[20]

Several studies have shown that attitudes on violence can be affected by what a person watches on television. In England it was found that the only significant predictor of attitudes toward violence on television was the amount of television watched on school days.[21] The more television watched, the more likely the child was to favorably regard violence on television.

A study conducted by researchers from the Institute of Psychology at the University of Regensburg, Germany, confirmed that watching violent films promotes violent behavior. Specifically it was found that "consumption of violent videos" had a causal relationship to "delinquency proneness."[22]

The film called *The Matrix* came out before the two teenagers in Littleton, Colorado, massacred their peers at Columbine High School. *The Matrix* features a computer fanatic who finds himself blessed with the power to choose any weapon he desires and kill with impunity. Not so ironically, he wears a black trench coat just like the now infamous "Trench Coat Mafia."

Timothy McVeigh, who was convicted and then executed for the Oklahoma City bombing, was reported to have seen a film titled *Blown Away* about a former IRA terrorist who baits a bomb squad before the bombing.[23]

The Columbine shooters and McVeigh, like millions of other young men, were raised on a steady diet of violence in the media.[24] By the age of 14, a child can have witnessed 11,000 murders on television. In just three hours of television, a child can see nine car wrecks, nine robberies, eight murders, and twenty-six insults. Some movies, such as *Die Hard 2*, have as many as 264 murders. Overall an average of five violent acts per hour are shown on prime time and eighteen acts per hour on children's weekend television.[25]

Countries with a lower level of violence depicted in the media have a correspondingly lower level of violence in their society. For example, Japan has long been noted to have relatively low rates of violent crime. Researchers at the University of Madrid, Spain, used ratings derived from the Index of Television Violence of viewers in Spain, the United States, and Japan. They found fewer scenes of physical or fatal injury on television in Japan than in either the United States or Spain.[26]

In July of 2000, six major national professional societies, including The American Psychological Association, American Academy of Pediatrics, American Medical Association, American Academy of Child and Adolescent Psychiatry, American Academy of Family Physicians, and the American Psychiatric Association, put forth a joint statement. They unanimously expressed concern about the danger of exposing children to violence in the media. Their statement read, "At this time, well over 1,000 studies . . . point overwhelmingly to causal connection between media violence and aggressive behavior in some children."[27]

Yet, like the cigarette company CEOs who have had the audacity to testify in Congress that they saw no evidence that their product causes cancer, the CEOs of the major media companies have argued that their product does not cause violence. They argue that the violence in movies and television only mirrors society. Yet as B. J. Bushman and C. A. Anderson of Iowa State University point out, only about .2 percent of the crimes reported by the FBI are murders, yet so-called reality-based TV programs feature murders 50 percent of the time. Bushman and Anderson, in their article on media violence and the American public, point out the metaphoric parallels between smoking and media violence. As with smoking, not everyone who watches violence in the media becomes violent. Yet tobacco CEOs and movie CEOs use this fact to argue that their products are not dangerous.

In fact, Bushman and Anderson see many parallels between smoking and violence in the media. Smoking is not the sole cause of lung cancer. Neither is violence in the media the sole cause of aggression. The first cigarette can nauseate a smoker, but repeated exposure reduces the sickening effects and leaves the smoker wanting more. The first exposure to violence in the media can make people—especially children—anxious and fearful but often leave viewers wanting more.

Just as the short-term effects of smoking are innocuous and clear up quickly, watching violence on the screen can result in short-term agitation. But long-term exposure can lead to destructive effects.

Companies who advertise in the electronic media know that not everyone will respond to their ads. In fact, if 1 percent of viewers are receptive to an ad, the ad is considered a success. Similarly, if 1 percent of the viewers of violence in the media respond, critics might say, "Oh, that is too small a percentage to worry about." Yet, Bushman and Anderson point out that if 10 million people watch a violent program, 100,000 people will become more aggressive.[28]

As a violence-saturated media spreads throughout the world, we can see a gradual erosion of civility. A decrease in cooperative behaviors has been demonstrated in as remote a place as the island of St. Helena in the South Atlantic. It was reported that there was deterioration in the behavior of children in two nursery schools since the introduction of satellite television there.[29]

Overall it appears that television watching results in the illusion of community and the degradation of the fabric of a society. Increasing levels of television viewing result in decreasing participation in the political process. Indeed, several studies over the past few decades have demonstrated that television viewing decreases social involvement.[30] Longitudinal studies have shown that increases in television viewing lead to detriments in physical and mental health.[31, 32] For example, people who report that they are energetic and happy when engaged in social contact report that they are bored and unhappy when watching television.[33] People who are lonely watch more television than people who are not lonely.[34] In fact, television watching can be viewed as both a symptom and a cause of unhappiness.

Television and motion pictures fragment our society by promoting the false assumption that we are actually being brought together as a community. This drift into an illusion of community is an insidious process whereby viewers participate vicariously in one another's lives. People fill the void of real social isolation by sitting in front of the television. As that void is masked over just as a drug masks over pain, people increasingly operate under the illusion that their loneliness and social isolation have been resolved.

SCATTERED IMAGES = SCATTERED MINDS

The Comedy Channel has referred to the channel-surfing Baby Boomer generation as the Grazing Generation. Indeed, by 1990 three-quarters of households used remote controls for their television sets on a regular basis. Only half of Americans report that they have a specific program in mind when they turn on the television. An amazing 30 percent try to watch two programs at once.[35] With remote controls available for most modern televisions, channel surfing has become common. Even Former President Bill Clinton confessed that he is a channel surfer. Viewers can surf to one channel to witness a murder. Once the murder is committed, they can go on to a car crash, a sexual encounter, or a shootout for continuing thrills. Thus channel surfing helps develop a short attention span and a need for sensationalistic stimulation.

The broadcast media have adapted to as well as contributed to the fragmentation of the consciousness of the Grazing Generation. The programming on television and the cinematography in motion pictures is replete with flashy images and quick scene changes.

Cartoon programs shown on Saturday and Sunday mornings are excellent examples of what has happened to the rest of television. Each cartoon is designed to rivet a child's attention to the television set by rapid-fire action. Each scene lasts no more than a few seconds. Television producers know that a child's attention span is shorter than that of an adult. To reach the largest possible viewing audience, they exploit the child's short attention span. However, the new programs do not just match the current low attention span level of children but shoot to the LCD. In this way, children's programming breaks new low ground, and few children escape the quicksand.

The popular cable channel Music Television (MTV) represents the new generation of media formatting. MTV offers its viewers samples—essentially commercials for musical groups. Flashy, often disjointed images of the singers pulsate on the screen as the soundtrack of their latest hit single is played.

An entire generation of television viewers came to age watching MTV. Indeed, as Michael Stephens has pointed out, this powerful new style of programming has been adopted by much of modern media: "Television advertisements helped influence Mark Pellington, who would help MTV develop its style in the 1980s and thereby begin the process of spreading the techniques of the new video throughout the universe—even as far as ABC News."[36]

MTV is the prototype for contemporary television. Its rapid-fire cuts appear similar to cartoon programs. Children's programming has therefore swept into television, geared for adolescent and young adult viewers. The television industry has adapted to the decrease in attention span by producing programs that train viewers with bite-size scenes and sound-bite news programs. Most programs offer a "quick fix" instead of promoting sustained attention by slowly unveiling a story with a coherent sequence of images. Consequently, the new LCD programming serves to further shorten the attention span of its viewers and exacerbate the symptoms of people with attention deficit disorder (ADD).

Our orientation toward immediate gratification fuels our inability to maintain attention. Though perhaps not directly a causal factor, there might be a strong correlation between excessive television viewing and a corresponding increase in the incidence of ADD. Perhaps it is no coincidence that in the mental health field we are seeing an epidemic of people wanting treatment for ADD.

Various television programs have ironically provided quick and easy rationalizations for these would-be ADD sufferers. Instead of asking probing questions of the program viewers about how they have had a difficult time concentrating, talk shows such as *Oprah* have featured entire shows on ADD. Following each of these shows, psychologists and psychiatrists receive a rash of calls asking for an assessment for ADD. These people often say, "I finally found out why after all these years I have had trouble in school." They fail to acknowledge that they rarely attended school or that their parents let them watch television instead of doing homework.

Television can also contribute to perpetuation of one of the most destructive causes of a short attention span. For anyone addicted to drugs or alcohol, television viewing can lead to relapse. Researchers from the University of South Carolina have demonstrated that certain types of cues seen on videos induce cocaine craving in addicts.[37] In Ontario, Canada, researchers demonstrated that alcohol cues from television induced the urge to drink heavily and kindled a loss of confidence in maintaining sobriety.[38] In a study performed by the Prevention Research Center in Berkeley, California, television advertising was found to instill a more favorable attitude toward alcohol consumption among young people and increased their intentions to drink as adults.[39] Subliminal and not-so-subtle inducements include advertising slogans and songs echoed by adolescents, such as "It's Miller time." If beer commercials feature sports figures, the inducement to drink is particularly powerful for adolescents.

Television and movies do not necessarily have to trigger relapse among substance abusers, induce violence, or reinforce a short attention span. However, when no one is abiding by national guidelines or mutually agreed upon ethics, the market will take us to the LCD and our entertainment will degrade our consciousness.

4
Infotainment

A good newspaper is never nearly good enough, but a lousy newspaper is a joy forever.

Garrison Keillor

An excellent measure of the change in American consciousness is illustrated in what we find worthy of being in the news. The news provides a window into what we regard as important. It is a weather vane of our cultural climate. If most news organizations run stories on O.J., Monica, Gary Condit, and Robert Blake, co-workers at the water cooler find convenient news stories to talk about.

Because many people in the LCD society live vicariously through compulsive television viewing, many memories and associations can be established from indirect experience. These memories are colored by filters of the programs presenting the information. For example, many people remember the war against terrorism in Afghanistan through their vicarious experiences achieved watching television news. Because each network packaged coverage of the war much like an ongoing miniseries titled "America Strikes Back," viewers remember the war as some kind of movie featuring Bin Ladin, George W. Bush, and Colin Powell. These images and symbolic characters make up the frames in which we construct our version of reality. They provide the backdrop for experience.

The past 30 years have seen a steady drift away from in-depth news stories explained with context and a corresponding increase in news stories hyped with sensationalism and voyeurism. The O.J. Simpson trial would have warranted some coverage 30 years ago but not daily reports that included descriptions of Marcia Clark's new hairstyle. President Clinton's affair with Monica Lewinsky would probably not have received any coverage. This dramatic shift has resulted in a parallel shift in the perspective and context in which we try to understand our neighbors. The more we discuss news stories that involve deceit and duplicity, the more we come to regard our neighbors with suspicion.

Because we have developed an insatiable craving for entertainment, the manner in which the news is delivered has changed. Stories about Monica were far more entertaining than stories about Milosevic. Accordingly, Monica was splashed across the front page while Milosevic's trial earned a Page Six story. Genocide has become less alarming because it occurs to people far away. Monica titillated our repressed thoughts and feelings about our own sexuality.

We have become desensitized to murder because we have witnessed thousands of murders and graphic depictions of violence in the movies and on television. We have become numb to Milosevic's campaign of genetic cleansing in Bosnia and Kosovo, but we remain highly sensitized to our own sexual cravings.

World events came to center stage only after those events involved our home turf. The September 11, 2001, terrorist attacks provided a brief wake-up call. The seemingly never-ending story of former Congressman Gary Condit and a missing intern drifted into our hazy memories. But eventually we tired of stories about terrorism, and another scandal broke when Robert Blake was charged with the murder of his wife. Meanwhile, one of the biggest influence-peddling stories of recent history, that of Enron's ties to the Bush Administration, drifted by with hardly a casual reference.

The rules for acceptable communication have changed, and the news media have perpetuated the change. The rules now read that it is acceptable to believe that conflict resolution can be achieved by violence and the imposition of superiority ensured by gunfire. Sex is seen as the expected goal of friendships, and compulsive materialism is the route to happiness.

The news media have contributed to a decrease in attention span and the death of curiosity, optimism, civility, compassion for others, and abstract and conceptual reasoning. To understand how titillation and sensationalism have become primary and many psychological skills dampened, we must first examine how the vendors of the news have been transformed in recent years.

CORPORATE NEWS

In the 15 years between 1982 and 1997, the monopolies of the media have consolidated into a powerfully select group of media empires. University of California at Berkeley Dean Emeritus Ben Bagdikian notes that the fifty media empires that existed in 1984 had shrunk to ten by 1996.[1]

The ten major players include Time-Warner, Disney, Viacom, News Corporation Limited (Murdoch), Sony, Tele-Communications Inc. (TCI), Seagrams, Westinghouse, Gannett, and General Electric. These media empires wield considerable power. Bagdikian writes, "By almost every measure of public reach—financial power, political influence, and multiple techniques—the new conglomerates have more influence over what Americans see and hear than private firms have ever before possessed."[2]

These mega-corporations simultaneously advance their own interests as they squeeze out the diversity and depth from the news. Their primary goal is to increase the profit margin. In recent years, profits have been secured by tapering stories to the LCD while simultaneously minimizing coverage of news stories that might go against corporate interests. By minimizing the depth of the Enron story, the corporations escaped the scrutinizing analysis needed to understand their pervasive influence on every aspect of society.

General Electric (a major defense contractor) and Microsoft own NBC, CNBC, Court TV, AMC, The History Channel, News Sports, and MSNBC. AOL Time Warner and Westinghouse (the largest defense contractor) owned CBS, several book publishers, HBO, and seven other television stations until Viacom took over CBS. Disney owns ABC, A&E, Lifetime, ESPN, AOL, and Hyperion Books, and Chilton Publishing. Finally, Fox is owned by media magnet Rupert Murdoch, who has the motto "Do what sells." Murdoch's motto is actually embraced by all the companies.

For many years, Murdoch's political rival was Ted Turner. Turner launched a media empire when cable television was developing during the early 1980s. With the advent of his Cable News Network (CNN), Turner envisioned constant access to the news no matter where you might be in the world.

Like other networks, CNN is a commercial enterprise and ratings are critical. News highlights are covered at the expense of context and depth. Producers do not want to give viewers a reason to channel surf. Consequently, despite Murdoch's claim that CNN has a liberal bias, the blandness of the coverage has earned CNN the nickname "Chicken Noodle Network."[3]

Ted Turner controlled seven television networks until taken over by Time-Warner. Murdoch controls the fourth largest international media empire: 128 newspapers, the Star Satellite, the Fox Network, and considerable political power. It was Murdoch who offered Newt Gingrich a four-million-dollar advance through HarperCollins, one of his publishing companies. Congress just happened to be considering a decision that would affect Murdoch's media empire. After Murdoch's tax problems and merger goals were settled in his favor, there was a public outcry over favoritism. Though Gingrich eventually had to decline on the advance, his book yielded a handsome profit and Murdoch received preferential treatment.

In 1996 Disney bought ABC/Cap Cities for an estimated 19 billion dollars. Many analysts wondered out loud what this takeover would do to the delivery of the news at ABC. Indeed, Davis Thompsom of the *Los Angeles Times Magazine* has noted that Disney has "done more than anyone in this century to legitimize the dumbing down of the American mind and establish the child as the ideal U.S. citizen."[4]

Even the companies that control the print news media are merging into mega-corporations. Gannett, Scripps Howard, Times Mirror, Meredith, and the Tribune Company orient themselves primarily around the profit margin. Their advertising departments increasingly influence what appears in newspapers. The *Los Angeles Times* editorial staff now invites advertisers to editorial meetings. The owner told the editor of the *Times* to move his office to the corporate floor.[5] Bagdikian reports that a California newspaper required its reporters to clear local stories with the paper's advertising department.[6]

According to a poll conducted by researchers at Marquette University, 93 percent of newspaper editors reported that advertisers tried to influence what was published as news.[7] A majority reported that the management of the paper is receptive to the pressure, and 37 percent admitted they had given in.

Bagdikian wrote the following:

Letting advertisers influence the news is no novelty in less respected papers, but in the past it was usually done by innuendo, or quiet editing, reassignment, or firing. It has seldom before been so boldly stated and practiced in ways that typify the new contempt that some news companies feel for the professional independence of their journalists—and for the news audience. The trend typifies a growing attitude that reporting is just another business.[8]

In recent years newspapers have come to function as large-scale ad sheets. The space allocated to commercial advertisements has proliferated. In many cases, whole pages are given to advertisements. One has to weed through hundreds of ads to look for actual news stories.

To compound this decline in the quality of news, corporate downsizing has struck the news corporations just as it has many other corporations. During the mid 1980s, when many networks were taken over by multinational corporations, several foreign bureaus were trimmed or cut altogether. Virtually every news corporation has cut its investigative reports and its reporters. With the number of news reporters slimmed down, news companies are less able to cover stories that require context and more prone to provide flashy headlines instead of actual stories. The coverage amounts to graphic images that shock more than they illuminate. This title shift in resources contributes to a trimmed-down view of what occurs in our world.

In his book *Jihad vs. McWorld*, Benjamin Barber has equated corporate capitalism and religious fundamentalism.[9] Both monopolize thought at the lowest levels. Barber writes, "Monopoly is a polite word for uniformity, which is a polite word for censorship, not as a consequence of political choices but as a consequence of inelastic markets, imperfect competition and economies of scale."

Bagdikian reviewed 84 studies of media content and found a strong pro-corporate emphasis in the stories. It is not in the best interests of a large corporation to allow its smaller media subsidiaries to produce stories that run contrary to overall corporate interests.[10]

Corporate interest and public interest often clash. For example, given the overwhelming evidence that has been accumulating over the years that media violence contributes to actual violence, one would assume that print and television news sources would report this information—or at least make note of it. Unfortunately, as Bushman and Anderson have pointed out, there has been a steady decline in reports. Thus, as it became increasingly clear that violence in the media contributes to violence in real life, the news coverage got weaker.

To make matters worse, some of these news sources have actually contributed to misinformation. For example, *Newsweek Magazine* claimed there was no solid evidence that exposure to violence in the media contributes to aggression.

We must ask why there has been a void in reports about the ill effects of violence in the media. The first obvious answer is that these companies are owned by parent companies that are the producers of violence in media. They produce it because it sells to the LCD. Wider sales yield wider profits. These parent companies are not regulated by any agency that actually tries to ensure that ethical standards are employed. Those in government who would presumably put pressure on these companies are the recipients of campaign donations from these very companies. Using the parallel of the cigarette companies once again, we could say that campaign donations have been essentially lopsided for the Republicans. Therefore, Republicans have done what they could to block any effort to make the cigarette companies accountable, to the point that Bob Dole, during the 1996 Presidential campaign, stated that it had not yet been proved that smoking causes cancer.

Following the debacle of the 2000 Presidential election, both President Bush and Vice President Cheney argued that global warming was yet to be proven a real threat. Not so coincidentally, both are former oil men who maintain close ties with the oil industry.

The Synergy Report on the reliability of journalism called to question whether commercial interests have so tainted journalism that objectivity is no longer possible. The television network news companies were described as not only owned by large corporations but also manipulated by them. Many newsworthy stories were suppressed or changed if they conflicted with corporate interests. The news programs were analogized as weapons of mass destruction because people assume we are getting unfiltered news but instead are being manipulated to believe what corporations want us to believe.[11]

Liberals have traditionally been suspicious of corporations. In contrast, Republicans have traditionally been strong supporters of corporations. Republicans have long claimed that liberals control the news media. The reality is that the far right wing has been involved in the consolidation and monopolization of the media. In a Roper Poll, journalists were surveyed about their political leanings. The results were reported in the *Wall Street Journal,* hardly a bastion of liberals itself; only 22 percent of the responders considered themselves liberal.[12]

Case in point, the most powerful media mongrel is Rupert Murdoch. His media empire is one of a growing number of conservative/pro-corporate media empires. Murdoch makes no secret that he requires a litmus test of all his new management employees. Liberals are purged, and conservatives have taken over in all his major media outlets, from newspapers to television. Even Ted Turner has referred to Murdoch as "Hitler." It is widely known that Murdoch influenced a British Labor Party defeat in 1992. Murdoch's London paper, *The Sun*, ran a front page on Election Day with the headlines, "If Kinnock wins today, will the last person to leave Britain turn out the lights," with Kinnock's face superimposed on a photo of a light bulb.

The major networks have also leaned toward conservative/pro-corporate interests. Danny Schechter, who once worked for CNN and ABC, notes that many of his former colleagues regard "ABC" to stand for "always be conservative."[13] During the 1976 Republican convention when Ronald Reagan made his first run for the White House, Frank Reynolds, then the ABC anchorman, actually cried on the air when Reagan lost the nomination to President Ford. Later, ABC helped the Republicans regain the White House from President Carter. They ran a series called *America Held Hostage* that highlighted the hostage crisis in Iran. That series was later morphed into *Nightline.*

Even Walter Cronkite, one of the bedrock icons of network news, spoke out against what he saw to be the increasing inability of network news to provide objective and in-depth news stories. Former NBC news correspondent Marvin Kalb, now at Harvard, noted that although the "quantity of TV news has expanded, the quality goes down. What we are dealing with here is a flattening out of journalism in America."[14]

Even Dan Rather, who took over from Walter Cronkite during the 1980s, complained when CBS became infused with infotainment: "We ought to be ashamed of ourselves. . . . They've got us pulling more and more fuzz and wuzz on the air, cop-shop stuff, so as to compete not with other news programs, but with entertainment programs."[15]

Against this backdrop of changes, morale among journalists has plummeted during the past few decades. A survey at Indiana University analyzing the job satisfaction of journalists found that in 1971, 49 percent reported to be satisfied. But by 1992, job satisfaction dropped to 29 percent. Perhaps this is partly why reporters sound so cynical: they are witnessing the degradation of their craft. *Harper's Magazine* reported that 54 percent of journalists believe that they have become more cynical than other professionals, with 45 percent of the public agreeing.[16]

The Nieman Foundation at Harvard, with help from the Gallup Organization, prepared a survey among journalists.[17] They found that most respondents felt the media is more concerned about profits than quality because of an increased emphasis on entertainment and celebrities.

As news reporting becomes increasingly flattened out, consumers have fewer options through which to base an understanding of the world around them. Coupled with the increasing complexity of the world (i.e., economic interdependence and terrorism), consumers are less able to contribute to the political process.

Equally dangerous is the degradation of the depth to which news organizations cover major social problems. News organizations run headlines such as "Teenage drug use climbs" rather than attempt to analyze the potential reasons for the climb. The public, therefore, is afforded little opportunity to become primed for introspection. We do not ask ourselves why our teenagers are using drugs at increasing rates. Instead, we respond by supporting policies that increase the penalties for drug smuggling and dealing and decrease the funding for prevention and treatment. This lack of insight results in placing a bandage on a compound fracture while the infection grows out of control and the news media applauds ill-fated treatment.

The trend toward monopolization and flattening out of the news to the LCD has not only steered us away from examining ourselves but has offered a narcotizing product—junk news. Just as a narcotic is a replacement for real experience in life, so too does junk news replace a hunger for real news.

JUNK NEWS

In the past 25 years we have seen an epidemic of tabloid publications. At the supermarket checkout stand, one can find an abundant supply of the *National Enquirer*, *Star*, and *Globe*. Typically the front page features sensational and mind-bending headlines such as "Elvis found on an alien spaceship." Occasionally the front page displays a doctored photo of a fish with an Elvis head or a UFO sitting on the White House lawn.

The phenomenon of the paparazzi was brought to the public's attention by the death of Princess Diana. The paparazzi photographers are paid six-figure sums for candid shots of celebrities engaging in their private lives, especially if those photos reveal love affairs. Though the initial blame for Diana's death was cast on the paparazzi photographers, little attention was focused on those who employ them or the customers who buy the tabloids that carry the photos.

This society has developed an insatiable appetite for petty voyeurism. As noted in the previous chapter, many people live vicariously. The lives of celebrities have become more important than our own lives. Consequently, we have seen a major shift in what is covered by the mainstream press.

So dependent are the networks on ratings that they try to pump up the ratings of their primetime programs through a seamless interface with their entertainment programs. For example, on Thursday nights the *Nightly News* might run a story involving emergency rooms. It is not by accident that the show *ER* will air later in the evening. Alternatively, during a commercial break of a primetime program, the news anchors break in to announce that you can continue watching the same channel to see an interview "with the real survivor of the Everest climb."

The network news programs have adapted well to the viewing public's fascination and obsession with the entertainment industry. The "Tyndall Report," a newsletter that reviews the evening newscasts, reported that the three major news programs on NBC, CBS, and ABC spent an average of 38 minutes a month on Hollywood-type entertainment stories during the 1980s. By 1990, the average number of minutes shot up to 68 per month.[18]

As if to emphasize the fact that news is commercially based, the news programs themselves are subtly punctuated by glossy commercials that look little different from the actual news coverage. What masquerades as news is packaged in bite-sized and sugar-coated clichés and flashing images. To match and reinforce the rapidly decreasing attention span of the viewing audience, the news stories have been formatted into obligatory commercials, as if the networks are saying, "We will be covering this story later in our news program." In fact, when a news program offers a preview of what they will cover later in the broadcast, we find that the actual story is rarely more in depth than the preview. The actual story is more of a repeat of that preview. In other words, the preview informs viewers that another preview is on the way. The promos are promos for more promos. It is not uncommon for the news anchor to say, "Now don't touch that dial! When we return, you won't believe what turned up today in the bay!"

Each news story is designed and tailored to fit into an overall format that skims quickly from one image to another, allowing viewers to whet their appetites but not satiate. The daily headlines are essentially the obligatory flash points in the news, which do not invite viewers into deep thinking. Instead, they promote a scattering of consciousness. Viewers are seduced into craving headlines over news stories.

Even the so-called 24-hour news channels feature essentially headlines at the expense of depth. One flashy story follows another. To adapt to the short attention span and hyperactive viewing habits of the audience, the bottom of the screen features sports scores, banner headlines, and weather reports. If you lose track of a story, you can shift your attention to the banner headlines or the scores of the latest games. By the time you shift back, another story will be featured. Viewers are left with an illusion that the program is so rich with information they do not need to surf to another channel.

ABC news hired David Barrent, one of the producers of MTV. He and others of like mind made MTV a rapid-fire collage of images. Barrent brought the "fast cut" (sometimes as many as four shots a second) to ABC. NYU professor Michael Stephens notes that though this type of production is creative, it promotes a dumbing down of communication. He wrote: I have suggested that the 'true' curse upon those who make images may be their difficulty communicating abstract thought.[19]

Due to the dumbing down of the news broadcasts, the LCD stories have become the same, whichever channel you watch. Each story carries the same emphasis, the same sarcasm, and the same flashy images. Even the order in which stories appear is generally the same on each channel. During the time slot designated for network news programs, television viewers need only to flip the channel to find that the story they left on one channel is on the next channel.

News stories are replete with sensationalism. "If it bleeds it leads," is a motto many news producers follow. They offer us graphic shots of wounded or dead disaster victims. The footage is crafted to offer maximum shock value. Apparently the networks assume their viewers will not be interested or stay on the same channel unless the stories are packaged with shock value. They assume viewers are asleep and can only be awakened by the LCD primitive emotions: fear, anxiety, and anger. Disaster stories exploit fear and anxiety; crime stories stir up anger and fear.

One technique employed by the news programs is voyeurism of grief. When a mother loses her child in a brutal traffic accident, the reporters rush to interview her. They shove cameras in her face and ask, "How do you feel?" This insensitive voyeurism offers viewers a vicarious opportunity to experience the loss without suffering the permanent consequences of such a loss. These stories are designed to grab viewers' attention by asking, "How would you feel if you lost your child?" Viewers are asked to be the mother for just a few seconds before they flash to another story. These vicarious experiences grab viewers' attention long enough to subtly traumatize them. After a bombardment of graphic images, viewers adapt by becoming numb, callous, and cynical.

So callous and cynical have we become that each news story, whether from the White House Press Corps or regional news reporters, often ends with a cliché sentence such as, "But that remains to be seen." This is especially the case when the reporter covers a positive political story. This style of reporting shows that it is much easier to appeal to viewers' cynicism than to their aspirations.

As cynicism and callousness are cultivated with each news story, viewers are conditioned to regard the important issues of the day with an equal measure of cynicism and callousness. As news stories are offered in bite-sized and glossy packages, viewers turn away from an attempt to present the news in any other format.

News consumers and those who produce the news reinforce one another. The trend toward junk news perpetuates junk news. News consumers adapt to the manner in which the news is offered, and news producers adapt to the changing consciousness of news consumers.

RATING FEVER

The emerging LCD society craves simple answers to questions that have complex answers. When we settle for simple answers, we misunderstand the major problems of the day. Simple answers to today's problems are found more readily in television news than in newspapers. Newspaper circulation has dropped consistently for the past two decades. This decline is largely due to the precipitous drop in evening newspapers. Nevertheless, another threat looms on the horizon: The audience for newspapers may be dying off. Although 71 percent of people age 65 or older read a daily paper, only 45 percent of people age 18–24 years old read daily.[20]

During the 1950s, 1960s, and 1970s, more Americans have gravitated toward television to get their news than to the print media or radio. Over the past few years, the network news programs feature the network logo in the lower right corner of the screen, just in case viewers forget what channel they are watching. The networks try to get you to buy their particular packaging of the news by suggesting that they provide just the right touch. The right touch often means they will entertain you more than provide in-depth reporting. If news is packaged in such a way that requires too much intellectual effort, viewers can simply change channels. Therefore news programs are increasingly entertaining to reach the largest possible audience.

Despite all the slicking up and dumbing down, the network news programs are still not achieving the high ratings that earn large profits from sponsors. In 1982, network news programs attracted 41 percent of the American viewing audience. By 1997 that percentage dropped to just 16.1 percent.[21] Network producers apparently realized they needed to do something to compete with entertainment programs. In many regional markets they opted to shift the airing time of news programs to an earlier slot to make room for the game shows and evening magazine programs that get a larger audience.

The television news magazines have become the most watched of all the news programs. The pioneer in this expanding field was CBS's *60 Minutes.* It took several years for the other networks to catch on that they too could produce a cash cow such as *60 Minutes,* which held very high ratings. ABC developed *20/20* and then CBS countered with a two-hour show called *48 Hours.* Eventually, there was a large-scale outbreak of news magazine programs including *PrimeTime Live* on ABC and *Dateline* on NBC. *Dateline* became so profitable for NBC that they run it four nights a week. Not to be outdone, *60 Minutes* now airs on a second night.

News magazine programs feature glossy stories by "star" reporters such as Barbara Walters, who have become so polished that their agents and promoters try to sell them to other programs. Walters and others have aired their own specials that highlight the latest hyped scandal. Whether it is Monica Lewinsky, Tonya Harding, or someone who knew O.J., the network and the star reporter milk every scandal to pump up the ratings.

More than anyone else in television, Walters has taken the trend of celebrity interviews and made them primetime events. In interviews with such people as Monica Lewinsky, Walters has legitimized the seamier side of life. As if to pretend to be above the tabloids, she is often heard to say, "You know I have to ask you this" or "My listeners would be angry if I didn't ask you why you had sex with a married man."

Danny Schechter, who once worked at *20/20,* noted that "staffers were constantly reminded that our programs were there to get ratings, which are there to get the advertising dollars, which are there to please the stockholders, who in turn reward management, and on and on."[22]

These news magazine programs offer sugar-coated and spoon-fed stories on subjects chosen to get maximum ratings. The packaging of news stories often includes stylized graphics, music, and quick pacing to keep viewers engaged. Schechter writes that the programs are not geared to offer depth but

. . . a kind of sameness and predictability to the story selections week after week. We did genres as much as stories—the limited expose, the disease of the week, the relationship problem, new technology, child raising, consumer rip-offs, celebrities or news maker interviews. Week after week, we cut and trimmed sliced and diced to ensure that segments fit the time allotted. The content was finessed, fine-tuned, even manufactured, to fill out the format.[23]

Simultaneous to the outbreak of newsmagazine shows we have seen an epidemic of the sleazier tabloid shows. Murdoch's *A Current Affair* stirred up like-minded scandal/gossip shows including *Inside Edition,* and *Hard Copy.* For viewers interested in the private lives of movie stars, *Entertainment Tonight* is aired several times a week.

These tabloid and news magazine programs have better ratings than the network news formats. They have yielded a powerful influence over traditional news programs. For example, the *NBC Nightly News* was in big trouble and losing money for years. The emergence of *Dateline* carried their news division. Then when *The NBC Nightly News* covered more of the O.J. trial than did ABC, the ratings went up and it became the leader in the ratings game. *Columbia Journal-*

ism Review called the transformation of the *NBC Nightly News* "Newslite." Overseas coverage was slimmed down and the "you news" of human interest stories went up.

Even the respected news magazine *60 Minutes* stooped in the quest to draw viewers by marketing sensationalism. One of its broadcasts featured the Dr. Kevorkian-assisted suicide of Thomas Youk.

CNN raked in an estimated 70 million over its usual profits because of its O.J. coverage.[24] So powerful were the O.J. ratings for all networks that the President's 1997 State of the Union Address was delayed because few would watch until the verdict for O.J. civil suit trial came in.

Many of the former O.J. trial stars went on to fame and fortune. Marcia Clark became the standby fill-in host for Geraldo Rivera's television program. Johnnie Cochran and Robert Shapiro became often sought after speakers and guests on talk shows. Mark Furman became a consultant for Linda Tripp.

The LCD trend is not limited to the broadcast media. Newspaper companies have crafted the format and the news stories to appeal to a wide audience. Many news analysts were surprised by the success of *USA Today*. When the *Los Angeles Times* announced it was shutting down its special sections with coverage on world affairs, media watch, and minorities, the stock in its parent company Times Mirror shot up.

In the past few years there has been a shift from viewing network news to local news. Over a quarter of respondents in a survey indicated they look to local news broadcasts for their news fix. There are a number of reasons for this shift. Many people in our society have become less interested in what goes on in the world and more concerned with such issues as "am I safe, can I get to work on time, and what are people wearing out there?" To this end, local news programs feature the latest shocking crime, up-to-the-minute freeway reports, and glossy stories on fashion and what is hot at the box office.

Most news teams feature attractive people. The assumption is that the ratings stay the highest if viewers can watch attractive people on the screen. Women are usually asked to cake on the makeup and look glamorous. A Bay Area news "celebrity" changed her entire style after she was elevated to the anchorship of the *Ten O'clock News*. Elaine Coral looked like an average American when she was a mere reporter, but once she was promoted to news anchor, she transformed her hair and make-up and began to wear expensive flashy clothes. In the end it wasn't enough, and she was passed over for a more attractive woman.

With budgets tight and news light, some networks such as CNN have opted to create the illusion of depth by running programs with pundit panelists. As Schechter has noted, these programs feature "not news but talk about the news, commentary not information. During the last 15 years the pundit shows such as *The McLaughlin Group* and *Crossfire* have featured staged fiery debates with one-liners. The cast of characters jumps from show to show offering the same pithy clichés that fail to describe the news of the day as much as they regurgitate it."[25]

Ken Auletta wrote in *The New Yorker* that the "news" talk shows have gravitated to a set format in which guests are coached and paid for a specific and narrow sensationalistic presentation.[26] The increase accessibility of these programs has resulted in a corresponding increase in banality and a decrease in depth of analysis.

These pundits function more as spin-doctors that push a particular agenda by using catchy phrases. They are not selected for their knowledge or even their intelligence but for how much they can render a characterization of a particular political position. Many of the pundits manage to expound sensationalistic views to shock and simultaneously entertain viewers. Patrick Buchannan became a national figure not because he was a low-level official in the Nixon and Reagan administrations but for the extremist views he argued on the pundit shows. His role drew such notoriety that he used the pundit shows as a springboard to run for President.

Viewers of these programs need not form their own opinions. As they watch the pundits spar with one another, viewers can chose an opinion based on the pithiness of the argument posed by one of the characters on the show, thus forming opinions vicariously. Viewers do not have to go to the trouble of reasoning out an opinion. Watching such programs perpetuates viewers' already decreasing ability to reason out opinions. They develop the tendency to gravitate toward opinions that are formed around clichés and posturing rather than sound reasoning.

What are television viewers to do if they want to receive news from television but avoid the pundit shows, news magazine programs, and network news? For many people the answer is to tune into public television.

"PUBLIC" TELEVISION

The government owns the airwaves. However, since the development of radio, commercial interests have outweighed public interests. During the 1930s there was a legislative effort in Congress to ensure that at least one-quarter of all radio stations are controlled by universities. Yet with the overwhelming success of programs such as *Amos 'n Andy,* corporations moved into exploiting the potential commercial opportunities radio programming yielded.

Years later, the Federal Communication Commission (FCC) required radio stations to devote time to public affairs and the news. Then, during the Reagan Administration, deregulation of radio occurred. The news and public service requirement was dropped. Stations jumped at the opportunity to work toward more profit and less public service. Numerous news programs were discarded altogether.

The 1996 Telecommunications Act slipped through Congress without significant debate and was protected by the seal of approval of the Republican Party. As *The New York Times* editorialized, "Forty million dollars worth of lobbying bought the telecommunication companies a piece of legislation they could relish."[27] This complicity of the government allows for more corporate consolidation of the media than ever before.

Marvin Kitman of *Newsday* called the Telecommunications Act of 1996 "the biggest giveaway of public assets in history. It makes the Teapot Dome scandal of 1921, the giveaway of oil reserves in Wyoming and California, seem like a tempest in a teapot."[28]

Congress has responded to the new digital technologies in the same manner. The digital revolution in television will surpass many of the previous advances. The government essentially owned the digital spectrum but gave it away to the corporations.

The Public Broadcasting System (PBS) was meant to remedy many of the shortcomings of the corporate networks. Indeed, when PBS was formed by Congress in 1967, the intent was to instill debate and diversity. Gradually, the debate has narrowed and the diversity withered away. What once looked like the British Broadcasting Company (BBC) and the Canadian Broadcasting Company (CBC) has come to look more like NBC, CBS, and ABC.

By the late 1980s the principal PBS news program, *MacNeil-Lehrer News Hour* (now simply called *The News Hour*), became less balanced. To reach a larger audience, *The News Hour* gives the illusion of a balanced opinion. Apparently, the producers of *The News Hour* have decided that if they offer opinions and perspectives "too" diverse, viewers might lose interest and switch the channel to one of the major networks. Consequently, the trend is to increase the acrimony and decrease the substance of the debate. Viewers are entertained by the debate but no more informed than before.

This shift toward the conservatives on *The News Hour* is understandable when one considers the fact that John Malone of TCI owns two-thirds of the program. Malone is widely known as being one of the most conservative media executives in the country.

Eric Alterman wrote in *The Nation* that several studies have indicated that the opinions aired in various PBS series have favored Republicans and conservatives over Democrats and liberals. For example, on documentaries, Republicans got 63 percent of the air time while Democrats got a mere 37 percent. Republicans also surpassed Democrats in percentage of appearances: 50 percent to 41 percent of the actual number of appearances.[29]

Because of consistent cuts in funds from the Republican-led congress, PBS and National Public Radio (NPR) air more "begathons." They have also carried commercials in camouflage before and after programming. For example, they often announce that underwriting for the program has "been offered by Mobil." Not only do large corporations get a tax break but they have taken the opportunity to advertise their product and convince a more intellectual audience that their corporation is looking out for our best welfare.

News programs on both public and corporate stations match and cultivate the LCD society. The less contextual information provided for each news story, the less able viewers are to develop the cognitive skills necessary to come to an intelligent opinion about news stories. Therefore, the infotainment industry perpetuates the LCD.

A question on one of the major intelligence tests asks "why is a free press important in a democracy?" Over the years, fewer people can answer this question. What the press has offered in recent years undermines democracy by fooling its consumers that they are being offered unbiased information.

The rise of infotainment has resulted in the overall degradation of many psychological skills. Curiosity is foremost among them. With the death of curiosity, Americans become increasingly myopic at a time when we should pay close attention to international events. When we should be deepening our reflection of current events, we have barely skimmed the surface.

As we sit back and consume sensationalistic entertainment in the place of context-driven information, we have replaced broad curiosity with a craving for titillation. Watching a never-ending barrage of news stories about Tonya Harding, Princess Diana, Monica, O.J., Gary Condit, Robert Blake, and Paula Jones, we convert broad curiosity to petty voyeurism.

We are essentially inoculated from the news. Because what we consume is a barrage of sound bites and "minimercials," our appetites have not only been satiated but also sealed off from further curiosity. Because we are offered immediate graphic images of disasters and calamities, we suffer from the illusion that we are better informed than ever. Knowing that you do not know is sad, but not knowing that you do not know is dangerous.

5
Retail Government

Politics is just like show business, you have a hell of an opening, coast for a while and then have a hell of a close.

Ronald Reagan

During the FDR administration, few in the country knew that their President could not stand without leg braces. President Roosevelt's aides orchestrated media events so the President could be wheeled in by a wheelchair and filmed only after the "set" was ready. Members of the press knew quite well that the President could not walk. During that era, there was a code of ethics prohibiting coverage of the private lives of public figures.

With the advent of television, politics changed irreversibly. Though the private lives of politicians were still off limits, political candidates could orchestrate image-enhancing television events. Political commercials replete with cute jingles such as "We like Ike" littered the airwaves.

Just before Richard Nixon made his famous "Checkers" speech 50 years ago, a consultant told him that his speech would work to regain the respect of the electorate and someday an actor would be elected President of the United States. He was right in both opinions.

The 1980s ushered in an era when an actor did become a popular President. Ronald Reagan served two terms and, despite the Iran-Contra scandal, remains a heroic icon among conservative voters. Since his administration, the pageantry and media promotion surrounding the Presidency have reached flamboyant extremes.

Eventually, however, news coverage of government became more about hype than pageantry. The tabloid media hype legitimized Kenneth Starr's witch-hunt. Former President Clinton's sex life carried the front page of most major newspapers and the top stories on network news programs. This scandal snowballed into impeachment.

Despite claims of denial, members of the emerging LCD society have grown to crave titillation by gossip about the private lives of our political leaders. Simultaneously, we have become increasingly cynical and politically illiterate. We believe our disdain for government officials is a sign of sophistication; but the truth is we are easily manipulated by well-crafted media productions. We have become more receptive to the politics of destruction than to elevated debates on the issues of the day.

How is it that in one lifetime we have gone from the hush-hush about FDR's leg braces and sex life to the astounding spectacle of impeachment because President Clinton lied about a sleazy affair? The first clue can be found in the synergy between corporate money and the media.

MONEY AND MEDIA = POLITICS

The United States was founded on the premise that democracy involves a frank discussion between diverse perspectives. Freedom to criticize the status quo is one of the strongest tenets of a true democracy. However, in recent years the debate has evaporated and the range of ideas has shrunk, partly because of the massive amounts of money thrown into political campaigns.

The media and the massive amount of money multinational corporations provide to politicians illustrate how closely the two "industries" have become intertwined. For example, donations from the broadcasting industry played a major role in the passage of the Telecommunications Act of 1996. In the year prior to its passage, broadcasters donated $871,115 in PAC money and large individual donations to congressional candidates who would soon thereafter be voting on the bill.[1] As noted earlier, this bill was a virtual giveaway to the large media corporations.

In the 2000 Presidential election, the Bush/Cheney ticket was by far the largest recipient of Enron donations. During 2001, when the Bush administration was developing their energy policy, Enron officials were present during closed-door meetings. When Enron collapsed in one of the largest bankruptcy scams in history, the Bush Justice Department managed to look the other way.

Despite all the rhetoric about campaign finance reform in recent years, the amount of money raised has continued to rise. During the spring of 2000 alone, a record amount of money was raised:

$70,034,834 by George W. Bush and $31,881,777 by Al Gore. By the end of the election, Bush raised $193,088,252 and spent $132,900,252, and Gore raised $185,860,812 and spent $120,369,160.

The amount of soft money that poured into the political system hit an all-time high in 2000. Political parties raked in $256 million up to June 2000. The single greatest donor was AT&T at $2.9 million. Business interests accounted for $208 million, or 12 times the amount coming in from labor.

Lobbyists continue to flood the capitol. Even the American Medical Association (AMA) has not been without monetary bias. It has been reported that the AMA spent $17.28 million in lobbying expenses in 1997, which is approximately $32,300 for every member of Congress.[2] Although the insurance industry was largely credited with defeating the Clinton Health Care Proposal, it was the AMA quietly working behind the scenes that killed it.

It is no wonder, therefore, that George Lundberg was fired from his position as the editor of the *Journal of the American Medical Association* after he allowed an article to be published that was subtly critical of the impeachment of President Clinton.[3] The AMA would not like to upset the Republicans in Congress.

The Philip Morris Company was the top Republican contributor at $2.5 million.[4] The CEOs from the major tobacco companies sat before a Republican-controlled committee while they were asked soft-balled questions about cigarette smoking. The CEO took the opportunity to claim that tobacco was not addictive.

During the 1996 presidential campaign, Bob Dole was asked whether he thought tobacco was addictive or caused cancer. Despite the well-known fact that nicotine is extremely addictive and that smoking has caused millions of deaths, he responded by saying he thought it had not yet been proven and more study would be needed. Dole did his job for one of his largest contributors.

The news media has not addressed the question "What are the large corporations buying?" Apparently the question does not garner enough LCD media hype to be appealing to the viewing public. In today's tabloid-saturated media, a President's private life gets more media coverage than the issue of corporate control of our government. If the President has a urinary tract infection, we are inundated with information about his condition, replete with charts and commentary. In contrast, stories are avoided about the effect of mega mergers occurring among media companies and corporate donations to politicians.

Politicians use the money invested in them to use the media to appeal to the LCD. Ever since the Kennedy Administration, politicians have learned to use the money they raise in television to market themselves. Today they employ media/marketing consultants who help them polish their messages to reach the LCD. Just like the large corporations who buy commercial space, politicians struggle to raise enough money to buy primetime commercials to sell themselves.

Unfortunately, these political ads have devoted more time to attacking opponents and less time to the promotion of specific policies. Negative advertising has become the LCD way of campaigning because it is much easier to smear the other candidate with distortion and innuendo than to explain and defend one's own views. Hot-button sound bites and negative characterizations of each candidate are much easier to remember than policy statements.

Sound bites mixed with negative advertisements have grown increasingly popular. The length of sound bites has been decreasing over the past few decades. Kiku Adatto of Harvard University reported that the average length of uninterrupted sound bites declined from 42.3 seconds in 1968 to 9.8 seconds in 1998.[5] Adatto also found a significant shift in how reporters covered candidates. By 1988, news of political campaigns placed significant emphasis on stagecraft. Specifically, Adatto reported that in 1988, 52 percent of the coverage was on how the campaign had orchestrated campaign sets to emphasize particular themes.

The late Lee Atwater ushered wholesale hit-and-run character assassination into the mainstream as a front-line campaign technique. Atwater was widely credited with the hit-and-run smear of former House Speaker Tom Foley. After implying that Foley was gay without actually saying it, he was able to send Foley scrambling to deny it without making reference to the smear. Later Atwater and the Bush (Sr.) for President team drew attention to the possibility that Michael Dukakis was once treated for depression. They also pressed the story that Kitty Dukakis was a prescription drug addict and a former flag burner.

When George Bush ran the Willie Horton ad during the 1988 general election, many people feared Michael Dukakis would let out thousands more Willie Hortons to plague our communities. Whether

Governor Dukakis had actually been involved in letting Horton go was not the point in the end. The damage had been done, and the uninformed electorate remembered Willie Horton's face associated with that of Governor Dukakis. With this ad, the Bush team was able to demonstrate that character assassination and veiled racism have entered the mainstream of American political campaigns.

Bush (Jr.) was essentially a protégé of Atwater. As he worked on his father's campaign in 1988, he learned a trade that paid off for his own run for the White House in 2000. Though he couldn't run directly against Clinton's sexual problem, he managed to tie Al Gore to Monica Lewinsky without ever uttering her name. He said he would "bring decency back into the White House." In the LCD society, Gore was guilty by loose association. Bush demonstrated how a subtle smear could work to his advantage as he exploited the shallow depth of public opinion.

THE SHIFTING TIDES OF PUBLIC OPINION

The manipulation of public opinion has a long history, and democracy is based on it. One of the first experiments with democracy occurred in Greece in approximately 400 BCE when Socrates was sentenced to death by hemlock. He was charged with inciting others to think out of the norm. For this reason, his student Plato distrusted the opinions of the masses and democracy. In his book *The Republic*, Plato proposed that only a "philosopher king" could be an effective ruler, because the masses are so easily manipulated by the whim of the moment. Even at this early date in history, it was evident that there is reason to be alarmed by how people can respond to the LCD fad sweeping the country.

The experiment of democracy did not reemerge until after two thousand years of autocratic rule. With the first large-scale democracy emerging in the United States, the rights of white males were expanded dramatically; however, the interests of the rich have always dominated government policy. The voting masses have not been difficult to manipulate. It is widely believed that the sinking of the Maine was staged. Not only did this event galvanize public opinion against Spain and trigger a war, but also the massive land grab fattened the wallets of many wealthy Americans.

Since the advent of television, manipulating the masses has become more complicated. Though corporations are pouring millions of dollars into the political system, the public has grown increasingly distrustful of politicians.

In the late 1960s, the Vietnam War marked a turning point in the media and politics. Every night on the evening news, we were offered graphic scenes of carnage. We saw Buddhist monks pouring gasoline on themselves and then setting themselves ablaze in protest of the war. We heard the horrifying details of the My Lai massacre. The war broke a pact the government had with its citizens. No other war in history had been as widely opposed as the Vietnam War. By 1973, over 60 percent of the voting public opposed the war. Many of my generation actively opposed the war in protest marches and debates.

Revelations of lying and obstruction of justice occurring during the Watergate incident served as another watershed in American politics. The Watergate hearings revealed how people in the government can deceive their constituents. Later, the Church Committee investigated the CIA, and the House Assassinations Committee investigated the assassinations of President Kennedy, Robert Kennedy, and Martin Luther King, Jr. and revealed hidden layers of intrigue. In 1988 we were exposed to the fact that the Reagan Administration had negotiated with terrorists and traded arms for hostages.

All of these events contributed to a general cynicism that citizens have about their government. The media has adapted to public cynicism by treating every story of potential impropriety as a scandal and attaching the suffix "gate" to the story. But the scandals became personal and salacious, more worthy of coverage on the pages of *The National Enquirer* and the *Star* than the *Washington Post* and *The New York Times*. For example, the firing of the White House travel office staff was dubbed "Travelgate," and other Clinton Administration hyped stories were referred to as "Filegate" and "Zippergate."

Reporters compete with each other to dig up the most amount of dirt in an effort to become the next Woodward or Bernstein. They chose stories related to Gary Condit rather than the full implications of the Enron debacle. When a story has the potential to raise eyebrows, it plays in the network news programs until the public loses interest. It is as if the networks are doing the Nielsen Ratings on news items, and when the numbers go down, they pull the coverage.

Politicians are uncomfortably aware of the sensationalistic power of television. Many believe Gary Hart would have been elected President in 1988 had he not been shown in a photo on television with a young blond woman on his lap. Hart knew his candidacy was doomed to defeat and pulled out of the race a few days after the story broke. Neither Hart, Condit, nor Clinton apparently understood the power of the LCD media. Nor did any of them seem to appreciate the fact that their dishonesty and their insensitivity to their wives would garner the national spotlight.

After the last three seasons of Presidential debates, news coverage has gravitated toward a concern over who looked good and how defensive he was, not who offered a coherent and compelling explanation of why his policies and proposals were more sensible for the nation.

It has been not uncommon for commentators to remark following a debate, "Well, there were no gaffes and no great one-liners that will make one remember this debate in the years to come." The implication of course, is "This was a pretty boring debate."

In the 1980 Presidential debates, instead of seriously discussing the issues, Reagan repeated "Well, there you go again" in response to President Carter, who was offering the viewing audience an in-depth analysis of the issues. Commentators announced that Reagan had "looked good" and apparently won the debate.

No longer are the masses waiting for a vigorous debate of the issues. The sound bites or gaffes are the fireworks we have come to expect. The performances of the candidates have become the sole focus of our attention. It is as if the characters in the debate are auditioning for a role in a movie called "The Presidency."

George W. Bush was widely regarded as having "held his own" during his debates with Gore because he made no major gaffes. Bush's handlers astutely prepared the viewing audience to expect Gore to be a formidable debater, Bush's lackluster performance took a backseat to attention on Gore. We were told that Gore was too whiney in the first debate, too meek in the second, and too late in the last.

An analysis of the transcripts of the 2000 debates reveals that Bush used language below a 7th grade level (6.7) and Gore below an 8th grade level (7.6). Bush was thought to talk to the "common man" while Gore "talked down" to them. This was a far cry from the debates of Lincoln and Douglas, who spoke at the 11.2 and 12.0 grade levels, respectively, in their debates.

Because the performance has become a high-stakes production, the spin-doctors are analogous to agents for actors who work hard to sign a contract with a movie producer. After each Presidential debate, network reporters rush to a room where spin-doctors for both sides await to offer their particular spin, such as, "I think our candidate certainly held his own" or "I think he really put the challenger on the defensive." Though the reporters sarcastically joke that each side "of course" distorts the truth, they nevertheless interview the spin-doctors as if each respective spin were a news story.

CONTRACTING WITH THE POLITICALLY ILLITERATE

Daniel Shorr of National Public Radio once noted that he met a woman in the Midwest who complained, "I'm tired of the government always wanting to tax me. Why don't they pay for themselves!"[6] Somehow this woman had grown to assume that the government funded itself or perhaps is a separate company funded by profits. Her confusion illustrates an alarming trend. Never before has there been such mass confusion and political illiteracy.

With the electorate becoming increasingly unsophisticated and media productions becoming an integral part of the political process, government officials rarely attempt to explain policy. Our public servants now employ pollsters and media consultants to help them portray the "message" that will appeal to the LCD.

The Republican Party has developed into a media-savvy party. The most poignant examples of a made-for-TV political commercial were the 1996 and 2000 Republican Conventions. The self-inflicted wounds of the 1992 convention stung the party. Few viewers could forget Pat Buchannan's self-righteous speech detailing his reasons for a "holy war" and his brutal condemnation of Hillary Clinton. Thus, the 1996 convention was a tightly crafted media event during which the party managed to stamp out any political debate. Ted Koppel of ABC News was so disgusted with the entire production that he packed up his crew and left town, saying, "There is no news here." Yet the press as a whole participated in the show. When Colin Powell spoke, cameras focused on a few African Americans in the audience. *Mother Jones* magazine revealed that one of the African American faces panned in the audience several times was a female reporter there on assignment.[7]

In the 2000 convention, people of color were paraded onstage and seemed to frequently stand in back of speakers who wanted to push the image of inclusion. My son dubbed them the "Color Guard." Jesse Jackson called it the "Inclusion Illusion." But apparently the American electorate got the message as evidenced by significance bounce in the polls after the convention.

As far back as 1994, Newt Gingrich "contracted" with pollster Frank Luntz to help put together the now famous "Contract with America." Despite the hyped promotion, only one-third of those who voted that year knew about the contract. This number is more striking when one considers that only one-third of the electorate voted that year. During that election year, Republicans took control of the House of Representatives and gained seats in the Senate.

The Republican Party even developed its own television channels, GOP-TV and National Empowerment Television (NET). Both are funded by the Conservative Free Congress Foundation. Two seemingly contradictory but typically Republican strange bedfellows, the National Rifle Association and the American Life League (an anti-abortion lobby group), produced NET. The Republicans have not limited their efforts to television. The Progress and Freedom Foundation, a think tank associated with former Speaker of the House Gingrich, orchestrated policy and produced an Internet website in addition to television.

So-called think tanks have contributed sophisticated assessments of the political consciousness of the electorate. While conservative think tanks are funded at $46 million on an annual basis, their progressive counterparts are funded at $10.2 million.[8] This lopsided financial arrangement is matched by the same disproportional contributions to the political candidates.

The electorate has dumbed down so far that many people do not know who their representatives are in Congress. In 1995 the *Washington Post* reported that fewer than half of those surveyed could not identify their own senators.

In the LCD society, politicians running for office find themselves in desperate need of name recognition. They try to pump up the rhetoric to appear different and novel. In many cases, this involves sophisticated polling and focus groups. Politicians work hard to find hot-button LCD issues to galvanize the electorate. They know quite well that if they campaign simply on the issues, it is possible that no one will remember them.

One story that received little attention during the 2000 Presidential election season involved an interview with Governor George W. Bush on ABC's *This Week*. Sam Donaldson asked candidate Bush his opinion of President Putin's agreement with the communists in the Duma. Bush refused to answer the question. Donaldson asked him again, reminding him that he was a candidate for the Presidency. But Bush refused once again. Perhaps he thought Donaldson was calling him a Dumya instead of asking about the Duma, the Russian Congress.

As if to illustrate a reading of the American electorate, George W. Bush accused his opponent Al Gore of being one of the thinkers in Washington. Reference to this accusation was made only in passing on NPR and was not covered at all by the major networks, as if a comment such as this was commonplace and acceptable. Certainly we do not want any thinkers in the White House. Bush went on to give a speech at Yale in the spring of 2001 saying that "who said C students can't become President."

TEFLON AND STEALTH CANDIDATES

The emergence of Ronald Reagan and George W. Bush as political leaders illustrates how vulnerable we have become to media productions. Prior to Reagan's election in 1980, few thought such an extreme candidate had a serious chance to win. Even *Saturday Night Live* did a spoof in 1976, joking about possible futures for the country, one with Ronald Reagan as President.

A number of factors combined to usher Reagan into respectability. To begin with, the exponential increase in oil prices led to "stagflation"—high interest rates and low growth. President Carter experienced something akin to Chinese water torture by the media coverage of the hostage situation in Iran. For over one year, Walter Cronkite ended each of his *CBS News* broadcasts by saying, "On the one hundred and ____ day of captivity, this is Walter Cronkite for the CBS Evening News bidding you goodnight."

Enter a man who acted like John Wayne and talked tough about hostages. After his acclaimed "performance" during the debate, Reagan went on to win the election. Many networks announced the defeat of President Carter before the polls closed on the West Coast. In retrospect political analysts now wonder if the media facilitated the landslide, as thousands of West Coast voters stayed away from the polls because of the early announcement.

After initially talking tough, Reagan secretly sold arms to the Iranian government. The Iranians were the prime supporters of the hostage takers in Lebanon. Yet Reagan remained popular. Reagan was truly the Teflon President. A poll during his administration indicated that most people did not agree with many of his policies but liked and trusted him as their leader.

According to Lou Cannon, biographer of Reagan, much of the Presidency had become more about perception than substance. In his book *President Reagan: The Role of a Lifetime,* Cannon argued that Reagan had become a "presidential performer." In fact, Reagan once told former NBC and ABC journalist David Brinkley that "There are times in this office when I've wondered how you could do the job if you hadn't been an actor."[9]

Reagan's performance made possible the Presidency of George W. Bush, for Bush had even less experience in government than did Reagan. The governorship of Texas is an essentially half-time job. Bush's job before the governorship was being a spokesman for the Texas Rangers baseball club. Much as Reagan was a spokesman for General Electric before running for governor, Bush's performance on television and the name recognition inherited from his father made him ripe for candidacy for governor—which served as the launch pad for the Presidency.

Media critic Marshall McLuhan predicted well before Reagan and Bush that the social climate would transform, making substance subordinate to image. He said, "Politics will eventually be replaced by imagery. The politician will be only too happy to abdicate in favor of his image, because the image will be much more powerful than he could ever be."[10]

Ross Perot garnered considerable initial attention and support. His appeal was possible because he did not have a clear public record to criticize. Indeed, Ross Perot led in the polls prior to the Republican and Democratic conventions in 1992 primarily because he was the least known candidate with the fewest known skeletons in his closet. He uttered cute little sound bites such as "It's time to clean out the barn." The public loved the idea of cleaning out the barn. He finally pulled out of the race, claiming that the "Republican attack machine" was poised to disrupt his daughter's wedding. Then just before the election, he decided to run again. He essentially did not allow the press time to produce detailed stories about him. His strategy paid off, because he received 19 percent of the vote.

The electorate has not only become politically illiterate and easily manipulated but also fickle. We want what we do not have, and as soon as we get it, we do not want it either. We want our leaders to be beyond human. As soon as a leader is found to be human and have faults, we toss that leader out like a throwaway cup.

RAW NERVES AND WEDGE POLITICS

Lee Atwater came to age working for Republican Senator Strom Thurman. He learned to use wedge politics and renamed the approach "value" politics. The issues of abortion, school prayer, and gun control galvanized and redefined Southern Republicans. By 1985 Atwater earned himself the position of Republican National Chairman.

Since government has become a high-priced media market, politicians have learned to strike raw nerves by appealing to one-issue voting blocks. These voting blocks have become the bread and butter for many politicians. The irony is that candidates can harvest voting blocks who in the not-too-distant past knew they had little in common with one another.

For example, the strange emergence of the Christian Coalition has been combined with the gun lobby and other right-wing groups. The Christian Coalition generally propose that school prayer be reintroduced and are often militantly anti-abortion or in favor of the "right to life." Interestingly, they are in an alliance with those who strongly advocate accelerating the legal processes leading up to the expansion of the death penalty. Somehow the Republican Party has been able to harvest this odd collection of voters.

The politically illiterate electorate is highly vulnerable to sound bites and slogans such as "You have the right to bear arms" and "Let's put prayer back in the schools."

Politicians have learned to galvanize voting blocks by using highly crafted, broad-based wedge issues that touch raw nerves. By performing with these ready-made scripts of sound bites, politicians can avoid an honest debate about the issues. When a raw nerve is touched by a well-crafted sound bite, few susceptible voters can resist the impulse to respond in the voting block.

For example, with much zeal, many Republicans exploited the sound bite that "big government" is bad and "small government" is good. Many voters now assume that big government is bad because it takes much of our hard-earned money through taxes to further itself with corruption and waste.

The Republican Party has built a bulk of their recent platform on the premise that all taxes are bad. Now that the existence of the Soviet Union is no longer available as a campaign issue, Republicans have combined the concerns of their largest constituency, voters in the high income brackets, and have carried the banner of less taxation and less government. Such political posturing is not hard to sell. The LCD-susceptible electorate craves the immediate gratification of a cut in taxes. Neither the news media nor many in the electorate have attempted to debate the potential long-term benefits of an investment into our infrastructure.

No one is pleased to see their gross earnings chipped away in taxes. Most people who pay income taxes by deduction from their paychecks have an opportunity to get detailed information on how much of each paycheck is withdrawn for taxes. The debate over taxes was fueled by revelations during the 1980s that we were financing thousand-dollar toilet seats and hundred-dollar nuts and bolts (charged to the government by large defense-oriented corporations). Yet for most people, the thought that there are people who do not work but receive payments from tax dollars is infuriating.

Though we as a society have debated intensely over welfare reform, corporations receive a much larger handout than do poor people. Corporate welfare amounts to $86 billion a year.[11] Corporate welfare includes $300,000 given to Disneyland to help improve its rocket show. IBM, General Motors, and General Electric received $268 million as part of the Department of Commerce's Advanced Technology Program. These same companies funneled $465,700 to Republicans and $154,000 to Democrats in soft money through third parties.

Corporate "aid" not only helps multinational corporations relocate jobs overseas; it also helps our burger companies sell Big Macs and Whoppers in Shanghai and Kuala Lumpur.

Meanwhile we have become less concerned with the fact that "big" corporations are taking over much of the media and having an alarming influence on government. We have acquired the simplistic frame of reference that "what is good for business is good for Amer-

ica." After the September 11, 2001, terrorist attacks, we were told
that buying was patriotic. Generally what is good for corporations
is a less effective government that would provide less oversight of
illegal activities.

Overall, the sanctity of business interests, the hype about big government, and the hype about taxes have contributed to what has
become a tax phobia. The dreaded "T" word—taxes—has come to
mean something terribly evil in our society. Never mind that taxes
are needed to pay for public education, pave the roads, repair the
bridges, and fund the police and fire departments, all of which everyone can agree are needed in a sane society. None of us seem to
think we are responsible to participate in paying for it all.

Many people continue to complain that their government does a
rotten job at what it does and should be smaller. From a positive
perspective, this position is part of the same political agenda:
namely, to promote a small, lean, and efficient government. Certainly, there will always be bureaucratic red tape to minimize, but
the only solution offered is to cut funding for programs. The government needs money to function, and money can only be raised
through taxes. What is needed is a thoughtful reform, not Draconian
cuts in funds that are called "reform."

Since the Reagan era, the term "liberal" has come to mean something akin to "communist." During the past several general elections,
Republicans have accused the Democrats of being liberal. In response to these visceral accusations, the Democrats have responded
with a flat-out denial.

During the 1988 Presidential election, President Bush accused
Governor Dukakis of not being patriotic. Within a week Dukakis
could be seen at election rallies surrounded by flags. As if to confirm
that he too was a patriot, he went to the extreme of being filmed
driving a tank because many have come to believe patriotism and
the military are two sides of the same coin. Dukakis only succeeded
in looking ridiculous. The tank episode was played over and over on
network programs as an example of the failure of the Dukakis
campaign.

President Bush went on to accuse Dukakis of being a card-
carrying member of the A.C.L.U. The symbolism was an effective
wedge position. Bush and his handlers realized that the term "card-
carrying" was last used during the late 1940s and early 1950s when

people were black-balled from society for being "card-carrying members of the communist party."

The use of the A.C.L.U. to call someone communist is ironic because the prime goal of this organization is to defend the constitution of the United States. The very fact that the Bush campaign was able to make use of these wedge issues illustrates how alienated patriotic Americans have become from the constitution to which they profess to swear their allegiance.

Subtle and not-so-subtle racism has also emerged in political advertising. The now infamous Willie Horton ad that the Bush campaign ran in 1988 tapped into this vast reservoir of racism. If Willie Horton were White and not Black, the ads would not have had as much punch. Later, in the hotly contested senatorial race in North Carolina, archconservative Senator Jesse Helms managed to turn the polls upside down two weeks before the election by playing on the LCD fears of Whites by running an ad depicting a White male who lost a job opportunity because of affirmative action.

In California, former Governor Pete Wilson held onto the governor's mansion by playing the race card. He campaigned against immigrants by promoting Proposition 187, which was designed to deny health care and education to the children of people who did not have proper immigration documentation. Few people asked whether denying services to these children would result in the loss of the opportunity to immunize them against carrying epidemic illnesses. Without immunization, they would be more apt to carry illnesses into public places where others come in contact with them. By denying these children education, we make them more vulnerable to becoming gang members and engaging in crime.

During his reelection campaign, Wilson saw a chance to tap into the same LCD raw nerve of racism and came out for another state proposition, this one against affirmative action. Wilson's effort was just the electoral boost he needed to survive an almost certain defeat.

But an actual debate about the ramifications of these propositions was not possible in the current environment of sound bites. Intelligent discussion has vanished in American politics. Television and the mass media have cultivated an emergence of LCD, regressive social attitudes. If a proponent of a political policy does not simplify an argument, the audience is likely to be offended and feel that the candidate is talking down to them. This is the kind of anti-intellectual tendency that Plato in Classical Greece and the framers of the American Constitution feared.

Ridiculing politicians who possess a great deal of education or intellectual capacity has also become commonplace. This is nothing new, but the trend is accelerating. For example, during the 1950s Presidential campaign, Adlai Stevenson was widely referred to as an egghead. As a result of this paradoxical label and the lack of a "hero" status, he was rejected for the presidency. In other words, people thought Stevenson was just too intelligent to be President. Eisenhower cruised to victory because he was a war hero. More recently, *U.S. News and World Report* ran a story titled "How Smart Do You Have to be to be President?"[12] The story was garnished with a picture of George W. Bush, who was reportedly referred to by his opponents as "George 'Dumbya' Bush." It is no wonder, therefore, that Bush (Jr.) took this one step further by bragging about his lack of intellectual vigor, noting that he was but a "C" student and complaining that his opponent was a thinker. Bush seemed to be saying that he meets the qualifications of the leader of the LCD society.

6
Lock and Load

My, my, such a lot of guns around and so few brains.
                    Humphrey Bogart in *The Big Sleep*

As we sleepwalk into the twenty-first century, we are far too often awakened to nightmares of gun violence. It has become increasingly commonplace to hear about a teenager who goes on a shooting rampage or someone "going postal." Are we in danger of growing numb to gun violence?

Every day, 13 children are shot to death in the United States. The same number of students were tragically gunned down in a single shooting at Columbine High School, Colorado. The Columbine tragedy got national attention for several days in contrast to many other killings that are referred to as "accidents" or "gang violence" or simply a murder of one child.

We lead the industrialized world in the rate at which children die as a result of gun violence. Americans murder each other with guns at a rate 19 times higher than the average of 25 of the richest nations. Overall, we lose an average of 87 people a day, or 32,935 annually, due to guns. According to a study reported in the *Journal of the American Medical Association*, gun violence costs $2.3 billion a year in medical treatment, almost half of which is paid for with taxpayer money.[1] Soon gun violence will be the leading cause of non-natural death in the United States.

We are drifting into the belief that gun violence is just a fact of life for which we need to arm ourselves. Not only have we grown to believe our country is a dangerous place, but we have convinced people abroad that when they come to the United States they put their lives at risk. Gun rentals to foreign tourists have risen in recent years.[2] The United States has become a country at war with itself.

ARMED TO THE TEETH

It has been estimated that there are approximately 192 million privately owned guns in the United States. The population is 270 million. In just a matter of years there will be as many guns as people.

From the time of the Revolutionary War in the late 1770s until 1850, approximately one-tenth of the population were gun owners. Now it is estimated that one-third of the population owns a gun. An FBI report indicates that between 1973 and 1993, more than 40 million handguns were produced in the United States, three times as many as were in existence between 1900 and 1993.[3] Gun sales in California went up 30 percent from 1998 to 1999.[4] Criminologist J. J. Mahoney has stressed:

The gun problem is not only the problem of guns, but the rapid proliferation of guns in a society far different than it was as recently as the 1950s. Back then a common handgun was a six shot revolver loaded with a lead bullet. Now, high-capacity semi-automatics are the norm (10 to 14 rounds is common), often loaded with a variety of hollow-point, or even frangible bullets (bullets that shatter into many pieces upon entering the body).[5]

Guns are available at gun stores, gun shows, and over the Internet and are sold privately. Guns sold over the Internet do not involve rigorous background checks such as those dictated by the Brady Bill. This law requires a waiting period for people wishing to purchase guns at gun stores. However, numerous teenagers across the country bought guns without delay.

Until just recently, the Great American Gun Show in Los Angeles County offered one of the biggest gun sales extravaganzas in the world. That massive supermarket of firearms, ammunition, body armor, and survivalist gear took place four times a year on publicly owned property at fairgrounds and convention centers. Surveillance by federal undercover investigators revealed that the gun show has also served as a market for illegal machine guns and assault weapons.[6] Only after considerable adverse press did Los Angeles County officials rethink their wholesale carte blanch to the gun show.

According to officials at the Federal Bureau of Alcohol, Tobacco, and Firearms (ATF), gun shows are often a favored means through which would-be assassins obtain their weapons of mass destruction. The Great American Gun Show was the site where the weapons were bought prior to the now infamous North Hollywood Shootout.

We are a society armed to the teeth. Even those who were widely assumed to be above the gun obsession have been caught with large caches of weapons. A Philadelphia psychiatrist legally amassed 287 assault rifles, shotguns, and pistols.[7] His collection included 29 AK-47s and 150 semiautomatic pistols.

EDDIE EAGLE

The National Rifle Association (NRA) placed an ad in the August 1997 edition of the *American Guardian* saying, "You already belong to the NRA, but what about your children? Did you know the NRA offers membership to them?"[8] Later the following spring they ran an ad showing then NRA president Marion Hammer with her grandson. The ad quoted her as saying, "The future of shooting sports will rest on the shoulders of our grandchildren and theirs. That's why, as NRA President, my major priorities are to reach out to American youth and to assure NRA's mission continues beyond the next 125 years."[9] At the NRA's annual meeting in Dallas in 1996, Hammer said, "It will be an old-fashioned wrestling match for the hearts and minds of our children."[10]

Just as cigarette manufacturers have actively tried to seduce children with Joe Camel, the NRA tries to prime the pump for new members with their gun-safety mascot "Eddie Eagle." Joe Sugarman, executive editor of the Violence Policy Center, noted that "Eddie Eagle is Joe Camel with feathers. . . . He is, in fact, a gun industry salesman in the front lines of efforts to create a youth gun culture."[11]

The NRA is quite open about the advertising utility of Eddie Eagle. At the 1998 convention in Philadelphia, official NRA products such as NRA bibs, infant sleepwear, and children's backpacks featured the picture of Eddie Eagle.

The NRA has also managed a legislative coup. Eddie Eagle has been selected by Oregon's legislature as the official mascot of the state's own gun-safety program. Certainly gun safety is important, but the Oregon legislature allowed a Trojan horse to enter their state government. Given that Eddie Eagle is essentially an advertising icon for the NRA, the state of Oregon now provides free advertising and a state endorsement.

So too do gun manufacturers use a variety of techniques to subtly and not so subtly try to convince people of all ages that guns are family-friendly toys. For example, in the 1989 Guns and Ammo

Handgun Annual Report, there was a picture of a teenage boy lining up the sights of an AP9 assault pistol. The caption reassures that "the gun was also easy to control, even when fired as a pistol, and young shooters . . . had no difficulty in shooting and handling the AP9."[12]

The October 1996 issue of *Machine Gun News* shows a boy in his early teens hunkered down behind a World War I vintage Browning machine gun. The caption reads, "For the first time."[13] The back cover of the 1990 edition of *Machine Gun News* offers an ad for Fleming Firearms titled "Short Butts from Fleming Firearms." The picture shows a two-year-old girl beaming while cradling an automatic pistol.[14]

In the December 1997 issue of *Gun World,* there is a picture of a father and his pre-kindergarten son, clad in matching camouflage outfits. A shotgun lies across the child's lap. The caption uses a biblical quote: "And a child shall come to lead them."[15]

Most gun advocates argue that owning a gun is their right, and some even argue it is their "God-given right." The fusion of theology and gun ownership represents a shift in the consciousness of our society. In the emerging LCD society, theology, interpersonal relationships, and our understanding of the Constitution have been turned upside down.

SELECTIVE INTERPRETATION

Gun-control opponents are fond of citing their "Constitutional rights" as justification for gun ownership. They tout the Second Amendment to the Bill of Rights, which states, "A well-regulated militia, being necessary to the security of a free state, the right of the people to keep and bear arms, should not be infringed."

The founders knew quite well that without a citizenry that possessed arms, the new country could be conquered by the British or some other colonial power. Thus the Second Amendment was written explicitly and exclusively to ensure the defense of the state from the potential reemergence of a tyrannical government. It was not written to ensure that people could own handguns to "protect" themselves from each other.

Some people even have bumper stickers that read, "This car is protected by Smith & Wesson." Gun advocates cite a study performed by Gary Kleck of Florida State University at Tallahassee as proof that our citizens actually protect themselves when they use guns.[16] He conducted a random telephone survey of 4,978 households and extrapolated from his results that 2.5 million Americans use firearms each year to defend themselves against criminals.

However, Mahoney has reevaluated this claim by using an FBI report and found that rather than 2.5 million, only 82,000 people have used a gun to defend themselves.[17] Further, 21,000 of these people were nonfatally wounded in the armed "defense." The conclusion of a 1986 study is that a gun owner is 43 times more likely to kill a family member than an intruder.[18] Many people who use a gun to protect themselves actually make the situation worse, as they eventually spark a shootout.

Mahoney has retold a story of a sobering example of how easily protecting yourself with a gun can turn deadly. Even a trained professional who knows quite well how to use a gun can encounter a situation that might result in self-destruction.

FBI agent Stanley Ronquest, 52, was talking to a woman he'd met at a bar in downtown Kansas City. The woman then drove Ronquest to his hotel. As Ronquest talked to the woman outside of his hotel, Richard L. Primm, a convicted felon was celebrating his 38th birthday, and looking for money to celebrate with, pressed a stick into Ronquest's back, pretending it was a gun, and announced a holdup.

Ronquest went for his gun, and Primm wrestled the .38 revolver away from Ronquest and shot him to death.

Primm, an ex-convict, could not legally own a firearm and he didn't have one. He had a stick. Ronquest, a 21-year veteran of the FBI, had a pistol. The ex-con simply took the pistol away from the FBI agent and killed him.[19]

Despite a highly questionable reliance on the Second Amendment and rationalization about self-defense, the NRA and other pro-gun groups have poured millions of dollars into the defeat of any form of gun-control legislation. The NRA donated $1.6 million in PAC contributions to candidates in the 1998 political cycle. They spent $2.25 million on lobbying in 1998. In 1999 the NRA spent $1.5 million during a four-week period to dismantle the Senate version of gun-control legislation.[20] Between 1991 and 1998, the NRA gave almost $9 million to candidates, parties, and PACS. In contrast, the largest pro-gun-control lobby group, Handgun Control, Inc., spent $146,000 during the same period.[21]

Following the 1999 season of gun-related violence, Congress took up the issue of background checks. The NRA and other pro-gun groups spent an average of $10,500 per Senator on those who eventually voted against the effort to close the background-check loophole. In contrast, Senators who voted for the measure received close to $300 from pro-gun control groups.[22] During the 2000 Presidential campaign, officials of the NRA boasted that if Bush were elected they would have an office in the White House. Their investment in Bush has paid off. In 2002, the president of the NRA boasted that they made Bush's election possible.

The NRA has maintained and apparently convinced Congress to echo their rationalization that if law-abiding citizens were prohibited from having guns, only criminals would have them. Many pro-gun proponents drive with an LCD bumper sticker reading "Guns don't kill people, people kill people." But the belief that all we have to do is prosecute people who use guns illegally is riddled with unrealistic assumptions. Yes, it is true that guns alone do not kill people. The fact is, *people with guns* kill people.

Even though the NRA has argued against virtually every gun-control law that was ever enacted, they often take the position that "We shouldn't pass new gun laws but rather enforce those that we have on the books already." This is precisely the policy of the Bush administration. However, many of the existing gun-control laws amount to placing a Band-Aid on a gaping wound. Though guns sold by licensed gun dealers are partially controlled, a criminal or would-be criminal need only to send a friend or family member to buy a gun and thereby evade the background checks. According to the ATF, during 1998 alone, 200,000 guns used in crimes were traced to "straw parties" who purchased the gun on behalf of the criminal.[23] Also, there is no federal legislation regulating the resale of guns. This is often referred to as the "great gun loophole." And what about stolen guns? The National Information Computer Center system contains information on two million stolen guns, of which 60 percent are handguns.[24] By mid 2001, reports of gun sales through venders regulated by background checks had gone down. Gun shows, private sales, stolen guns, and Internet sales provide a gaping loophole.

GUNS AND RAGE

Over the past 20 years, some people who are walking time bombs have gravitated toward a fascination with automatic weapons and assault rifles. These guns are designed with one purpose in mind, to kill as many people as possible before the shooter is in danger. They are ideal for drive-by shootings or spraying bullets into a crowd of people to kill indiscriminately. In other words, assassins can kill people they had not intended to kill, assuming they had in mind specific people in the first place.

The turn of the century was marked by a horrific epidemic of people opening fire in crowded buildings. Some of these gruesome massacres were performed by children at their schools.

Following each killing, there is a brief and superficial debate about what might be causing children to go on the rampage. Legislatures debate the merits of trying children as adults, the NRA takes the position that it is not guns that are a problem but the people who use them, and the fury dies out until the next carnage.

In 1999, in an attempt to appear to do something about gun violence in our schools, President Clinton ordered a million-dollar study of whether media violence contributes to the problem. Most analysts are quite aware of the towering mountain of data from studies showing that violence in the media is, in fact, one of the contributors to violence in the community. But Clinton needed a way to put pressure on the movie industry without forcing any changes. For their part, movie and television executives postured in defense, with some calling the probe a witch hunt.

Meanwhile, more than 6,000 students were expelled from schools in the United States for bringing guns to school. Government officials were proud to report that the number actually decreased in 1999 from the number of students caught in 1998. Yet they did not report that many schools have installed metal detectors and hired security guards.

Some schools have come to resemble high-security camps. Because of the gun violence in schools, some administrators have installed metal detectors and surveillance cameras and hired armed guards. Public address systems are used to announce security advice. One school principal in Chicago reports that now "They know that if I come on the P.A. and say, 'We're in lockdown situation' . . . to clear the hallway and get down on the floor."[25]

The NRA is partially right in maintaining that we should look at the people who use guns because it is not guns alone that are the problem. When Timothy McVeigh blew up the Federal Office Building in Oklahoma City, killing 180 people, he was armed with home-made bombs, hate, and paranoia—not guns.

Timothy McVeigh had seen a movie titled *Blown Away* about a terrorist who evades the bomb squad before he has performed his own bombing. Also, McVeigh timed his bombing to coincide with the second anniversary of the government's ill-advised attack in Waco, Texas, on the Branch Davidians and on the same day that Richard Snell, a leading figure for a number of far-right groups, was executed for murder.

On August 10, 1999, an avowed racist named Buford Furrow Jr. opened fire with his Uzi semiautomatic and Glock 9 mm handgun at a Jewish Community Center, spraying 70 rounds and wounding several children. On his run from the crime scene, he shot and killed a Filipino American postal worker. When finally apprehended, Furrow wore a smile on his face and commented to the police officers escorting him that he was pleased with all the media attention. He claimed he thought his attack would induce others to rise up against Jews across the country.

The day the Columbine High School students returned for their 1999–2000 school year, three swastikas were found etched on school buildings. Though racism has been around for a long time, what makes it more frightening today is that it can erupt into a violent rampage.

More important still is that all the factors that have led up to many of these rampages are now endemic to our LCD society. The assassins are playing out expressions of violence almost as if they are on automatic pilot.

Indeed, the teenage shooter from Jonesboro, Arkansas, who killed five schoolmates wrote a friend from detention that he "was not mad at anyone. I was honestly happy. I had a very loving family." He added that things are not all that bad in captivity; in fact, he gets to watch Jerry Springer, eat fast food, and listen to his favorite rap song, "Shoot 'Em Up" by Bone Thugs-N-Harmony.[26]

We must, therefore, understand the epidemic of gun violence in context. We have now entered the twenty-first century loaded to the teeth with a mix of guns, hate, and a media drenched in violent images. Thousands of murders are shown on television and in motion pictures. By the time the average child in the United States turns 18, he or she has seen 40,000 dramatized murders and 400,000 acts of violence on television or in the movies. Many children also play video games and computer games replete with gratuitous violence.

After the Columbine shootings, Hollywood executives braced for the government reaction. Many decided to weather the brief political storm. One director told the Writers Guild conference, "They are sanitizing violence. . . . They are afraid of what the kids are going to do, but not what the government is going to do?"[27] The storm has passed until the next eruption of gun violence. But perhaps we are growing numb.

Meanwhile, movies remain infused with gratuitous violence. Trailers for movies are often designed to entice an adolescent audience. One moviemaker noted, "The objective of nearly every trailer is to get teenage boy's butts into seats . . . and that means going for as much violence and sex as you can jam into 2 1/2 minutes." One trailer-maker noted that "Littleton hasn't taken away from my cutting style. I'm still hearing, 'That's a great cut but it could use more guns, more pain!'"[28]

Movies serve as an advertising medium for the gun industry. The Smith & Wesson Model 29.44 Magnum was not especially popular before Clint Eastwood played Dirty Harry. After the series, sales of the Model 29 exploded.[29] In fact, many gun makers make their products available at low cost to Hollywood prop houses, which oblige by putting them on camera.

Psychiatrist Robert Jay Lifton has referred to our society as a "gunocracy." He noted that the gun has become a sacred object revered by many as the essence of American life. In the gunocracy, guns represent an icon of "freedom and power." According to Lifton the gun has "filled much of the psychological vacuum created by the absence of a traditional American culture."[30]

Guns are used in 60 percent of suicides in the United States. For teenagers younger than age 16, there is a 30-percent increased risk for suicide if there is a gun in the home. Presumably these guns were kept in the home for "protection."[31]

The explosion of gun ownership throughout the country reflects regression to an Old West mentality. Today if someone cuts you off on the road, it is advisable not to honk your horn. The other driver could easily pull a gun from the glove box for "protection."

For those overwhelmed with feelings of alienation and hate, they can express their rage in ways only imaginable in our nightmares or seen on television or played out on our computers. We can now, therefore, rephrase the bumper sticker "It is not guns that kill people" to "Guns + Alienation + Violent Movies + Shoot 'em up computer games = Rampage."

7
The Bottom of the Barrel

We are born princes and the civilizing process makes us frogs.
                                                    Eric Bern

In recent years, people who were once marginal have been coming out of the woodwork. These people have carried their bottom-of-the-barrel interests into the general society and in some cases have become respectable. A half-century ago these people would have existed only at the margins of society. Today, however, with the mass gravitation toward the LCD society, the range of possible points of view has shrunk and moved toward the right of the political spectrum.

Though there have always been fringe groups such as militias, radical religious groups, and cults, they have grown less marginalized in recent years. We now hear about them with regularity, discussing the merits or demerits of their views on talk radio and as standard fare on the evening news. The Waco and Ruby Ridge stand-offs became battle cries for the militias. Children armed with guns and explosives massacred 13 fellow students in Littleton, Colorado, on Hitler's birthday. Timothy McVeigh blew up the Federal Office Building in Oklahoma City on the anniversary of the Waco fiasco.

McVeigh received favorable coverage in a *Newsweek* article. His interview gave an opportunity to legitimize his cause. According to the interviewer, "McVeigh looked a lot more like a typical Gen-Xer than a deranged loner, much less a terrorist."[1]

DRAGGING LOW WITH THE BARELY CONSCIOUS

During the past 15 years, talk radio has exploded over the radio waves. This modality has been referred to as "shock radio" because it highlights extremist and inflammatory viewpoints. A cast of flamboyant characters including Rush Limbaugh, G. Gordon Liddy, Oliver North, and Howard Stern provide a vehicle for those of like mind to cultivate bigotry and paranoia. They stir up blind anger toward people not of the same class or race and disguised as patriotism. All these shock jocks have built their careers around marketing crudeness and have profited from doing it.

Oliver North made a notorious name for himself because of his performance in the Iran Contra Hearings. He said of trading arms for hostages and using the profits to fund terrorists in Nicaragua, "I thought it was a pretty neat idea." After his near-successful run for Senate in Virginia, he has made a handsome living as a radio talk show host.

Rush Limbaugh (before and after his hearing loss) cultivated primitive emotions with an audience estimated as large as 20 million on 643 radio stations, including Armed Forces Radio. Limbaugh became a conservative hit with comments such as "Feminism was established so that unattractive, ugly broads could have easy access to the mainstream" and "The poor in this country are the biggest piglets at the mother pig and her nipples."[2]

Howard Stern is often misjudged to be a liberal, probably because he has long hair. However, he has strong beliefs in conservative and libertarian themes. He, like the others, banters sexist and periodically racist comments. Stern and Jerry Springer have late-night television programs that push the limits of censorship. Stern often features scantily clothed women who talk about taking off their clothes as men tease them about the size of their breasts. Springer features couples who in their off-screen lives engage in kinky sex or prostitution and then argue about their relationships on the show.

Radio shock jocks such as G. Gordon Liddy and Rush Limbaugh exploit an increasingly frustrated cluster of people who fear the loss of their power in society. Those listening to these inflamed shows need a fix of anger and distortion to jar them out of the psychic numbness of the meltdown in our society. Unfortunately, the fix results not in an awakening but in a nightmare.

They believe that the government is some kind of foreign entity that threatens our freedom. Across the country, militias have been formed that use this government phobia as one of their prime reasons for existence. In these extreme cases, we see largely White, uneducated men dressed in fatigues, accumulating automatic weapons and preparing for the day when the government will come and take their freedom away. They often cite Ruby Ridge and Waco as evidence of the government's diabolical intentions. Occasionally, an incident such as the Oklahoma City bombing erupts from this primitive stratum of our society.

Many of these people are ardent opponents of the Brady Bill. Politically powerful lobby groups such as the NRA share their position on guns. The NRA distributed a fund-raising letter that referred to federal law enforcement officers as "jack booted government thugs" in an ironic reference to Nazis. Even George Bush Sr., once "a card-carrying member of the NRA," had to renounce his membership. But with the ascent of Bush Jr. into the Presidency, we hear again of the necessity to protect the rights of gun owners. It is no wonder that the president of the NRA claimed they helped him gain office.

The rising spectacle of militia groups across the country provides paranoid fringe groups with an opportunity to share their nightmares with the nation. Often these groups are composed of White, uneducated males who feel inadequate in the rapidly changing economy. Membership in the militias gives them a chance to feel the power of self-righteousness instead of feeling powerless.

A novel by William Pierce titled *The Turner Diaries* has become a favorite among members of racist groups. The book tells about a revolutionary martyr who helps overthrow the "Zionist-controlled" American government and exterminate all non-Whites. The destruction of most of the world's population is achieved by a "nuclear cleansing." Oklahoma City bomber Timothy McVeigh was known to have been influenced by *The Turner Diaries*.

One White-Supremacist group took its name, the "Order," from *The Turner Diaries*. Robert Matthews, founder of the group, is regarded as having been martyred and is now revered by other racist groups. William Furrow, the gunner at the Jewish Community Center in Los Angeles, married Matthews's widow.

The two teenagers who gunned down their classmates in Littleton, Colorado, in April of 1999 absorbed many of these extremist attributes. Eric Harris and Dylan Klebold were like so many other teenage assassins over the past few years. They felt shunned and humiliated by the popular kids on campus, most notably the jocks. Less than two years earlier, the two boys had been members of the Boy Scouts and played fantasy baseball. Then, in the year before their rampage, they expressed their angst through an obsession with guns, violent computer games, and Nazi garb.

Harris and Klebold formed the "Trench Coat Mafia" and were fond of addressing each other in German and at times giving the "Heil Hitler" salute. They were also interested in the beliefs and fashions of the racist skinheads. They adorned their trench coats with swastikas and wore steel boots (for maximum damage in a fight) with red shoelaces symbolizing the "master race."

One year before the massacre, Harris and Klebold made a video that was essentially a dress rehearsal, in which they hunted down their friends to simulate a mass murder. Then on the day of the massacre, they gunned down their fellow students, just as they had rehearsed. They were armed with a semiautomatic pistol, a carbine, and two sawed-off shotguns.

They asked one girl if she believed in God. After she responded that she did, they shot her execution-style. Before they shot themselves, they laid out 30 pipe bombs and other explosive devices.

This tragic scene has been played out many times in schools from Kentucky to Texas, Arkansas to Oregon. As societal LCD rage leaches up from the bottom of the barrel, the combination of guns, racism, and bigotry plagues our society as a whole.

A CULTURE OF ADOLESCENCE

Racism, bigotry, violence, and mayhem are not the only symptoms of the LCD society. Examining trends in humor can reveal many insights into the psychological health of a society. We can surmise that the more complicated or subtle the humor, the more sophisticated the culture. This premise is based on the concept that what people find humorous lies on the borders of psychological comfort areas.

A glance at comedies on television reveals an erosion of our sophistication in humor over the past 30 years. Clear racial stereotype humor, sexual jokes, and even poop jokes have emerged as commonplace.

One way to examine humor is from a developmental perspective. In other words, if we examine how people at varied aged groups respond to humor and compare these attitudes to the humor most popular in our society, we find an alarming trend.

The humor most appealing to preschool children often involves poop, bathrooms, and underwear jokes. In recent years, a rash of cartoon and late-night comedy programs have featured this type of humor. Adolescents respond to put-down jokes and humor involving sexual connotations. Many of the most popular motion picture comedies coming out of Hollywood involve humor of this type.

Motion pictures such as *Dumb and Dumber* and television programs such as *Ren and Stimpy, South Park,* and *Beavis and Butthead* are cultural expressions of the day. The motion picture *There's Something About Mary* features the main character with semen hanging from his ear. Mary grabs the semen and uses it as hair gel. Twenty to thirty years ago, base humor such as this was only on the margins of society. Even the Three Stooges of the 1930s and 1940s refrained from comments about semen, farting, and vomit.

The collective deterioration of humor illustrates that we have plunged to a pre-adult level of psychological development as a common denominator. Producers of entertainment have to go to the LCD to yield a profitable return for their investments.

The extension of adolescence also reflects how poorly our society trains people to be independent. Children have become superfluous to the economy other than as consumers. A child on a farm prior to the Great Depression knew he was vital to his family's survival. Today adolescents look at the world around them and suspect that consumer society is only intent on selling them products. When they grow into adulthood, they convert the suspiciousness into cynicism.

Adults are increasingly having a difficult time shaking this attitude. Children as young as eight are being taught by television sitcoms to be disrespectful toward their parents and cynical about life. Instilling distrust of a child's parents tears at the family structure. If this trend continues, the long-term consequences of lack of respect for authority figures and cynicism about life will undermine the fabric of society.

Many factors contribute to the public rancor and cynicism. These include a general sense of political malaise resulting from major government scandals such as Watergate, the Arms for Hostages/Iran-Contra Deal, and the Impeachment of President Clinton because he lied about his affair. Civility is a social trait long since eroded away by exaggerated rancor and public discontent.

The culture of cynicism emerging in recent years is also a byproduct of the psychological reaction to stress, chronic fatigue, and commercial overstimulation. As our culture melts down into a cynical LCD, many people find it much easier to communicate in negatives than in positives, to poke fun at what we dislike rather than focusing on what we like.

Though apparent throughout history, sarcasm and cynicism as humor have proliferated in recent years. This sarcasm and cynicism is not only expressed by our comedians but also is becoming endemic in our news media. Reporters express themselves in a style that is common to the society at large. Reporters often close a positive story with the sarcastic spin, "It will remain to be seen if this can continue."

When a scandal splashes across the front pages of newspapers, talk show hosts sarcastically comment on that scandal with vulgarity. During the impeachment investigation of Clinton's affair with Monica Lewinsky, David Letterman and Jay Leno almost nightly started their monologues with a few Monica Lewinsky jokes that highlighted her sexual skills, only to move on to jokes about President Clinton's zipper. Now they have President Bush's lack of intellectual skill to ridicule. However, the degree to which they actually joke about his intellectual limitations is tempered by the fear that they will be also poking fun at the audience.

Meanwhile, rancor has increased in the legal system. There has been an explosion of litigation over the past 20 years. As a barometer of the level of legal discord, lawyer jokes have led the way in sarcastic humor. The jokes themselves reveal what little insight we have developed about ourselves. For example, "What are three reasons lawyers are used by researchers more than white rats? Answer: 1) They breed faster. 2) You don't grow as attached to them. And, 3) There are some things white rats won't do." Although there are elements of truth in these answers, people in the LCD society employ them to represent them.

During the 1980s we witnessed a dramatic shift toward "looking out for number one." Our society lost its community focus, turning toward greed and personal needs against the benefit of the many. The wave of social narcissism that took over in the 1980s neutralized the social idealism of the preceding two decades. Now the word "liberal" has come to mean something the masses do not want to be. Most people have come to believe that making a fortune at the expense of others is "getting ahead." Ethics and social responsibility do not factor into this equation.

The narcissism of the 1980s became the management attitude of corporations in the late 1990s and early 2000s. "Downsizing" became a buzzword for the corporate world. With downsizing we see an effort to cut corners to increase profits. As a result, there is a corresponding decrease in the quality of services.[3] Meanwhile the corporate culture has provided itself camouflage for its excessive concern with the profit margin. Terms such as "partnering" and "leveraging" have been brought into the dialog but only provide window dressing for the hidden dynamics of winners and losers.

The social narcissism marked by such legislative proposals as English-only laws or black-balling of particular immigrant groups polarizes our society. Not only is racism still alive, but there is a resurgence of it. However, the United States is a country of immigrants. With fewer Anglo immigrants coming into the country, English—or for that matter, Northern European—immigrants are now in the minority. The wide diversity of ethnic groups converging in the same country is an opportunity to gain the best of all cultures. Instead, we appear to be throwing away this opportunity into the depths of old LCD fears and bigotry.

In the emerging LCD society, what you wear and drive are more important than what you think. Adolescents are overly concerned with style and posturing and have not developed a sophisticated ability for reflective insight. They focus on primitive black-and-white viewpoints. Adolescents center their comments on "I like" and "I hate." They are notorious for their rebellious attitudes. Their developmental challenge is to learn to differentiate themselves from their parents as individuals and develop a sense of identity. They consider their parents incapable of understanding their plight. They often talk about their hometown as one that is never good enough, saying they "can't wait to become old enough to get out of this place." Carried into adulthood, this attitude has infected our media, our politics, and even our relationships.

We are losing our ability to fully appreciate the full complexity of life and see beyond the black and white—good and bad. We need to move beyond the concepts of in-groups and out-groups that are usually assigned sound-bite labels such as conservative and liberal. To see shades of gray is the main task of moving beyond adolescence into adulthood, but many people never move out of the adolescent developmental phase. "I like" and "I hate" leave nothing in the middle. We do not love or hate everything, yet there is an ever-increasing trend toward thinking in black-and-white frames of reference. We focus on winning the Superbowl, the World Series, or a gold medal. Not winning is thought of as a failure. The morally righteous win and the sinners lose. What the winners win is the right to accumulate massive amounts of material possessions. But as we shall see in the next chapter, heightened materialism has not brought us happiness.

8
Shopping and Dropping

There is so much plastic in this world that vinyl leopard skin is becoming an endangered synthetic.

Lily Tomlin

Popular bumper stickers seen in suburbia today read "Shop until you drop," "This car stops at all malls," and "I'd rather be at Nordstroms." Together these bumper stickers reflect a rapidly emerging belief: "buy more—feel better." After the September 11, 2001, terrorist attack, shopping was touted as a patriotic duty.

Never before in the history of the world has consumerism reached the extreme it has in the United States. Buying and selling not only bind our economic system, but Americans have grown to overidentify with what they buy. It is not uncommon to hear someone say, "I'm a Chevy sort of guy."

The major corporations pay close attention to the buying habits of American consumers. Millions of dollars are spent by corporations researching and trying to convince potential consumers to buy their products. Corporate manipulation of the American mind has forever changed the landscape of our culture. We have become more oriented toward identifying ourselves by what we buy than by what we think. And now during the early years of a new century, our thoughts are increasingly dictated by the products we buy.

SKIPPING THE WATER OF CONSUMERISM

As a society, we have legitimized the belief that excessive material gratification is healthy and have simultaneously lost a sense of rootedness with our families, subcultures, and ethnicity. In the place of the secure sense of rootedness, we numb ourselves with the immediate gratification of buying products we do not need.

The initial concept of Christmas has long since eroded in the LCD of commercialism. After the family drifted away from being the center of the world for most Americans, gift-giving at Christmas reflected a compensatory effort to bind the loosening ties. Christmas became Xmas. There is little evidence that Christmas still represents humility and compassion.

The LCD society is deluged with ads and television news stories about the latest gizmos and toys people are craving or told to crave. Preceding Christmas, local newscasters say, "Well, it's 20 more days until Christmas and have you done your shopping yet?"

Many recent news stories have highlighted what days are the busiest shopping days before Christmas. The shopping traffic is described much like weather patterns. A reporter might begin a story by saying, "Our Eyewitness News van had to be double-parked at the Sunsearch Mall today because there were no parking slots left."

Reporters try to interview shoppers to gain a human-interest touch. The shopper is asked, "Were you able to find everything you wanted?" The interviewee might respond, "No! Here it is one month before Christmas and the stores are jammed and all I was hoping to buy is already gone!" If the reporter presses on and asks what the shopper had hoped to buy, the response could be, "My son saw the Jumping Jo Jo GI Commando ad on TV, and he decided that he simply had to have it. Oh, he is going to be so disappointed because I couldn't find one and all his friends will have one. I'm so depressed!" A woman requested a crisis appointment at the Department of Psychiatry where I work because she had a panic attack after not being able to find a Beanie Baby at the toy store for a Xmas present.

Some people have become so seriously addicted to shopping that they sink into major debt. Thousands of people have become overdrawn on their credit cards and forced to declare bankruptcy. Personal bankruptcy filings have climbed steadily since 1980.[1] Meanwhile, millions of credit card applications are sent out like junk mail to would-be consumers. I receive at least one credit card application a week, and I'm sure that I am not out of the norm. Even my twelve-year-old son received an application.

The rate of personal savings has plummeted in the past few decades. The average annual percentage of dispensable personal income was 5.6 percent in 1975 and fell to 1 percent in early 2001.[2]

Not long ago I was served in a restaurant by someone who confessed that being a waiter was his third job. He worked 40 + hours a week at his first job and drove three hours in commuter traffic. When I asked why he worked so much, he did *not* say "I'm having a hard time making ends meet." To my astonishment, he said, "When I come home and look at all the things I've bought for my family, I feel real good!" I asked him what he did to relax, and he responded, "Washing my car twice a week—it's my time—I take great pride in my car!"

Many people have grown to believe they "deserve" to gratify themselves by buying material goods. I have even heard therapists reinforce this consumption frenzy by saying, "Oh good! You are taking care of yourself."

According to a University of Michigan study, most people cite increased wealth as the primary means to happiness. Yet studies assessing the effects of winning the lottery indicate no corresponding increase in happiness. Studies measuring citizens in countries with a high GNP indicate that such citizens are actually more depressed than people in countries with a mid-range GNP. Children of upper-middle-class parents in the United States were found to be more depressed than children of lower-middle-class parents.[3] In short, happiness declines as prosperity increases. Wealth orients people toward a primary focus on material possessions. Perhaps this is what Jesus meant when he said, "It is easier for a camel to go through the eye of a needle than it is for a rich man to enter the Kingdom of Heaven."

BROUGHT TO YOU BUY:

The LCD society is saturated with corporate advertising. When we go to a sports event, watch television, or even drive down the highway, we are bombarded by advertisements. Children wear tee shirts with large designs advertising what company made the shirt. Many shirts and jackets worn by latency-aged children (ages 7 to 12) are walking advertisements. It is extremely common to see jackets or sweatshirts with bold letters plastered on their backs saying "Levi" or "Bugle Boy." No one bats an eye; it is all considered a natural part of the environment.

The amount of money spent on advertising mushroomed during the latter half of the twentieth century. In 1950 American companies spent $5.7 billion on advertising; by 1960 that figure doubled and then almost doubled again by 1970. By 1986 the figure spiraled to $100 billion and then rose to $187 billion in 1997 (see Figure 8.1).[4]

According to the *Wall Street Journal*, brand-name products dominate the retail economy. Companies such as Coca Cola, Pepsi, General Mills, Folgers, and Crest dwarf their competitors in sales. The *Wall Street Journal* put it like this: "The American consumer's heart still belongs to big-name brands. While people are buying more store brands in some categories, private-label merchandise accounts for only about 14 percent of the total packaged-goods sales in food, drug, and mass-merchandise stores."[4]

As early as the 1950s, advertisers were researching how companies can influence customers by tapping into their "hidden persuaders" and motivational "subsurface desires."[6,7] Louis Cheskin had explored how color can influence the buying habits of potential customers.[5]

Twenty years later, advertising researchers were exploring the degree to which commercials affect brain-wave patterns.[6] By the 1980s, marketing researchers began to explore how potential customers embody specific life styles that could be targeted with ads. Now marketers have begun to sell databases of membership and subscription lists to one another that enable companies to target customers with ad mail.

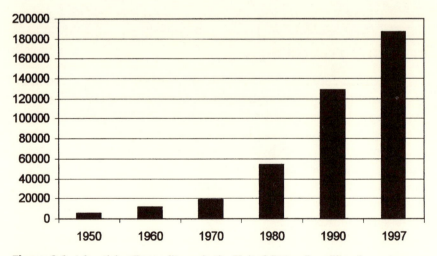

Figure 8.1 Advertising Expenditures in the United States (in millions)
Source: 1999 Wall Street Journal Almanac, p. 210.

The number of commercials shown on television varies with the time of the day. The average number of commercials during prime time is 37; during daytime television, that number shoots up to 50.[10] Producers realize that the majority of people who watch daytime television are women who buy the majority of products for the house.

Marketing consultants have especially targeted children ages 4 to 12, most of whom watch television in the late afternoon. More than half a million dollars a year is spent on advertisements for children. It has been estimated that the average child sees 20,000 thirty-second commercials a year. By adolescence they will have seen 200,000. Children have a sales potential of $9 billion of their own money and influence $130 billion of their parents' purchases annually.[11]

Many studies suggest that children younger than seven do not understand that the advertisements they see on television are directed toward trying to convince them to want the products. Adolescents, however, are more suspicious. Advertisers have learned that if they bind their product to the image of a sports or entertainment star, sales increase. For example, sports stars such as Michael Jordan, Tiger Woods, and Dennis Rodman and actors such as Jerry Seinfeld and Paul Reiser provide endorsements from telephone service to soft drinks. This practice has resulted in millions of dollars spent by consumers.

The binding of corporate products and entertainment figures creates an increasingly seamless boundary between products and entertainment. Indeed, many entertainment figures have become icons for products. When seen in their roles as entertainers, these figures carry with them the association to a particular product. For example, when Candice Bergman is seen on her television show, she represents a subliminal association with Sprint. Thus, when viewers of her television show receive comic relief after a hard day at work, they also develop a positive view of Sprint. Similarly, when Dick Clark hosts the New Year's Special every year, he carries with him an association to the Publisher's Clearing House contest. Viewers of the New Year's Special are vulnerable to the binding of their hopes for a prosperous new year and signing up for the Publisher's Clearing House contest. Signing up for the multimillion-dollar contest could be hard to resist.

Many commercials and ads have long since abandoned the sole goal of convincing would-be customers that their product is of good quality. Increasingly, products are sold for image enhancement. Neil Postman noted that "The television commercial has oriented business away from products of value and toward making consumers feel happy."[12]

A common practice on commercial television is to splice the commercial messages into the programming near the climax of a particular scene. For example, during a television program in which two lovers are about to be united and kiss, we are offered a commercial. Not only is the viewer motivated to stay tuned, but the vicarious feeling of affection they felt before the commercial break is carried "piggyback" into the commercial. In other words, viewers are set up to have affectionate feelings for the product displayed in the commercial.

Advertisements can be obvious or subtle. Psychologists and advertising consultants know that people are more vulnerable to manipulation if they are distracted or otherwise already saturated with a bombardment of stimulation. In such situations the person is less capable of fully analyzing or developing a critical eye to advertising ploys. For example, a type of hypnotic induction taught by the late Milton Erickson involves distraction and confusion. Those of us that practice this type of hypnotherapy refer to it as an "indirect" technique. The client does not muster together a defense against going into a trance, because the hypnotherapist has done an end run around the client's defense system or resistance. Similarly, the influence of advertising can be set up to do an end run around the customer's critical eye. A commercial flashes by and the customer might be left with only attractive images associated with a product or a catchy tune to hum while climbing into the shower. With the media saturated with sophisticated and hypnotic advertisements, members of the LCD society can become consuming automatons.

CORPORATE HOMOGENIZATION

Commercial chains are accelerating the homogenization of modern society. Consumers are experiencing an ever-increasing comfort with sameness and familiarity. When traveling to another community, loyal consumers can go to the same brand restaurant they usually frequent in their own communities. For example, if you often dine at Coco's, Denny's, or Lyon's, you can count on the same menu wherever you travel. The competition between these chains homogenizes the customers' palates because they offer similar menus. As Denny's offers a Santa Fe chicken sandwich, so do Coco's and Lyon's.

The current fast food mania not only provides quick fills for empty bellies but also drives the American palate into banality. This homogenization narrows our appreciation for a wide diversity of possible foods and contributes to the tendency in people to desire the expected. In other words, when you travel across the country, you can go to a McDonald's fast food restaurant for a sense of security and familiarity. This need to know what you are getting narrows imagination and creativity for both you and the proprietors.

Though we now have increased contact with cultures around the world, our opportunity for a broadening experience is flattened by commercialization. Instead of an adventure in new curried or chili tastes, we are offered McIndian or McMexican sandwiches. Not only are our taste buds dulled by sameness, but we are also inoculated against explorations into nonconventional tastes.

Most major boulevards in the United States feature McDonald's, Wendy's, Carl's Jr., Arby's, Jack in the Box, Taco Bell, and Burger King in the same city block. They all have followed the same marketing plan and have "kid's meals" and an increasingly similar menu. Soon there will be a McJack Jr. King in every Taco Box.

The proliferation of retail chains has so homogenized style, food, and general merchandise that people have grown fearful of purchasing outside of these chains. It is not uncommon to hear someone say, "Well, I go to that store because I am familiar with what they have."

Although interest in gourmet cuisine is increasing in select pockets of American society, the mainstream consumer is knee-deep in corporate cuisine. Large food corporations have exploited the term "gourmet" and have offered gourmet brand-named TV dinners.

Similarly, interest in "organic" and "natural" products has melted down into sound bites and inaccuracies. The subculture I have called "organos" pioneered an interest in completely organic foods in the late 1960s and early 1970s. By the late 1970s, large commercial companies realized they could make huge profits by attaching the term "natural" to their products even though that label did not describe the authenticity of the product. Unsophisticated customers bought millions of dollars worth of foods labeled natural from which just one common preservative had been withdrawn.

Because corporations and advertisement agencies compete with one another, their ads look more and more alike. The long-term result is a homogenization of tastes and style. As Macy's carries ads of men's suits with thin or wide lapels, so does the Men's Wearhouse, Lord and Taylor's, and Nordstrom's.

Fads blow through the LCD society at lightning speed as dictated by what is seen in the entertainment industry. Commercials on television advertise these new fads, and people try to dress as though they are in a commercial. This conformity narrows creative expression.

Fads are also seen in the automobile industry. The vehicle we buy expresses the image we think we should have. For example, in the American automobile industry in 1957–1959, fins around the taillights became a must-have. The dawning of the space age drew the public's attention, and consumers were convinced they ought to buy a car that looked "modern." Many automobiles are modeled after the Mercedes/BMW motif. The reason for this most current style appears to be emulation of the rich and successful. Because people with money are the icons of the LCD society, drivers want to look like those they admire.

Another auto fad involves the 4-wheel drive "sports" vehicles. These "assault cruisers" (ACs) often have very large engines and consume twice the gasoline of most automobiles. ACs can weigh 5,000 pounds and are often as long as 17 feet. ACs take up to 1.4 percent as much space as most automobiles. They spew as much as five times more pollution and one-third more carbon dioxide into the air than other vehicles. Some ACs get as little as 9 miles to a gallon, and they consume as much as 43 percent of the gasoline in the United States.

One of the most popular of these ACs is the Chevrolet Suburban, which has morphed into the Yukon. The irony is that many of the people who drive this AC never need to engage the 4-wheel-drive capability. These are essentially suburban vehicles most often bought in areas where it does not snow, yet many AC owners want to look as though they go to the mountains to ski.

The ACs have been the greatest moneymaker for the American automakers over the past few years. The Ford Expedition and the Lincoln Navigator have been among the most successful brands, capturing between $36,000 and $43,000 per vehicle. Ford Expeditions bring in a profit of $3.5 billion, one-third of Ford's global earnings for 2000.[13]

In 2002 Congress passed the energy bill, which deliberately avoided making ACs more energy efficient and less polluting. This omission earned only a passing reference in the news.

Opulence has taken center stage as people with money are more inclined to spend ostentatiously than ever before. The top 20 percent of the population accounted for 42 percent of the car sales in 1980, and by 1996 they accounted for 55 percent of the sales.[14]

Approximately 16 million Americans have bought "home theaters" that cost up to $100,000 and are essentially home movie theaters. There are waiting lists for $65-million Gulf Stream aircraft and $15,000 Hermes bags. According to Dan Philips, publisher of the *Robb Report*—one of the increasing number of magazines dedicated to the "luxury lifestyle," there are more $10,000 to $50,000 watches being worn on a daily basis than ever before.[15]

MARKETING NICHES AND THE ILLUSION OF PLENTY

The power of corporate control over the LCD society has resulted in a tendency for consumers to look, speak, and want to be like one another. In our corporate-dominated society, the diversity and complexity of our culture cannot be addressed. Corporate ads attempt to promote the illusion of increasing diversity in our society. Television programs, for example, target certain markets to achieve maximum ratings. A great deal of effort is made to research these markets and offer messages (commercials) to their viewers. For example, beer commercials are often aired during football games. However, because the people in various markets watch more than just the targeted programming (football), the commercials are becoming less unique and more blended into a homogenous format. Therefore, commercials are being made that have a broad appeal by featuring attractive people, such as beautiful women enticed by a man sipping a particular brand of beer. These women speak with no identifiable accent and could come from anywhere in the country. They do not want to risk offending a man in Alabama by featuring women speaking with a Boston accent.

Corporate advertising not only influences what people buy but also how they paint and restructure their bodies. Today's cosmetics sales amount to $20 billion.[16] Cosmetic surgery is a $1.76-billion-a-year business.[17] Not only do many modern American women feel compelled to undergo face lifts but also bone-sculpting and liposuction. The popular fixation on breast size has resulted in thousands of breast implants. Only later did we find that the most prevalent type of implant, silicon gel, resulted in an outbreak of health problems.

MAKING IT?

People have always fantasized about wealth. However, in our media-saturated LCD society, we believe that money is the solution to all things. The expansion of lottery programs throughout the country and the proliferation of casinos attests to this trend.

An adequate income undeniably makes life more tolerable, but people rarely limit their dreams to such humble goals. Rather, most people are more enticed with the fantasy of being a multimillionaire. When one has thoughts of "making it," the "it" is regarded as a fortune, not wisdom or enlightenment.

Mihaly Csikszentmihalyi of the University of Chicago has researched American's quest for happiness. He found that wealth is inversely correlated with happiness. When he compared reports of happiness and depression of people from countries of varied levels of wealth, he found that the people in the wealthiest countries had the lowest levels of reported happiness and the highest levels of depression.[18]

With an exaggerated focus on material comfort and immediate gratification comes a greater degree of hollowness. It is difficult for extremely wealthy individuals to maintain interest in the immaterial aspects of their lives. Many such overly gratified individuals lose incentive and a sense of accomplishment.

Though striking it rich has always been a dream, in recent years greed and gluttony have become noble pursuits. The credo imported from Adam Smith, the guru of capitalism, is "take it all." We saw the outbreak of the societal narcissism in the 1980s when figures such as Ivan Bosky pronounced that "greed is good." The beliefs that we must take it all and that greed is good have become mantras in the LCD society.

Greed and "taking it all" have wide-ranging destructive consequences for every fabric of society. Tax breaks for the rich became institutionalized during the Reagan years and once again in the George W. Bush years. It was rationalized that making the rich richer would be good for us all.

Fame is another dream of "making it." Fame is often believed to be as lofty as becoming rich, hence the phrase "becoming rich and famous." However, fame provides considerable narcissistic gratification. In other words, someone who makes it because of fame holds the admiration of many people. People who have become pro athletes, royalty, or movie "stars" are among the most famous, admired far more than scientists and caregivers. Princess Di's funeral received more press coverage than did Mother Teresa's. People in the general public so admire entertainers that they deify them. Ironically, in centuries past, actors and athletes would have been court jesters and gladiators, but in media-saturated societies they have been given immortality.

The salaries of actors and athletes reflect how we value the most superficial aspects of our society. When their salaries are compared to those of public servants such as teachers, social workers, and college professors, we find a bizarre discrepancy. Public servants don't fare well. In contrast, the athletes or movie actors are rewarded with the wealth commensurate with having "made it."

Fame can be a destructive influence on one's mental health. Many of these individuals do not have the psychological resources to cope with fame and fortune. So overblown is their interest in how they appear that many become jaded and hedonistic on the outside and hollow and empty on the inside.

People who receive both overblown praise and wealth are set up for psychological self-destruction. When their pumped-up egos are not gratified and the praise they are accustomed to receive is not available, they experience a withdrawal metaphorically not unlike a drug withdrawal. Their addiction and dependence on praise sets them up for a psychological crisis.

Just as some entertainers and athletes possess a hollow self, we too may have invested an inordinate amount of energy in maintaining our exterior selves. What we regard as healthy has become distorted. Indeed, even the spectacle of athletic games has become more glitz than muscle, as we shall see in the next chapter.

9
Men and Women Are from Earth

If love is the answer, maybe I should have reframed the question.
Lily Tomlin

In recent years relationships between men and women have been trivialized. Efforts by mental health professionals to help remedy marital turbulence have gravitated to LCD solutions whereby images of what it means to be a woman or a man in modern society are reduced to commercial concepts.

We have been invaded by images of extraterrestrials. Female Venusians and male Martians have cluttered our minds and reached the bestseller lists. Martians are told they need to understand that Venusians need to chatter. Venusians are told that Martians need to go off to their caves. Yes, there are differences between men and women. But the exaggerated differences have served to polarize as much as help couples trying to make sense of their relationships.

How has the omnipresent forces of the LCD society affected our relationships with our most intimate partners? How have we come to understand ourselves as men and women? Why are many relationships doomed to a short life? In this chapter the problems facing Venusians and Martians will be brought down to earth.

DISPOSABLE RELATIONSHIPS

Many people in postmodern society have moved several times during their lives. This mobility contributes to a sense of impermanence and lack of rootedness in human relationships. Similarly, the trend toward consumerism has also shaken the foundation of the old phrase "Til death do us part." In a society replete with fast food restaurants and the insatiable need for instant gratification, men and women have come to unconsciously regard relationships with one another as if they are consumers looking for the best fit during a particular phase in their lives. In this throw-away society, people can change relationships as if merely changing clothes. When either our clothes or our relationships wear out, we can shop for new ones.

In many states, over 50 percent of marriages end in divorce. The divorce rate in the United States has doubled since 1960.[1] Overall, 50 percent of children have experienced the effects of divorce. Approximately 60 percent of these children will grow up and experience their own divorces.

During the early 1960s, if couples lived together without being married, they probably kept it a secret from their respective parents. They were thought to be "shacking-up" or "living in sin." Today it is common for couples to live together. By 1990, the number of couples living together was six times what it was in 1960. As much as a quarter of all adults have cohabited with a sexual partner at least once in their lives. Most of such cohabitations last an average of 12 months. Only about half of these cohabitations result in marriage, but one-third of those end in divorce. The bottom line is that fewer couples are getting married.[2] Thus, the mobility and lack of a sense of rootedness in our highly mobile and consumer-oriented society is matched by a lack of depth and commitment in our intimate relationships with one another. Intimate relationships are now based on convenience, sensation, and whim.

Yet there have been some positive developments in how we conduct and maintain our relationships with one another. Fifty years ago couples stayed together despite gross incompatibility. Many women stayed with an abusive husband for fear of being ostracized by society. There were no domestic violence programs and no laws protecting the victims. In less aggravated marriages, incompatibility rarely factored into grounds for divorce. Today there is greater equality between the sexes, and both partners expect fulfillment. The growth of marriage seminars and counseling services testifies to the increased importance of compatibility.

Despite all these efforts, the number of divorces has dramatically risen in the past 50 years. Have we come to expect the impossible in our relationships, or has the pace of the emerging LCD society so transformed our lives that we are numb to our intimate partners?

LOVE, THE MYTH AND THE REALITY

The LCD consumer society has also embraced the belief that the emotional experience derived from an intimate relationship is similar to eating a chocolate éclair, to be consumed for its short-term joy. The high one receives is counterbalanced by the low of a broken heart. Indeed, the experience of being in love has been mythologized and is thought of as an all-or-nothing experience.

Many people assume that all you need is the love that was somehow immaculately conceived and "meant to be." If the fruit dies on the vine, the partners might say, "Oh, well, I guess we weren't meant to be together after all. The spark is gone. I guess it's time to move on."

Such a loss of interest in a relationship often occurs after the early phase of the relationship has passed. This honeymoon phase is analogous to the glitz and superficiality endemic in our culture. Just as the motion picture industry has gravitated to the LCD of sensationalism and away from plots requiring reflection and thought, so too does our fixation on the excitement of the honeymoon phase of a relationship.

The honeymoon phase of a relationship has much to do with infatuation. Infatuation provides a high not unlike a drug high. When it wears off, both people in a relationship run the risk of becoming sour and disappointed. Many relationships do not survive the aftermath of the infatuation phase. In fact, the early part of a relationship, often referred to as "falling in love," could be better described as falling into infatuation. During the infatuation phase, the partners might perceive each other as "ideal" mates. This idealized perspective emerges not only because of the heightened effort both partners are making but also because we might project the mythic image of a soul mate onto the partner. Both partners are trying their best to show how great they can be by acting totally present, generous, and loving. This is one of the reasons the infatuation phase is vitalizing and described by most people as euphoric.

Neither partner wants the other to quit trying to be that "perfect" lover, but neither is able to continue to maintain a 100-percent effort. We all want to have our cake and eat it too.

Once the relationship is "safe" from the threat of ending prematurely, there is slow erosion of the effort expended by both partners.

Both partners become lazy and expect the other to keep trying to be that perfect lover. When the other partner is revealed as mortal after all, with faults and limitations, both partners might feel that "maybe this is not the partner I thought he/she was."

It is not uncommon for people to say, "I fell out of love with so-and-so." Inherent in this mindset is the overly simplistic idea that love occurs on its own accord or through some act of God. Love can be subtle. Infatuation is sensational. Love requires commitment and humility. Infatuation requires no such commitment, because it captures our consciousness.

Many people in our LCD society are taught through social modeling on television and in movies that intimate relationships happen on their own accord. We are taught to be lazy in our relationships with one another. Because television viewing is a passive process, so too do we regard our intimate relationships.

As we watch actors engage in dramatic relationships, we vicariously experience the thrills of the love affairs without getting off our couches or uttering a word. Many relationships featured on the screen are laced with intrigue. We run the risk of expecting the same kind of relationships we see in the movies or on television.

Movies often feature a couple that has suffered a misunderstanding but, in the end, finally come together and live happily ever after. This motif drives home the point that permanent happiness can be reached without further work on the relationship.

In the LCD era, long-term relationships run the risk of being derailed by unreasonable and even silly expectations. Perhaps more than ever, the emerging LCD society jeopardizes our understanding of and involvement in our most intimate relationships.

DIFFERENCES AND SIMILARITIES

Men and women are both from Earth, despite the recent popular series of books describing us as metaphorically being from Mars and Venus. The differences between men and women are not as great as assumed. Some of these differences can be traced to cultural influences and others to biophysiology.

In some cultures—such as the Navajos of the American Southwest, for example—women are raised with high status. Thirty years ago, while traveling late at night through a Navajo reservation, I encountered a vivid illustration of the status of women in Navajo society. On the reservation at that time, there were no barbwire fences to keep cattle off the road. Because of the "open range," cattle would often wander onto the road and cautious driving was necessary. That night we traveled in a remote part of the reservation to reach an ecological research site. To our instantaneous horror, we ran into cattle crossing the road, severely wounding one of them. A Navajo family descended on the crash site, seemingly coming out of nowhere. A middle-aged woman directed the men to bring a butcher's knife from their nearby hogan. Within minutes she slashed the cow's throat to put it out of its misery. Then, very calmly, she turned to us for our insurance coverage number and disappeared with her entourage.

In cultures such as the Navajo, kinship is traced through the matrilineal line—that is, the line of heritage is traced through the woman's family. However, most cultures are patriarchal and men have a dominant role. In such patriarchal societies, women have a subordinate role and are essentially second-class citizens. In China, for example, parents are allowed only one child. They hope and pray that their child will be a boy. Some extremely desperate parents abandon their baby girls lest they be disqualified from another chance of having a boy. This trend is largely responsible for the massive exportation of baby girls from China to adoptive parents in the United States.

Women in patriarchal societies behave, think, and feel different from women in matriarchal societies. Women in matriarchal societies might appear more like Martians than women in patriarchal societies. Within either patriarchal or matriarchal societies, each woman's position within her society has a great deal of influence upon her experiences.

The differences between men and women cannot be attributed to cultural factors alone. There are structural differences in the brain between men and women. The band of nerve fibers between the two hemispheres (called the corpus callosum) is denser in women's brains than in men's brains. This means the two hemispheres communicate more readily in women than in men. Accordingly, when women use words, they hear and feel more of the emotional content. In contrast, men generally feel less of the emotional content and look instead toward the logic and facts the words express. It is based loosely on this fact that the book *Men are from Mars and Women are from Venus* stressed the LCD concept that women (Venusians) need to talk for the sake of talking. In contrast, men (Martians) are thought to gravitate to just wanting the facts.

But the cultural and biophysiological factors co-evolve. Consider the fact that during much of our evolutionary history, men were the hunters and women were the gatherers.[3] The residual influence of these evolutionary factors can be seen in how differently boys and girls mature. Girls acquire language and fine motor skills much earlier than do boys. Boys, in contrast, learn gross motor skills much earlier.

Against this backdrop of our hunter-gatherer evolutionary history, men have evolved keen spatial skills to excel at hunting and women have acquired superior detail-oriented, spatial-location memory. It has long been believed that men and women differ in several aspects of intellectual abilities, including verbal, qualitative, and spatial abilities. Some researchers have pointed out that these differences decrease over time.[4] In other words, modernization and the blending of gender roles increasingly make sex-role differentiation less pronounced. Yet most researchers agree that men have greater ability in visual-spatial abilities and math skills and women have greater ability in verbal fluency.[5]

Because of our evolutionary past as hunter-gatherers, men developed greater upper body strength by perfecting hunting. Women who bore children necessarily stayed close to camp and did the gathering. Therefore, masculine traits have evolved to be more aggressive, and feminine traits have evolved to highlight cooperative traits.

Men competed for access to females. Women learned to choose a mate who could provide for them while they performed the responsibilities of nursing the young and preparing food. Because men were not restricted to these responsibilities, they could be relatively promiscuous. And from the point of view of some evolutionary psychologists, this promiscuity corresponded to the drive for men to spread their genes. Also, according to this model, men evolved to exert control over women and developed sexual jealousy.

Alice Eagly of Northwestern University and Wendy Wood of Texas A&M summarize the prevailing perspectives of evolutionary psychology:

Because men competed with other men for sexual access to women, men evolved a disposition favoring violence, competition, and risk taking. Women in turn developed a proclivity to nurture and a preference for long-term mates who could support a family. As a result, men strived to acquire more resources in order to attract women, and women developed preferences for successful, ambitious men who could provide resources.[6]

In a study of over 10,000 individuals from 37 countries, it was found that women place great emphasis on finding a mate with good financial prospects.[7]

Some researchers have stressed that physical differences between men and women factor into the development of social customs that result in an economy based on these differences.[8] The resulting social structure with sex role assignments produces a division of labor and psychological sex differentiation. In other words, people adjust to the sex roles assigned to them and develop either "male" or "female" psychological traits assigned to those roles. Women have acquired roles regarded as nurturing and oriented toward acquiring resources. They have been more readily oriented toward domestic skills and interpersonally facilitative traits.

Males evolved to control their reproductive success by being better able to control the social environment through dominance, whereas females evolved to cultivate reciprocity. These characteristics have an influence on what occupation people choose. Women are represented in proportionally higher numbers in the helping professions. Men are over-represented in occupations that require less reciprocity and emotional expression, such as physics, engineering, and biology.

Because of the tendency on the part of men toward dominance, women have been suppressed in the workforce. Though women have made significant gains during the twentieth century in the world's industrialized countries, they are still under-represented in the highest levels of organizational hierarchies. Women also earn comparably lower pay and are over-represented in service occupations such as food service and professional jobs such as teaching and nursing.

When women compete with men in occupations that men have traditionally dominated, the women have to become more assertive. Unfortunately, men who feel threatened by the competition regard those women as aggressive or "bitchy."

Traditional marriages built around the male breadwinner and female homemaker favor an age spread whereby the man is older than the women. In such arrangements, men who are older have had time to accumulate income and resources to provide more security than younger men. Younger women are better able to bear children and are more apt to succumb to the dominance of older men. Support for this view comes from cross-cultural studies that have surveyed as many as 37 cultures.[9] In modern industrialized societies, these tendencies play out less dramatically, yet a consistent theme is that women seek out men who are potentially good breadwinners. Men generally seek out younger, attractive women.

In recent years, as people approach gender equality, these lop-sided preferences break down. However, in the LCD society, the residual influences of these evolutionary traits have resulted in the tendency, for example, for older men to seek out "trophy wives" who are attractive and young.

The impact of feminism on the study of differences between men and women has resulted in the emergence of a group of theorists who favor the view that biophysiological differences are negligible and cultural conditioning influences are paramount.[10] Much effort by these theorists has been directed toward mitigating the belief that women are inferior. Their gender-neutral strategy of making no distinction between men and women has been directed toward the political goal of gender equality. Some feminist writers have accepted a belief in the traits of feminine nurturance and masculine aggression. Their position has been that as civilization matures, sex role differentiation neutralizes.

Over the course of evolutionary history, sex roles have changed and diversified. Though residual biophysiological differences between men and women still play a role in psychological experience, these differences are expressed differently in each culture. Further, within each culture there is tremendous variation in the differential expression of femininity and masculinity.

In recent years men have felt alienated by the many changes that have occurred in sex roles. That is, many men have been threatened by the shift toward equal rights between the sexes. In an effort to resolve these feelings, men have taken part in men's groups and retreats.

It is true that the important changes in the women's movement have put a strain on the old model of how men are defined. The crude and simplistic model of the patriarchal controlling figure of dominance conflicts with the new assertive image of women. Social philosopher Sam Keen has challenged men to become more in touch with their feelings and find "fire in their belly."

The Promise Keepers movement has emerged from Christian fundamentalism to offer men a comradely sense based on fundamentalist tenants. The Promise Keepers have jammed stadiums in the name of recapturing the "morals" of a truly Christian society. Unfortunately, much of the program is clothed in a thin veneer of sexism.

Similarly, more left-leaning men have been encouraged by poet Robert Bly to "find the inner warrior" by sitting and beating on drums. This is an effort to resonate with that part of themselves that has been buried by civilization. The inner warrior is imagined to be an archetypal powerhouse of vitality and strength long since exiled from modern society.

Is the simplistic gravitation to resurrect the warrior needed to accomplish this social and spiritual transformation of equality between the sexes? How is being in touch with my "warrior" self (if I have such a self) going to provide me with sensitivity? Such a simplistic perspective seems to conflict with the challenge of cultivating sensitivity. Yet, with all their faults, the wide variety of retro men's groups attempt to offer their practitioners a semblance of connectedness with other men and an identity long since lost in the postmodern society.

The popularity of the Warrior seminars and Promise Keepers conventions reflects rather than resolves the void between men and women in the LCD society. This void has resulted in an increasing discontent between men and women and a cheapening of intimate relationships. They have embraced archaic concepts such as the warrior self. In this sense they have provided little beyond the LCD concept of a Martian needing to go to his cave.

Men and women are from Earth, and now in the twenty-first century we have the opportunity to move beyond the Martians and Venusians and Warriors of LCD pop retroism.

10

Hyped Sports

You're a child still playing a game. You're a superhuman hero.
No wonder we have a hard time understanding who we are.

Billie Jean King

Sports stars and the games they play are part of the surreal world of entertainment and the commercialized LCD society. Many stars have become so deified that their names overshadow their humanity. The name Michael Jordan is known the world over, and his image is worn on tee shirts from Moscow to Bangkok.

Professional sports have become a massive market of promotion and commercialized production. Major corporations have moved into the professional sports marketplace by buying up teams, stadiums, and endorsements from athletes. Sports promotion has become a $3.8 billion enterprise.[1] The sports industry generates millions of dollars for corporations. Television coverage of sports events has become a lucrative way for networks to capture millions of dollars from sponsors.

Corporations have learned that even the "nonprofit" Olympic Games are a means by which to make millions of dollars. Cities have scrambled to entice the Games into their sphere with the hopes of pumping money into their infrastructure through investments and tourism.

MEDIA/SPORTS MONOPOLIES

Corporations have looked everywhere to maximize profits. The new San Francisco Giant's stadium is "Pac Bell Stadium." It joins the ranks of Busch Stadium in St. Louis, the Mariner's new field in Seattle named "Safeco Field," and the old Jack Murphy Stadium in San

Diego now referred to as Qualcomm Park, all of which function as giant advertising icons.

Professional sports teams were once owned by wealthy families. Now an increasing number are owned by large corporations. Most pro teams are selling for between $150 and $250 million dollars, but media mogul Rupert Murdoch paid $311 million for the Los Angeles Dodgers. He will promote the Dodgers on his Fox Network. Such a move competes with the Atlanta Braves, promoted on TNT. The Atlanta Braves and Atlanta Hawks are also used as a means to promote Turner's WTBS cable television channel. The Disney Corporation has controlling interests in the Anaheim Angels, Anaheim Ducks, ABC television, and ESPN. Seattle billionaire John Crow owns the Mariners, the NBA Vancouver Grizzlies, and the NHL Canucks. The Tribune Company in Chicago owns the Cubs, cable "superstation" WGN, a number of local television stations, and the *Chicago Tribune*. The Tribune Company also extended itself in other sports markets by broadcasting the Dodgers and Angels on KTLA (before Murdoch and Disney), the Phillies on WPHC, and the Rockies on KWGN.

Many of these corporations and owner/media tycoons seek tax write-offs and "spinoffs." The tax write-offs occur essentially as tax shelters whereby the owners of the teams hide profits made from their other enterprises. The spinoffs create benefits for other corporate interests. As they go after the sports contracts, the owners increase the prominence of their networks. Fox, for example, demonstrated it was a major player in national television. By purchasing the rights to air NFL football, Fox demonstrated that there were no longer three but four national television networks. In so doing, they encouraged viewers to watch other Fox programs.

Disney produced a remake of the movie *Angels in the Outfield*. This seamless interface between movies and sports ensures the profits of both enterprises. Disney was so successful with its movie *The Mighty Ducks* that they bought a National Hockey League franchise. By such cross-merchandising, the promotion of movies promotes teams and vice versa.

Because the owners of media and teams control the only access to the pro teams, they maintain a monopoly on sports entertainment. Fans have nowhere else to turn to see professional sports. Not only do they give in and watch their teams, but they are also inundated by scores of commercials.

Sports franchises have earned millions from commercially endowed television and radio. Back in 1980, Major League baseball took in $80 million. Ten years later the take was $600 million. Even after the public relations disaster of the baseball strike in 1994, each team took in $28 million by 1996. The profit increase was even greater for NFL football. In 1960 the income from the media was $36 million. In 1980 the figure jumped to $167 million. Then in 1990 it jumped again to $948 and in 1996 to $1.29 billion. In 1998 the national television contracts were signed for an eight-year stretch for $17.6 billion, yielding $73 million per year for each team through 2005.[2]

The consolidation of media and sports franchises, therefore, meant millions of dollars for those mega corporations. They put pressure on the teams to draw superstar athletes to keep the teams competitive. Simultaneously, with the rise of the unions and free agency, the salaries of star athletes shot up to the level of movie stars.

Indeed, James Quirk and Rodney Fort argue in their book *Hard Ball* that one of the main reasons for the rise in salaries is that star athletes are part of an entertainment industry controlled by monopolies.[3] The owners and the leagues they compose are essentially cartels that prohibit competition from outside. They negotiate directly and exclusively with television and radio interests, all of whom are oriented around one central goal: to maximize profits.

The owners of the teams have risen to such stature that they are powerful leaders in their cities and influence public policy for their own financial gain. For example, the 1980s and 1990s saw an increase in the construction of publicly financed stadiums and arenas. Because the owners were so powerful, they were able to co-opt politicians into "supporting" the local team. Owners could threaten politicians with being blamed if the home team left the city because a new stadium was not built. No politician wants to be blamed for being against "the team." In Seattle alone, taxpayers had been on the hook for $1 billion to subsidize their sports teams. Between 1992 and 1999, 34 new stadiums or arenas came on-line at the tune of $6.3 billion, 70 percent of which was public money.

Many of the supporters of publicly financed "sweetheart" deals with the teams argue that they are trying to keep the team from leaving. A departure would not only result in low morale for the region but in a loss of jobs. However, according to a study conducted by Robert Baade, there was no correlation between the construction

of a stadium and growth in income for a city.[4] Even the jobs of vendors at the stadiums are seasonal and only relevant for a few hours
a day on game days. The minor benefits of the part-time jobs are
overshadowed by massive amounts of public monies spent. To add
insult to injury, the teams often receive a deal in which they are not
responsible for paying taxes.

Very few people pay attention to the disparity between the costs
and the benefits of publicly financed stadiums. What has, however,
received attention is the exorbitant salaries of the star athletes.

In recent years the combination of sports/media cartels and superstars has produced winning teams such as the Atlanta Braves and
the New York Yankees. The smaller franchises such as those in Kansas City, Cincinnati, and Pittsburgh have not been able to compete
the way they did just 20 years ago.

The carry-over effect of seeing the superstars' teams defeat the
less endowed teams serves to work against the model of "teams." In
other words, the emergence of highly paid and mobile superstars
clustered in sports/media empires takes the air out of the sails of the
smaller-market teams. Fans in the smaller markets see their teams
disenfranchised by money and the media. Some of the fans in Kansas City, Cincinnati, and Pittsburgh can watch TNT and switch their
allegiance to the Atlanta Braves. They can watch more games and a
winning team. Children are taught that team-building and teamwork
are less important than money and greed. They might see their local
team raided by the super teams just as a player on their team reaches
stardom.

The practice of leaving home and not looking back is legitimized.
The belief in personal gain over community membership fits well
into the LCD mobile society. Even the illusion of community with
the belief in "our team" can't make it to the centerfield bleachers.

DEIFIED STARS

Star athletes have reached an epic deification. More people know
the names of these stars than know the names of major authors,
scientists, or their representatives in government. The stars have become iconic role models for our youth or even politicians. Jim Bun-
ning from baseball, Bill Bradley from basketball, Jack Kemp from
football, and Jesse "the body" Ventura have all made their way into
government.

With that reverence comes a weighty responsibility. However, most stars have not tried to develop a persona outside the sports arena. When one of them misbehaves, it is immediately highlighted in the evening news. Wife beatings, drug arrests, and DUIs teach lessons better not taught.

The stars have grown to such a high stature in the LCD society that many lose the courtesy of social grace. Following the 1997 World Series, the victorious Florida Marlins were invited to the White House for congratulations. Only half the players showed up for the event.

These athletes are rewarded for their stardom by ridiculous amounts of money and public adulation. The average Major League baseball salary is $1.5 million per year, but the "big" stars make considerably more. Albert Belle and Gary Sheffield earned $10 million each for the 1998 baseball season. At the $8 million level, we have Barry Bonds of the San Francisco Giants, Greg Maddux of the Atlanta Braves, Roger Clemens of the New York Yankees, and Mark McGwire of the Saint Louis Cardinals, who will command more in the years to come. Michael Jordan earned $30 million for the 1997–98 season and then $33 million in 1998–99. Kevin Garnett, the 22-year-old forward for the Minnesota Timberwolves, has a six-year contract for $126 million. In NFL football, Brett Favre of the Green Bay Packers and Steve Young of the San Francisco 49ers both earned $6.5 million. And these salaries have not stopped all of these players from doing a multitude of commercials to earn more money.[5] Well into the 2002 baseball season, Barry Bonds was featured with Hank Aaron in a frequently aired television commercial. Despite not having played for a few years, Steve Young still sells cars.

An endless barrage of television commercials feature star athletes wearing Nike running shoes or using an American Express credit card. Many of these stars have earned millions cashing in on their promotional appeal. Tiger Woods earned $30 million. "Sport stars, especially professional basketball players, are far more visible on television than entertainers," says David Vadehra, President of Video Storybook Tests, Inc., who conducted a recent study demonstrating this fact.[6]

Given that star athletes are significant role models for children, the salaries paid teach a lesson hard to unlearn—namely, "To be great is to earn a great deal of money." Then when the players ask for more, the lesson becomes "Greed is good and gluttony is honorable."

GO FOR THE GOLD

During the nonprofessional international athletic event, the Olympic Games, sponsors for both television and on-site media coverage poured in millions of dollars to influence would-be customers into buying their beer, snack foods, and assault vehicles. When NBC went after the Centennial Olympic games, they spent two million dollars to buy the exclusive rights to cover the games. They earned $70 million in profit from their heavily commercialized coverage.

Of the businesses present at the Atlanta 1996 Summer Olympic Games, the *Wall Street Journal* reported that "there were more than 100 licenses, 20 sponsors, and 10 Centennial Olympic Partners, contributing to the $1.6 billion Olympic budget."[7]

NBC assigned researchers the task of discovering what might best sell their products. Nicholas Schiavone, research director, told *The New Yorker* that "viewers want narrative momentum, a story that builds. . . . what they really want is not live but alive; not sports but stories about sports."[8]

NBC made a calculated effort to target women by featuring many personal profiles of the major American athletes, many of whom were women. The actual coverage of the Games themselves continues to thin out at best. More time is spent on the glossy story-telling promos than on any event. Viewers were subjected to promos instead of being able to see complete coverage of the games themselves.

To capture the wide audience necessary to reap millions in sponsor dollars, the Olympic coverage featured "GM Moments"—touching background stories of people in the background of the Olympics, such as the Australian woman who won a gold medal years before she developed multiple sclerosis. These GM Moments spliced sympathy and compassion with their product, teaching us all that corporations really do have a heart.

One of the staples of the coverage has been melodramatic "personals" of athletes who hoped to win the gold. These personals are imbued with tightly crafted scripts, crisp editing, and dramatic poses of the athlete in romantic settings.

By the 2002 Winter Games in Salt Lake City, there were seamless segues between the commercials and the glossy coverage. It was often difficult to know at first whether we were viewing the coverage of the game or just another commercial. The personals and the commercials seemed interchangeable. Viewers were enticed into a dreamlike blur in which the products and the games were part of the same commercialized imagery.

The coverage of sports events matches the sensationalism found in the rest of the entertainment industry. We have seen an almost obsessive focus on winning. Intense competition is nothing new, but in recent years our society has perpetuated the idea that if you do not win, you fail. Take for example the go-for-the-gold attitude bantered by the media during the coverage of the Olympic Games. Commentators are heard to say, "He has gold in his eyes—can he do it?" Silver or bronze Olympic medalists know all too well the greatly increased dollar value they would have possessed had they "brought home the gold." By the 2002 Olympics, the cliché was "He's mining for gold." And many of the gold-medal winners actually do "strike gold" in promotional fees for decorating a Wheaties box or selling Nike running shoes.

When Lenny Krayzelburg won gold medals for his backstroke races, the announcer said he had the "package." Presumably he meant that Krayzelburg had the story as a devoted son and an immigrant from a previously communist country. Add a few gold medals and he becomes an advertising icon.

Winning a gold medal does not necessarily result in a positive outcome for athletes. A study of gold-medal winners in Australia indicated that they had a number of negative experiences. They reported difficulties with coping strategies and found themselves little prepared to deal with the media attention.[9]

The obsession with winning is also seen in the coverage of the World Series and the Superbowl. Commentators say, "After making it all the way to the Superbowl, they have come so far, only to go away empty-handed." To emphasize the dichotomy between winning and losing, during the last game of the World Series, close-up shots of the jubilant "victors" and the sullen "failures" are featured after the last out is made. The victors celebrate by piling up on one another, while the "failures" sit in their dugout with sad faces and sometimes even tears. The athletes described as failures obviously have not failed. They have managed to play extraordinarily enough to be in the championship games, but in the LCD atmosphere we think of them as just not good enough.

We have also become dependent on viewing the reactions of other people to feel emotion ourselves. A new technique in sports broadcasting has emerged: "the reaction shot." Because television viewers are not actually playing the game, a reaction shot can stir up viewers' emotions by displaying the intense reactions of the players. When a batter gets a game-changing hit in a baseball game, the camera zooms in not only to show how the batter himself felt but also to reveal the reactions of both teams, including the pitcher, who stomps his feet in disgust. Viewers are invited to vicariously feel the tension of playing the game: "the joy of victory and the agony of defeat."

AMERICA'S PASTIME

Professional baseball began in the late nineteenth century as a slow contemplative game played out over many hours. By the mid-twentieth century, baseball retained the interest of millions of Americans. At the beginning of the massive migration to the suburbs and the proliferation of television in the 1950s, baseball was still referred to as American's pastime.

NFL football games were played in baseball stadiums. For example, the Chicago Bears played in the Cubs' Wrigley Field. By the 1990s most NFL football teams played in their own stadiums. But baseball in the beginning of the twenty-first century is a game that needs to compete with the quick action of basketball and the gladiator sport of football. Television viewers do not want to waste time watching a pitcher at bat, thus designated hitters (American League), juiced balls, lowered pitching mounds, and revamped playing surfaces (artificial surfaces) move balls more quickly.

Because baseball is not as physically violent as football, people often say, "Baseball is too slow—not enough action." Indeed, the ratings for baseball games do not compare to those for football. Baseball promoters have decided they need to grab the attention of viewers lest they turn to another channel to watch football or a Sylvester Stallone movie. Given that baseball is sometimes referred to as the chess game of all sports, subtle strategies such as throwing a curve ball instead of a change-up are always below the surface. But in our LCD society, we are losing interest in that depth—thinking takes too much effort. Therefore, to compete with the rising prominence of the NFL, Major League baseball began a campaign to convince would-be viewers that baseball is really as exciting as football. One commercial features all-star catcher Mike Piazza being rammed at home plate by a base runner. The narrator goes on to say, "Try telling Mike Piazza that baseball is not a contact sport!"

The Chicago Cubs signed a college pitcher who threw a ball at a player in the on-deck circle and hit him in the head. The pitcher complained that the player was timing his pitches. The assaulted player incurred damage to his sight. Apparently, the pitcher's crime was not enough to dissuade the Cubs, or perhaps it was his notoriety that drew the team's attention.

Over the past 30 years, NFL football has far surpassed baseball as the American pastime. In fact, though football audiences were once assumed to be male, 40 percent of the viewers of football games are now women. But football has not become gentler because women are tuning in.

Just as we have seen the motion picture industry gravitate toward violence and aggression, so have we seen the coverage of football shift from finesse to scenes of violence. Especially heavy hits are shown over and over in "super-slow-mo." The most sensational hits are collected and strung together and made part of the NFL commercials. Even commercials for later football games feature rock music played over the scenes and the sounds of pounding physical contact.

Many Americans have become addicted to the sensationalism of contact sports. Interestingly, in the rest of the world the most popular sport internationally is football—not the football we know, but soccer. International football (soccer) is a game of finesse, agility, and stamina. In contrast, American football is arguably a game of brute force, aggression, and significantly more serious injuries. In American football, the players wear helmets and pads over much of their bodies to protect them from the violent collisions that can take place on each play. Such protection does not prevent frequent injuries, which are often the close-up focus of television coverage.

During the 1999 NFL playoff game between the Atlanta Falcons and the San Francisco 49ers, the referees made a questionable call. One of the announcers said, "I can't believe it! That was a pathetic call." Still upset about the call ten minutes later he said, "If anyone tells me that call was okay, I will cram the ball down their throat." In years past, announcers were expected to demonstrate impartiality and describe the games with objectivity. In the emerging LCD society, acrimony and sensationalism have replaced impartiality and sober objectivity.

It is not uncommon to witness players being carried off in stretchers due to the brutal combat. The former quarterback of the San Francisco 49ers, Steve Young, incurred a concussion from being hit by rushing linemen. After just a few weeks of recuperation, he was back out on the football field, and a lineman hit him again, intentionally. This lineman attempted to put Young out of the game by "head butting," and when confronted on his outrageous behavior by one of Young's teammates, the lineman shouted back and spit on the player.

Just as American violent blockbuster movies are shown worldwide, NFL football is growing in popularity throughout the world. Prior to each season, many teams play exhibition games in countries such as Great Britain and Japan.

The changing world of professional sports reflects the loosening dynamics of the LCD society. The increasing violence in society as a whole and the increasing violence in sports are symptomatic of the massive regression we now find ourselves within.

Identification with a group of people such as a team represents a milestone in developmental experience. Just as adolescents overidentify with a particular style of dress or music to build a sense of belonging, so do fans identify with a particular team. Fans display the team colors on their jackets, sweatshirts, and caps. When the team wins a game or championship, the fans feel that they have won. It is not uncommon that after a Superbowl or a World Series victory, fans flock to the center of the city to honk their horns, drink beer, and party. Such exhibitions represent a residual tribalism of our evolutionary past. The pounding-of-the-chest ritual at the center of the city is their victory celebration. Acting almost as if warriors from their tribe have defeated warriors from another tribe, the fans burst into a spontaneous expression of violence. In Denver, after the 1998 Superbowl victory, cars were turned over and police were dispatched to quell the uprising. In an ironic twist, the police became representatives of the other team as the rioters threw back tear-gas canisters. In today's deepening LCD society, this expression of periodic jubilance mutates into rage. For most of the year, however, the deified sports stars tell us what to buy while they simultaneously model how to be truly "free agents"—free of humility and community affiliation.

11
Waging the Soul

Adventure upon all the tickets in the lottery, and lose for certain: and the greater the number of your tickets, the nearer you approach that certainty.

Adam Smith

Throughout history people have gambled as a sport and pastime. As the LCD society begins to pick up steam, gambling is becoming one of the fastest growing industries in the United States. In 1976, Americans legally wagered $17.3 billion, and that number grew exponentially to $586.5 billion by 1996.[1]

During the same period, the means of gambling changed dramatically. While horse racing, which had been one of the icons of gambling, decreased in popularity, casino gambling grew in popularity. Horse racing is infused with social and ritualistic trappings. Many gamblers studied the statistics on the horses and discussed the merits or demerits of each race. From the 1960s on, sports betting became more popular than betting on horse races. Although football, basketball, and baseball games were televised, horse races were not.

With a licked finger in the breeze, racetrack officials began to realize they would entice more gamblers by introducing slot machines or card tables to their tracks. These efforts to transform racetracks into casinos proved profitable. The Prairie Meadows Racetrack in Iowa now reaps more profits from slots than from bets on the horse racing.

Indeed, casino gambling has become dominant. Betting in casinos grew by 395 percent. The casino business amounted to 85 percent of legal gambling in the United States in 1996.[2] The casino industry today wields considerable political power. *Mother Jones* magazine reported that the gambling industry spent $100 million on lobbying and political donations between 1992 and 1996.[3]

According to the Center for Public Integrity, the casino industry spent $4.5 million supporting political candidates between 1991 and 1996. Much of that money went to Republicans—to Bob Dole in the 1996 Presidential election. As if to emphasize its political bias, the casino industry hired former Republican National Committee chairman Frank Fahrenkopf to be president of the Gaming Association.

It appears that these investments have paid off. The public has been convinced that gambling is just another form of entertainment. The gambling industry has succeeded in convincing the government to agree with their semantics. They have taken the letters "b" and "l" out of the word gambling and now use the sanitized term "gaming."

GAMING THE CITIES

During the economic turbulence of the early 1930s, Nevada came close to bankruptcy. Unlike most states, Nevada did not enjoy a broad-based infrastructure or a diverse enough population to survive the Great Depression. The Nevada state legislators decided to roll the dice and depend on taxes generated by gambling.

By the time Benjamin "Bugsy" Siegel and the Mob arrived in the small desert town of Las Vegas in the late 1940s, two casinos were already doing well financially. The Mob worked hard to transform that sleepy little town into a gambling playground.

As Los Angeles mushroomed in population, so did Las Vegas. Las Vegas became the decadent playground for Los Angeles. The influence of Hollywood transformed Las Vegas into an entertainment and gambling carnival. The so-called Rat Pack of Frank Sinatra, Dean Martin, Joey Bishop, Peter Lawford, and Sammy Davis Jr. enlivened the hotels on the strip. Thousands of tourists from outside the region flocked in for an "adult" vacation.

Las Vegas became the archetype of gambling and glitz, regarded as sin city, America's playground, and an adult Disneyland. Many resort towns throughout the country offer the backdrop of a beach, a mountain lake, or even mineral hot springs, but not so with Las Vegas. The fact that Las Vegas emerged from the harsh flat desert of Southern Nevada underscores the reason it became a vacation destination. Gambling and entertainment are its primary features.

With the advent of the Caesar's Palace hotel/casino, Las Vegas set the pace to develop into a decadent fantasyland. This elaborate simulation of ancient Rome established a new standard for future hotels to follow: the more garish, the better. Later, tourists were offered ancient Egypt—The Luxor, Medieval England—Excalibur, and seventeenth-century Caribbean—Treasure Island. Customers at each hotel can enter a fantasyland with the casinos as the centerpiece.

In the black glass pyramid of the Luxor Hotel, most of the interior space is dedicated to the casino. The rooms are on the exterior walls in terraces, and the restaurants are in either the basement or the loft. The clanging of quarters in the slots and dazed, wandering gamblers permeate the cavernous extravaganza.

The promoters of the casino/hotels learned that wrapping gambling up in these fantasy costumes means it can be seen as a lark, just fun and games. By providing a simulation of plastic nirvana, they presented gambling as just entertainment, no less harmful than throwing rings at a carnival in hopes of winning a stuffed bear.

Up until 1968 most of the money made in casinos was from high rollers. Then the Circus Circus hotel/casino introduced more gambling options to low rollers. By the mid 1970s, the operators of Circus Circus found they could make more money from low rollers by pushing the tables aside and featuring slot machines as the primary gambling game. Until then, most casinos placed their slot machines on the periphery. Slot machines were considered just a means to "keep the missus occupied" while her husband did the serious gambling at the tables. But soon most hotels followed the lead of Circus Circus.

During the 1950s and 1960s, 75 percent of a casino's take came from tables. By the late 1990s, 62 percent or $4.4 billion in Nevada's casinos came from slots. In 1985, there were 90,612 slot machines in the state; in 1995 that number rose to 160,083.[4]

The prominence of the slots illustrates how widespread and mainstream gambling has become. Any adult or un-carded adolescent can play a slot without being watched and scrutinized by other people. Middle-aged and senior citizens are particularly susceptible to slot-machine use. Video poker slots are considered some of the most addictive gambling games. It is very common to see seniors sit for hours, entranced by the process of emptying their buckets of quarters amid the gong-gong and clank-clank.

Millions of people come to Las Vegas each year. Promoters of Las Vegas often boast that 12 of the 13 largest hotels in the world are found in their city. Indeed these hotels are major draws for the casinos. Gamblers lose an estimated $330 to $430 million annually.[5]

The state of Nevada has grown so dependent on the casino business that approximately 40 percent of the State's revenues come from the casinos.

Nevada's success in the gambling business did not go unnoticed. In the early 1990s, several Mississippi River states, including Iowa, Illinois, Kentucky, Mississippi, and Louisiana, began to put wagers on the gambling business. Many of these states decided that riverboat gambling could provide the revenues needed for their state coffers. The gambling revenue from Biloxi has made Mississippi the state with the third largest casino earnings. But after gambling was legalized in Tunica County, Mississippi, crime shot up despite the increase in tax revenues.

Atlantic City also weighed in with several large hotel/casinos. Its casinos drew thousands of day visitors coming in on buses and cars during the weekends, but the bankruptcy rate in Atlantic County, the county of Atlantic City, grew to 71 percent higher than in the rest of the state of New Jersey.[6] Students in the Atlantic City school district have also not fared well. The dropout rate is high and test scores low. The unemployment rate grew 15 percent, two and a half times the average for the rest of the state.

Las Vegas, too, reflects many of the social problems of gambling towns. The actual depth of the city infrastructure is thin. The schools are overcrowded, the dropout rate and juvenile delinquency is high, and there are approximately one hundred street gangs. Nevada's crime rate is 50 percent higher than the national average. Whereas 1.14 percent of the general public suffer from compulsive gambling, in Las Vegas the figure is 12 percent. According to interviews with casino executives and managers, upwards of nearly 80 percent of the gambling revenues come from 20 percent of the gamblers.[7]

The graft and corruption from the practices of skimming and money laundering drew the attention of many U.S. government officials. The government passed the Gaming Control Act, which established Gaming Commission to oversee Gaming Control Boards. However, in Nevada the Control Board functions as no more than a rubber stamp.[8]

For all the LCD hype and promotion of gambling as a means to save the budgets of states and communities, it appears that at best it is a double-edged sword. The casino industry bolsters employment numbers only in the service industries. Many service workers suffer from problems associated with living in towns with casinos as its main industry. For example, the percentage of casino employees with compulsive gambling problems is 15 percent of the estimated 55,000.[9]

In short, cities built around the casino industries are providing quicksand for gamblers to sink into. Many casinos offer automatic teller machines so their patrons can draw money on impulse. In Las Vegas, pawnshops are open 24 hours a day and will easily accept the signing over of vehicles.

Many gamblers are also parents, but some bring their children to the casinos and park them in the video arcades. In 1997, a 7-year-old girl was raped and murdered in a restroom in a Nevada casino. This horrifying crime is vivid testament to how the destructive power of gambling can so obsess people that parental responsibility is put on the back burner.

THE NEW BUFFALO

In the novel *The Bingo Palace*, Louise Erdrich told a story about a community of Chippewas who ran a bingo operation on their reservation. In fact, for many years reservations have turned to bingo games to produce income. But just as many cities have promoted casino businesses, so have many reservations moved to expand their operations to include casinos.

The Seminole tribe in Florida sued the government to expand the $100 pot limit in their bingo games to $10,000. The Cabazon tribe of the Mission Indians outside Palm Springs opened a card room in 1980. In the next ten years they expanded their enterprise to a variety of gambling games.

One of the pioneers in Native American casinos was the Mashantucket Pequot casino in Connecticut. But the Mashantucket Reservation had just a few members of the tribe still living in the area in the early 1970s. Through the efforts of a few members such as Richard "Skip" Hayward, tribal members began to drift back to the reservation with hopes of developing a business. By 1975, Hayward was Tribal Chairman of 55 people. Most of the Pequots living on the reservation today are the descendents of one of nine sisters who lived on the reservation at the turn of the century. These "reunited" Pequots are from a diverse racial mix. Some look distinctly African American while others look distinctly European American.[10] Eventually the Pequots developed a casino known as Foxwoods. Strategically located halfway between Boston and New York City, Foxwoods brought in approximately 45,000 people each day in 1996. Their casino grew larger than the largest Las Vegas casino, the MGM Grand.

Native Americans began to refer to the casino business as the "new buffalo."[11] Indeed, between 1988 and 1996, approximately 110 of the 554 federally recognized Indian tribes in the nation opened 230 gambling operations. Native American casinos made $121 million in 1988, which rose to $5.3 billion by 1996.[12]

Indian gaming became so lucrative that by the late 1980s Congress passed the Indian Gaming Regulatory Act, which requires the tribes to negotiate compacts with the states. These compacts were meant to provide a working agreement between the states and the reservations over how much the casinos can expand. But in California in 1998, the tribes managed to lobby for and pass a state proposition to give them more freedom in their expansion requests. Twice, Indian casinos came up in California elections. Both times, the Indian right to self-sufficiency packaged in a state proposition won easily.

The tribes argued that reservations were sovereign nations. Though the Nevada-based casino industry poured in millions to defeat the proposition, the Native Americans were able to tap into the deep stratum of guilt left over from nineteenth-century genocide of tribes. Many voters agreed that because Native Americans were so horrifically treated in the past, they should be allowed to operate outside of state law.

Indian-based casinos have also been wielding considerable political power. The Pequots donated $500,000 to the Democratic National Committee in 1994. Following the donation, Skip Hayward was invited to the White House.

Even decisions made about Indian casinos can easily turn into scandal. Like casinos throughout the country, reservation-based casinos create social graft. According to the *San Francisco Chronicle*, the Cabazon group has maintained suspicious ties to organized crime.[13]

And like casinos everywhere, reservation-based casinos draw people not well served by the expense of gambling. Indeed, a friend of mine was asked to testify in front of the New Mexico State Legislature in her capacity as the State Director of Mental Health and Substance Abuse regarding the effect of the reservation-based casinos on the population of New Mexico. A significant portion of the customers of the reservation casinos in New Mexico are low-income Hispanic women who gamble after dropping their children off at school. Many of these women receive Aid to Families with Dependent Children.

In 1996 a Massachusetts couple was arrested for locking their child in their car for several hours while they gambled at Foxwoods. It was 22 degrees outside, and another customer found the boy shivering. Even after the boy was in the custody of the police, the couple did not return for an additional seven hours.

LOTTO MANIA

Lotteries have a long history. They were used in ancient Greece, Rome, and China. They were used during the Middle Ages to fund government projects and in the fifteenth and sixteenth centuries to finance some explorations, including the Columbus voyages. Lotteries were used in the United States until they were outlawed in the early twentieth century. Now they are more prevalent here than they ever were.

By the 1930s the Mob was operating a very lucrative numbers business. Then in 1958 *The New York Times* reported that a Harlem numbers ring had been taking $300,000 worth of bets a day.[14] States began to notice that the numbers racket was a way of bringing in considerable revenue.

In the early 1960s, New Hampshire opened the gates for the reintroduction of the lottery as a government enterprise. Rather than implementing a sales tax or raising existing taxes to fund the school system that was dealing with increasing numbers of baby boomers, the state chose to "protect" its citizens from the "punishment" of taxes by depending on lotteries to fund programs.

Governor Nelson Rockefeller of New York gave up his opposition to the lottery and came out instead to promote it as a means of funding the school system and other government projects. Gradually the New York ad program transformed from messages such as "Help your schools" to "Get rich quick."

By 1975 the New Jersey lottery system offered its gamblers the opportunity for immediate gratification by computerized betting. New Jersey's innovation illustrates the problem lottery systems had in competing with casino gambling operations. Because we are a culture increasingly oriented to immediate gratification, lottery players have been offered a way to quench their thirst for gambling with a quick fix. Just as slot machines let gamblers know immediately if they have won, so scratch-off lottery tickets give that instant feedback. Lottery players can know immediately whether they have three aces and are entitled to an instant reward.

States such as New York have been offering instant games at interactive video lottery terminals (VLTs). These VLTs have been dubbed "video crack" because they are extremely addictive. A player can play blackjack, poker, or quick-draw keno.

Up until the 1980s, the lottery constituted just a fraction of the gambling in the country. But then the massive federal deficits brought on by the Reagan and Bush administrations meant the federal dollars the states so depended on were cut dramatically. For states still on the fence about lotteries, this budgetary crisis was just enough to push them over the edge. Between 1984 and 1996, bets on lotteries grew by 950 percent, and 37 states and Washington, D.C., moved into the gambling business.[15]

The largest lottery had been in New York. In 1996 it was estimated that people were betting $10 million a day on the New York lottery. The big Lotto games drew considerable attention. Then the states in the Northeast combined their efforts to pump up the jackpots by offering the multi-state Power Ball drawing.

It is now considered perfectly legitimate to fund programs by operating lotteries. This LCD concept undermines the notion that paying taxes is a responsibility of every citizen. The very premise that citizens should not be burdened by having to pay taxes but should be allowed to support the government through betting on the lotteries tears at the fabric of society. Many politicians participate in reinforcing this LCD belief and stay in office by railing against taxes while turning a blind eye to the destructive influence of gambling.

Government supporters of the lotteries have served to subvert the consciousness of citizens. Consider the following poster ad for the Massachusetts lottery:

How to Make Millions.

Plan A: Start studying when you're about seven years old, real hard. Then grow up and get a good job. From then on, get up at dawn every day. . . . Do this every day for 30 years, holidays and weekends included.

Plan B: (a picture shows two lottery tickets)

Many such ad campaigns to sell lottery tickets reflect not only a crude attempt to reach a public consciousness long since gravitating to the LCD but also the apparent belief that gambling is a perfectly legitimate activity.

The expansion of state lottery programs reinforces the belief that striking it big at gambling is the road to happiness. Yet, as noted earlier, several studies have shown that winning at the lottery does not equate with happiness.

Understandably, many people who bet on the lotteries do not consider the bet a form of gambling. Winning it big at the lottery is believed to be the answer to one's problems.

Timothy O'Brien describes a Connecticut lottery ad:

A 1980 television ad for the Connecticut lottery portrayed a solitary fisherman sadly admitting that he could have saved for his children's education or his own retirement, but he neglected to be so responsible. He then soberly confided to viewers that he had played the lottery instead. Then, after a slight pause, came the kicker. The fisherman shouted for all to hear that he was rich! rich! rich! It was a sales pitch with a perennial appeal.[16]

Most people who buy lottery tickets are people with low incomes.[17] Wealthy lottery gamblers bet a much smaller proportion of their income than do lower-income gamblers. *Newsday* reported that households with an annual income of less than $20,000 per year spent an average of $420 a year on the lottery.[18]

The primary reason lotteries were implemented was to support schools and other programs. But a study of state lotteries by Thomas Jones and John Amalfitano found that lotteries do not, in fact, help the schools.[19] Often these monies are siphoned off into the state's general fund.

NAMBLING

Though private Internet services have been around since the late 1980s, the government did not allow businesses to market themselves until 1991. Since then, Internet gambling sites have spread over cyberspace. The Internet has made physical remoteness no obstacle for those wishing to satiate their hunger for gambling. Internet gambling is now referred to as "nambling" by many of its operators.

Nambling companies offer their customers accounts through the use of their credit cards, wired funds, or deposits in specified banks.

In 1994 the Virtual Vegas nambling site opened up in Venice, California. Its operators estimate that approximately 100,000 people play Black Jack, the slots, sports betting, or craps.[20] It is difficult to determine precisely how much gambling is taking place on the Internet. By measure of the number of sites open all over the world, it would be safe to assume that the number is extraordinarily high. A trade publication named *The International Gaming & Wagering Business* estimates that $143 million worth in sports bets were made in the United States over the Internet in 1996. That figure jumped to $760 million by the year 2000.

In the United States, federal law prohibits transmitting bets across state lines, accept for horse racing. Because of this law, many nambling companies are setting up shop outside the United States. Many are going to the Caribbean. Nevertheless, because the Internet has no boundaries, Americans gamble over the Internet via servers in the Caribbean and elsewhere.

Most of the Caribbean nambling businesses are actually American. Interactive Gaming and Communication Corporation has its corporate headquarters in Blue Bell, Pennsylvania, but maintains its server in Grenada. The company known as World Wide has its corporate office in Santa Anna, California, but maintains its server in Antigua. In fact, World Wide has touted its undersea fiber-optic link with the United States.

Interactive has publicly sold stock in its company; therefore, we are able to know its business report. They reported that in one year they handled $58 million in bets and lost only $695,920.[21]

The nambling site known as Centrebet offers gambling to anyone in the world from its home in Alice Springs in Australia's outback. Centrebet began accepting bets in 1996. Its operators estimate that $35 million worth of bets were made in 1997.[22]

Much of the nambling business is devoted to sports betting. In fact, Interactive Gaming & Communications Corporation maintains a sports-betting unit called Sports International. Austria's Interlope offers sports betting, as does Australia's Centrebet.

Nambling is rapidly becoming mobile. Many airline companies, including Swissair, Singapore Air, British Air, and Lauda Air of Austria, have tested nambling services for their in-flight entertainment.

The growing phenomenon of nambling demonstrates that as the gambling business goes high tech, what little public scrutiny still exists will evaporate in hyperspace. Nambling will render obsolete what few societal controls we maintain to protect those who have not yet fallen into the quicksand of compulsive gambling.

Gambling has legitimized and intensified the lust for money. The intermittent reinforcement the gambler experiences, so well described by Learning Theory, strings the gambler along for another rush of excitement. Gamblers know that if they play long enough they will eventually be rewarded by an enticing hors d'oeuvre. But rarely if ever do they enjoy the main course—the big win. In his book *Chase: The Compulsive Gambler,* Illinois State University Professor Henry Lesieur points out that compulsive gamblers strive for a "continuous stringing together of action."[23] Many compulsive gamblers get a rush from the risk and excitement of the "action" of gambling.

A Harvard University Medical School study indicated that 1.14 percent of the adult population in the United States and Canada are compulsive gamblers. Even more alarming was the finding that 5.77 percent of adolescents are active compulsive gamblers. Problem gamblers—those who often bet beyond their means but still are not addicted—amount to 2.8 percent of adults and an astounding 14.82 percent of adolescents.[24]

It has been estimated that approximately $88 billion is bet illegally on sports each year. As much as $5 billion is bet on just the Superbowl alone.[25] A University of Illinois study of college students found that 20.5 percent of a sample of students from six colleges identified themselves as having a gambling problem.[26]

Even athletes themselves admit to gambling problems. According to a 1995 University of Cincinnati study conducted for the NCAA, 25 percent of the athletes gambled, with 4 percent betting on the games they played in.[27]

There is every reason to believe that gambling and the problems associated with it are becoming an increasingly widespread problem in the emerging LCD society. For example, the Iowa Department of Public Health reported that the calls they receive from people seeking help for gambling problems went from 3,700 to 14,000 in just one year.[28] It just so happened that riverboat gambling was expanding in Iowa and Illinois on the Mississippi River during the same period. With the expansion of nambling and its easy access, we find the prevalence of gambling and its associated problems proliferating into the twenty-first century.

DAY TRADING

The stock market is a sophisticated form of gambling. Because investing in stocks is tied to the very fabric of our economy, the stock market is considered respectable and even a lofty enterprise.

The phenomenon of day trading resembles sports and horse race betting. Indeed, someone who engages in day trading cannot rationalize that it is an investment. An estimated 4,000 to 5,000 people put in as many as 35 trades a day from their computer terminals. Most of them lose money.[29]

Day trading has become such a source of recklessness and loss that in mid 1999 the North American Securities Administrators Association (NASAA) warned that major problems include questionable loan schemes, misleading marketing, and poor screening of customers.

Perhaps not so ironically, the NASAA report came out just as Martin Barton, a 44-year-old day trader, shot to death nine people in two Atlanta brokerages. He was reported to have lost $450,000 in day trading in these very brokerages.

There are over 100 day-trading firms in the United States. Clients are expected to have no less than $50,000 in their accounts. The NASAA found that day-trading firms misrepresented their customers' potential income from day trading. The TCI Corporation was dubbed as a "power high profile income opportunity" with "unlimited income opportunity." In fact, some firms promote and arrange inter-customer loans to help losing traders meet margin calls.

By some estimates, the number of people who have quit their jobs to gamble full-time at day-trading firms grew to over 5,000 by 1999. But the number of people who take a break from meetings or trade on-line at home is approximately 5 million.[30] Only 15 percent of these people actually make money.

Day trading, like casino gambling, provides players with instant gratification often followed by grief. All such forms of gambling offer the illusion of the opportunity to get rich quick.

Now the erroneously assumed boundaries between gambling and stock market trading have been neutralized. We have come to the point where we can say that as we sleepwalk through the first few years of the twenty-first century, our economy and the people who participate in it are part of a massive crap shoot.

12

Punching the Clock

During the past 20 years we have seen major changes in our work-force and working conditions. There has been an increase in work-place violence, more workers out on stress leave, and a surge in corporate takeovers with subsequent downsizings. Workers have been asked to perform more work for less pay.

Many workers do not possess the skills critical to adapting to the changing economy. Also they have been ill prepared psychologically for these changes. Much of the general degradation of the labor force can be attributed to the emerging LCD society, as there have been several cultural shifts among our workers. To examine these changes, we need to first examine the large-scale sociopolitical changes incurred by our labor force.

THE RANK AND FILE

As we shifted from an agrarian economy to an industrial economy, thousands of people left farms and moved into the cities to find work. The Industrial Revolution produced tremendous tension between la-bor and management. Initially, this oligarchic gap was between the rich owners of large companies and the badly paid and exploited workers.

Thousands of people found jobs in large sweatshops and unsafe factories. The pay was low and the hours long. Many families had great difficulty making ends meet and asked their children to work alongside them. No child labor laws existed, and children were abused and exploited.

Gradually, socially conscious public officials opposed these de-plorable conditions. Theodore Roosevelt shocked his Republican colleagues when he sided with workers instead of company owners during a major strike. Workers' rights were finally becoming part of the national discourse.

By the 1930s, unions expanded in response to gross exploitation by large companies. Essentially, the unions emerged because com-panies were not looking out for their employees' welfare. As unions emerged, their leaders negotiated with management to secure eq-uitable contracts for wages, safer working conditions, and benefits. By the 1960s a consortium of unions under the umbrella of the AFL-CIO maintained considerable political and economic clout. If con-tract negotiations did not go well, the unions reserved the right to call crippling strikes and force the corporate management back to the negotiating table to concede a better deal for workers.

Wages rose dramatically for many union workers. During the 1970s it was not uncommon for members of the United Autoworkers to earn $30 an hour. However, union workers assumed these condi-tions would go on into the future. Workers supported their union's attempts to bargain for higher wages without concern about the fu-ture. They ignored the necessity to develop clauses in the contracts that included severance pay and retraining.

As the international economy began to transform, multinational corporations began to rethink their relationships with the unions. Corporations began to export thousands of jobs to countries whose workers were paid a fraction of what American workers earned. Thousands of Americans, such as steelworkers, lost their jobs. The exodus of factories sent abroad struck whole towns. The rust belt began to symbolize the economic transformation of our economy.

Just as the unions were losing their clout, the newly elected Rea-gan administration crushed the Airport Controllers' Union. To add insult to injury, Reagan inflicted heavy damage to existing labor laws.

Ironically, millions of blue-collar workers had contributed to their own demise. Thousands of them became the so-called Reagan Dem-ocrats. Dazed and confused by layoffs, they felt that Reagan's tough talk about terrorists and communism was just what America needed.

Few had prepared themselves for the economic transformations of the 1980s and 1990s. When many of the blue-collar workers lost jobs they thought they would have until retirement, they found themselves in a transformed economy without marketable skills. Many laid-off union workers did not know what hit them.

By the mid 1990s, the labor market changed again. The economy began to expand, and unemployment shrank. What was a skilled workforce has now become a burgeoning service industry. Indeed, the largest gains in the growth of new jobs have been in the service industries.

Though the unemployment rate decreased during the late 1990s, a segment of the population was no longer counted by the Labor Department. This segment of the population was referred to not as "unemployed" but rather as "jobless."

Then came the recession of 2001–2002. Tech companies went bust and many of the bellwethers were cut by half. Mergers and the downsizings continued. Workers scrambled to keep their jobs.

There has also been a widening of disparity between people in the higher incomes and those in lower. Those with higher incomes now fare better, but the 40 percent at the bottom have fared very poorly since 1970.

When the economy expands again, the growth in new jobs will further strain our already stressed educational system. One measure of our preparedness for these new labor demands is the growing tendency to recruit abroad for skilled workers. It has become increasingly difficult to fill positions for highly skilled computer analysts, engineers, and programmers. A friend of mine quit his old job to become a headhunter for computer companies. So desperate are the computer companies to fill positions that they pay my friend $25,000 per person for their first year of employment. He has looked to Europe to find the talent the companies need.

The emergence of the LCD society is set on a collision course with the demands of the twenty-first century. Unfortunately, this looming labor crisis is not being debated or covered by our news media. Just as the laid-off union workers in the rust belt did not know what hit them, so today we face a crisis without awareness of the danger ahead.

WORKER ALIENATION

Against this backdrop of demographic change, workers have experienced increased feelings of alienation and anger. One result of the antagonistic relationship between labor and management is the loss of pride felt by workers in the quality of their work. Many workers find that their goals are different from company goals. Companies generally are oriented toward profit, while workers' goals are typically centered on increasing wages and benefits. Not often enough do the two goals coalesce.

Although unions have been critical advocates of the preservation of wages for their members, they have also underscored the impression that the company is an adversarial entity. For their part, many companies have downsized or merged with other companies, reinforcing the impression that they are not friends of the workers. With all the downsizing and corporate mergers, work conditions have deteriorated. Workers are asked to stretch themselves for the new company, to do more with less time and less support.

Many workers regard the time they spend at work as the company's time. Accordingly, they don't consider the product they produce their own. This lack of ownership has disastrous effects on the quality of work performed.

During the 1970s and 1980s, many Americans began buying Japanese, German, and Swedish automobiles because the quality of American vehicles plummeted. They became convinced that the quality of American craftsmanship had withered away. Ironically, many Americans who bought foreign goods were the producers of American goods. They not only saw what their peers produced but also understood how hard they themselves had worked.

Yet it is not as if Americans are working fewer hours to produce these goods. According to Harvard economist Juliet Schor, Americans are working longer hours than 50 years ago but finding it harder to maintain the same standard of living.[1] Corporate downsizing has meant that workers are responsible for more tasks but have not received significant pay increases associated with the new demands. The number of hours worked has increased by an average of 47 percent. The American workforce is now working 49 hours per week. The average now is about eight weeks longer per year than in 1969 for the same income.

Not only has inflation required that both parents in families work, but there is a general belief among these workers that they need more material possessions than in previous generations. As a result, today's workers are stuck in an obsessive cycle of working and spending.

For the past several years I have led a job-stress psychotherapy group. Not only have I seen an increase in referrals of people who have experienced stress related to corporate downsizing and harassment by supervisors, but I have also seen an increase in clients who harbor an attitude of entitlement. It is not uncommon to hear people say that because they feel exploited, they do not take the initiative to extend themselves. Employees sometimes respond to assignment requests by saying, "I don't believe that is in my job description." Although there is certainly a positive side to workers' feeling empowered enough to respond to management, many managers believe that workers have become increasingly combative.

Job stress has resulted in increased use of sick time and disability leave. The National Institute for Occupational Safety and Health (NIOSH) has produced a report citing psychological disorders as one of the 10 leading occupational diseases and injuries. According to NIOSH, the growth in job stress correlates to widespread downsizing. Companies that have downsized are now likely to have an increase in disability claims and to see decreased morale and productivity in the workforce. The director of NIOSH estimates that all this translates to billions of dollars of economic loss in terms of the whole area of work stress.[2]

Between a quarter and a third of workers in the United States report high job stress and feel drained at the end of the day. But it is not as if workers feel they can just switch jobs. In the past 10 years, the number of workers who fear job loss has doubled. Job burnout is the highest it has ever been.[3]

Due to the surge in temporary work, people are put into positions that do not offer security, a chance of advancement, or an opportunity to use their creativity. There has been a corresponding decrease in reported job satisfaction. Workers are finding that jobs fall short of their expectations.[4]

We have also seen an increase of drug and alcohol use in the workplace.[5] In response to this epidemic, many organizations now require random drug testing. Indeed, the federal government requires transportation companies to regularly test their drivers, pilots, and captains.

Many employees who use mind-altering substances regularly work in nonregulated industries and do not receive a sophisticated degree of scrutiny. This is especially the case if they consume drugs and/or alcohol on the weekends or after work. These employees do not know that drugs and alcohol impair concentration, memory, and energy levels for days after their last use. Though the employees might not be intoxicated on Monday morning, their cognitive abilities are not up to par. It is quite common to see deficits in motivation, optimism, and energy level. Other symptoms of drug and alcohol abuse include increased rigidity and difficulties with abstract and conceptual thinking. Finally, drug and alcohol users have often been noted to have difficulties in their interpersonal relationships. They are inclined to misread social cues and overreact to social stress. Together these symptoms contribute to major limitations in the quality of work produced by individuals who use drugs or alcohol on the weekends or after work.

For employees who use drugs or alcohol in the work environment, interpersonal conflict might become dangerous. The recent cliché "going postal" describes the all-too-common occurrence of disgruntled employees coming into work for lethal revenge. Going postal is not isolated to violence among postal employees. Murder in the workplace is rapidly becoming one of the fastest growing types of violence.[6]

Still, for the vast majority of workers experiencing job stress, violence is internalized into depression. Over the past several years, the number of people applying for workers' compensation for stress claims rose dramatically—so much so in California that the requirements for being approved have tightened considerably. Despite the tighter regulations, the number of applications has not dropped off.

It is not uncommon for workers to file claims for workers' compensation for stress and then wait out the process before deciding what they will do about moving on with their lives. Instead of looking for another job or enrolling in a retraining program, they suffer the illusion that there is a pot of gold at the end of the rainbow.

Similarly, it is very common to encounter people who want their state disability payments extended when in fact they are quite capable of working. This increasing trend represents an attitudinal shift whereby workers regard employment as a necessary nuisance, better circumvented than embraced.

If workers and the companies that employ them continue to regard one another with suspicion and cynicism, the LCD culture they collectively produce in the workplace will continue to motivate people to anesthetize themselves with the world of entertainment. That entertainment will reflect the same dynamics they are trying to escape.

13
McMedicine

There are more doctors in a single North Shore medical building than in one entire West Side ghetto.

Jack Starr

Medical care has gone aggressively retail in the marketplace. Over the past five decades, the health care system in the United States has become big business. Health care exists as a significant part of the national economy. In 1960, 5.1 percent of the gross national product was spent on health care; by 1980, it was 8.9 percent. By the late 1990s, health care spending in the United States climbed over the trillion-dollar mark and was 1.6 percent of the GNP.[1] Meanwhile, the number of people without health insurance expanded.

DOWNSIZING HEALTH CARE

Until just recently, there was a large-scale trend toward specialization in medicine. Most physicians newly graduated from medical schools chose specialized fields in medicine, partly because the financial rewards were greater than in primary care. As the number of specialists increased and the number of primary care or family physicians decreased, referrals to those highly paid specialists moved up.

According to the *Wall Street Journal*, in 1975, 3.3 percent of physicians entered anesthesiology. That rose to 4 percent in 1985 and then to 4.5 in 1996. Simultaneously, in 1975, 10.8 percent of physicians were in family practice. In 1985 that number plummeted to 4.9 percent, and in 1996, it dropped again to 2.3 percent.[2]

The health care system has changed dramatically over the past decade. Since the early 1990s, multiple efforts were made, including downsizing, to cut costs and stabilize prices. Many of the highly paid specialists lost as much as half of their salaries, and many nurses were laid off and replaced with aides. However, the downsizing cuts have taken many companies to the bone and left the health care industry less able to actually manage health care. The Draconian cuts made during the downsizing craze in health care produced only short-term savings.

Then in the mid 1990s, there were large-scale financial losses. Kaiser Permanente announced a $270-million loss in 1997. The United Health Care Corporation posted a $900-million loss in the second quarter of 1998. According to Intrastudy, a managed care research firm, 75 percent of health plans lost money in 1997.[3]

Partly because it's an integrated system with high customer satisfaction, Kaiser Permanente emerged from the restructuring years with a budget in the black in 1999 and 2000. Other health care systems have not been so fortunate. Harvard Pilgrim Health Care has been forced into receivership by its home state of Massachusetts. Two of the largest nursing home chains, Sun Healthcare Group Inc. and Vencor Inc., declared bankruptcy. In California alone in 1990, there were 22 major health plans. By the end of that decade, the number had shrunk to seven.

DAMAGED CARE

Corporate mergers and downsizing of retail health care has mutated the United States health care system; what has emerged has come to be known as "managed care." But managed care is an oxymoron. To generate large profits within the health care industry, care has been degraded. Managed care should be renamed "managed dollars"—or "damaged care," as dubbed by the San Francisco Mime Troupe. The only way big profits could be made was to take the care out of managed care.

For clarity, however, let us continue to use the oxymoron. Managed care has turned all aspects of health care upside down. Managed care is, in fact, a euphemism for "limited access." In the manic effort to save money and generate profit, insurance companies are asking their providers to trim the care delivery to brief and inexpensive office visits.

Corporate control over health care decisions has also driven the quality of care downhill. The insurance industry has taken control of the providers and has aligned itself with the demands made by PACs and large employers for lower insurance premiums.

Insurance companies sell their plans to employer groups, who in turn try to convince their employees that they are getting a great deal. The employer groups have demanded cheaper care while providing the illusion of ongoing excellent coverage. They insist that health insurers should give immediate access to patients. The result is McMedicine health care that gives relatively quick access for short, cheap doctor's office visits.

The "feel good" message about turning to managed care stated that medical groups would stress preventive care to keep group costs down. However, the reality became limiting patient access to keep costs down.

Many physicians have found that if they continue to work at the same pace as before managed care, their incomes would drop by one-half. To maintain the same standard of living, they have to work twice as hard. In other words, they have to see twice as many patients as they saw in the past. Where a primary care physician might have had approximately 12 minutes to see each patient 10 years ago, they have 6 minutes to see a patient now. Not only do they have less time to spend with patients to accurately diagnose and prescribe a treatment, but also these shorter visits tend to focus around single symptoms. Patients have to schedule another appointment if they have multiple problems or if their illness is complex. But many physicians have to leave their paperwork until later. During the perhaps two hours of paperwork at the end of the day physicians might have difficulty keeping all the patients straight in their memory. Charting becomes more cryptic and potentially inaccurate.

The health care industry has increasingly relied on medication as the sole answer and cure for our ailments.[4] Antibiotic medications are being prescribed at an alarming and inappropriate rate. It is not uncommon for a parent of a child with a simple cold virus to walk away from a pediatrician's office with a prescription for antibiotics. This prescription is made despite the fact that antibiotics do not cure the common cold. The fault lies with both the parent and the physician. The parent wants "something" and the physician wants their brief consult to result in at least the appearance of help. As a result, antibiotics are now becoming increasingly ineffective because of overuse. There is evidence that approximately 70 percent of antibi-

otic medications are inappropriately prescribed for upper respira-
tory infections.

Against this backdrop of overreliance on medications, premiums
for an HMO's pharmacy insurance products have risen 4 to 6 percent
annually over the last few years. Meanwhile, medical expenses have
jumped 16 to 18 percent each year. In 1997, drug costs were up 14
percent. Then in 1998 the costs shot up another 12 to 17 percent. Out
of the approximately 60 new drugs to emerge in the health care system in the past few years, very few cost under $100 per month.[5]

Many HMOs are requiring physician organizations to assume risk
for the rising costs of drugs. In 1996, just 26 percent of HMOs had
used this Draconian cost-containment strategy. According to the
1998 Novartis Pharmacy Benefit Report "Trends and Forecasts,"
there has been a 40 percent increase in the number of HMOs plan-
ning to use pharmacy risk pools.

Now physicians are concerned about financial risks and they are
pressured to choose the least expensive medication. Weighing financial risks and treatment efficacy can be very difficult. In other words,
a physician might be biased in favor of a cheaper medication and
have less time to thoroughly investigate its efficacy in the research
literature.

Thus, given the rise in costs for drugs, physicians are forced to
think twice about what medication they prescribe. If antibiotic medication A is more effective for a particular infection than is antibiotic
B but A is more expensive, the physician might be pressured to use
B. But use of antibiotic B might make the cure less probable. Addi-
tionally, because antibiotics are overprescribed in general, the use
of antibiotic B might contribute to less effectiveness when it is appropriately prescribed later.

In many HMOs, certain medications do not make it on the for-
mulary despite the fact that they are the recommended treatment.
This is because certain drugs are extremely expensive. Despite their
efficacy, the insurance companies do not want to pay for providing
these medications.

Not only is drug choice moderated by financial concern, but also
referral to an appropriate specialist is controlled under managed
care. The waiting time to see specialists has increased. Consequently, a patient with a heart disease who sees an overworked primary care physician might receive inadequate, untimely treatment,

and a referral to a cardiologist, if medically indicated, might be delayed.

Physicians have been told they should limit certain types of treatments and restrict access to specialists. So pervasive has this trend been that several states have moved to legislate a lift of the "gag order" on physicians to permit them to recommend appropriate options, including access to specialists. Lifting the gag order might be more therapeutic for the patient but more expensive for the insurance company.

As the specialists feel the squeeze, they become frustrated with the marked drop in referrals. When patients do reach a specialist, the specialist might vent to the patient that the referral should have been made earlier. The patients, already concerned about their medical conditions, not only lose confidence in their primary care physicians, but some might use the comment as grounds for a malpractice suit.

Meanwhile, overcrowding in emergency departments is reaching a critical level. According to a study published in the January 2000 issue of the *Annals of Emergency Medicine*, Robert Derlet and John Richards of the University of California, Davis, Medical Center report that "unless the problem is solved in the near future, the general public may no longer be able to rely on emergency departments for quality and timely emergency care, placing the safety of people of this country at risk."[6]

My own aunt sought the care of a physician in an emergency room with complaints of chest and shoulder pain. She was told to go home and rest her sore shoulder. That night she died of cardiac arrest. Had her physicians been given time and resources to fully assess her symptoms, they would have correctly found that she suffered from the early signs of an impending heart attack.

PROFIT SHARKS

In the late 1980s, 27.7 million people belonged to HMOs. By the late 1990s, 145 million people received their care through HMOs, PPOs, and similar programs. A few years ago it looked as though the less cost-effective PPOs would fade away in the face of managed care and the HMOs. However, it appears now that PPOs are taking market share from the HMOs. As a result, physicians are experiencing a cut in reimbursements; yet somebody is reaping the profits.

Some have characterized the current business situation for those in charge as a gold rush until something is done to curtail the huge salaries and payoffs. The Columbia Corporation, infamous for takeovers of small hospitals, quietly paid "salaries" to board members of community hospitals to conscript them into supporting Columbia's takeover bid.

Pharmaceutical companies have also been participating in the gold rush. To ensure high profits, companies have tried to induce physicians to prescribe their particular brand of medication. A recent accounting of the money spent in promotion by pharmaceutical companies indicated that $13,000 was spent per physician. One company paid primary care physicians $5,000 per patient to research its medication's lipid-lowering efficacy.

The pharmaceutical companies have also begun to market directly to patients. For example, Claritin ads feature a beautiful alpine scene and other "clean air" views on television and in magazines. These ads have been responsible for a significant boost in sales of the drug. Meanwhile, Viagra is now being marketed to the general public despite an increase in the related death rate.

Genentech touts its +PA at $2,500 a dose for stroke victims, and the general public believes it is a cure for strokes. However, almost all studies have shown that the medicine can be dangerous for most stroke patients.[7] As Genentech puts out their own studies of support, Canada meanwhile prohibits the use of +PA.

Among the pharmaceutical companies' never-ending promotional programs, they offer HMOs a discount if physicians prescribe a selected list of drugs. HMOs, pressured to keep costs down, have a difficult time resisting the savings. In September of 1998, Bristol-Myers Squibb proposed a deal to Foundation Health Systems whereby the HMO was to receive $1 million per month for adding five Bristol-Myers Squibb drugs to its formulary as the only medications in their therapeutic classes.

The New York Times reported that some physicians, in exchange for money, have allowed pharmaceutical sales representatives into their examining rooms to meet patients, review medical charts, and recommend medicines to prescribe.[8] Some of those salespeople have even recommended that doctors prescribe drugs not approved by the Federal Food and Drug Administration.

While, on the one hand, the pharmaceutical companies are hiking prices and contributing to escalating health care costs, they are also offering an ethically challenged way for physicians and HMOs to make and save money. Many physicians watch in dismay as their power to effectively treat patients is overridden by economic interests.

SINKING LOW WITH THE PROVIDERS

Job satisfaction and morale have plummeted across the country. With the increase in downsizing, we see an increase in work-related stress. It has been estimated that up to one-third of people who have taken off work have done so because of work related stress; this is true for all workers. The nation's health care workers are not an exception.[9]

According to a survey of 1,053 doctors and 768 nurses conducted by the Kaiser Family Foundation and the Harvard School of Public Health, 87 percent said their patients had been denied health care coverage by their HMOs during the previous two years. None of these health care providers were from Kaiser Permanente.[10]

Health care employees have become overworked, and morale has sunk. And patients themselves have experienced the subtle effects of the low morale. Not only are patients disappointed that routine tests are avoided and appointments with specialists limited, but also their confidence in the health care system has plummeted.

Providers are not only treated badly and asked to do more with less help; they have also been attacked by the very organizations that pay them. Providers are less likely to stretch and go the extra mile to provide a comprehensive assessment of your health problem. Consequently, as providers become pessimistic, your exam results will be seen with pessimistic eyes: "Well, Ms. Smith, there is not much we can do for your condition." Alternatively, the overworked but optimistic provider might say Mr. Jones is fine when in fact he might be seriously ill.

No wonder patients are becoming more concerned about the medical system. According to a survey in the early 1990s of people from 10 different countries, respondents from the United States rated their health care system the most poorly. Specifically, only 10 percent of the people surveyed in the United States reported that their health care system on the whole worked pretty well and required only minor changes to make it work better.[11]

Because the emerging McMedicine system relies on quick and often inappropriate use of medication at the expense of thorough ex-
aminations, we have damaged medical care. Though thousands of
hard-working, dedicated physicians provide quality care for their
patients, we have created a system that ties their hands and relegates
them to being a "doc in a box."

We have come full circle. In our efforts to repair the health care
system, we have created a health care crisis. While attempting to
keep health care costs down, we have cultivated the dynamics for
which the quality of care plummets to the LCD and ironically costs
can rise again.

If the "care" is taken out of the health care system, the contradiction in meaning fuels the already surreal social fabric of the LCD
society. Under such conditions, actors who play doctors on TV can,
in fact, sell over-the-counter medicines in television commercials.

14
Shrink Wrap

Show me a sane man and I will cure him for you.

Carl Jung

In this rapidly changing society, LCD perspectives have tarnished the public's understanding of the mind. Not only have the concepts of sanity and insanity been oversimplified, but mental health professionals have also responded to simplified frames of reference.

One would assume that our LCD society would not affect those who have been trained in the mental health fields, YET these practitioners have not been insulated from the meltdown. The economic and societal pressures have been too overwhelming to withstand. Along with significant gains in our understanding of the mind have also come setbacks in the development of a viable mental health system because of cutbacks in funding. These cutbacks have forced mental health practitioners into political jockeying and posturing replete with hollow clichés.

CLINICALESE

As the professional mental health community has become increasingly established as a viable part of the general health care industry, we have embraced simplistic clichés that parallel the public's gravitation toward LCD concepts such as the medical model.

Currently two doctoral-level providers exist in the mental health field: psychologists with a Ph.D. and psychiatrists with an M.D. The field of psychology has fragmented into specialties. Organizational psychologists specialize in consulting to large companies, neuropsychologists evaluate people with neurological disorders, forensic psychologists treat and evaluate people in the criminal justice system, and the list goes on and on. The American Psychological Association has 51 divisions.

Psychiatrists still hold the medication bag and a significant degree of power in the system. Consequently, the mental health system remains stuck in a one-dimensional medical model that parallels the LCD embraced by the general public, namely that psychological problems are the result of bad genes and can only be treated by medication.

Psychiatrists, accordingly, have centered their training and practice solely on psychopharmacology—prescribing psychotropic medications. They are trained in three-year residency programs that amount to on-the-job training. If they are fortunate, they might receive a day a week of actual didactic training. Though already miniscule, many programs are being cut almost out of existence. Recently the psychiatric residency program at the University of New Mexico, like many other residing programs, was threatened with a cut of their remaining three hours of didactic training a week. Thus psychological theories are given only lip service.

Joining psychologists and psychiatrists in the mental health field are master's-level social workers and marriage and family counselors. In California, the marriage and family counselors (formerly referred to as MFCCs) have lobbied the state legislature to strike the unclinical term "counselor" and replace it with "therapist." They are now called marriage and family therapists (MFTs). Many master's-level practitioners tend to feel inadequate because they lack the title "doctor," so they refer to themselves as clinicians. The clinical posture is essentially a defense against being thought of as inferior. Those who have donned themselves in clinical garb have also embraced the LCD medical model adopted by psychiatrists.

Many of these clinicians speak in a cliché language of the medical model that I have called "clinicalese." For example, they might preface an opinion by saying, "Well, clinically speaking . . ." or "It is my clinical opinion that. . . ." It is as if they are saying, "I really don't feel confident, but I do have credentials and I can call them a term we all agree means something." Confident therapists do not need clumsy qualifiers to hide behind. The clinical qualifier is an oversimplification that negates the complexity of the mental health field and provides an LCD facade of legitimacy.

Social commentator James Thurber once commented, "In an extensive reading of recent books by psychologists, psychoanalysts, psychiatrists, and inspirationalists, I have discovered that they all suffer from one or more of these expression-complexes: italicizing, capitalizing, exclamation-pointing, condition frankly, Rhetorical-Over-Compensation."[1]

Downsizing in the mental health system has fueled the LCD jargon during the past 15 years. Many mental health practitioners fear for their jobs as insurance companies shrink benefits and the numbers of staff in provider agencies. Speaking in clinicalese provides camouflage for practitioners who fear their competency will be questioned and, as a result, their jobs eliminated.

As administrators try to stretch decreased budgets to pay for staff positions, the qualifications expected for these positions have dropped. For example, in community mental health centers, psychologists are now virtually extinct. When a psychologist leaves a position, it is converted to a master's-level "clinician" position. The same trend is underway in the HMO system. This trend follows the downsizing trend in health care in general, whereby LVNs replace RNs, and the quality of care plummets.

If qualifications for providing services in the mental health system continue to go down, so will the sophistication of the assessment and treatment of patients within that system. Patients will be misdiagnosed and treated inappropriately. Downsizing of the mental health system has therefore not only contributed to clinicalese but also to a narrowed view of the range of psychological problems and possible treatment strategies.

DIAGNOSTIC FADS

During the past 20 years, practitioners in the mental health community have overdiagnosed personality disorders. Personality disorders are enduring patterns of behavior and emotional responsiveness (or lack of it) that the person has little insight about. Though the concept of personality disorders has been helpful, it can be a double-edged sword. Many practitioners describe those they do not like or understand as a person with a personality disorder. This becomes a way of writing the person off and avoiding any responsibility for helping them. The most common example is the term "borderline"—basically meaning that the person has a tendency to split and put down his or her helpers or, alternatively, idealize them. The term borderline has been used countless times by clinicians who have trouble describing a client who is not consistently compliant with the treatment goals established by the clinicians. Gravitating toward the borderline tag seals therapists off from further analysis and prohibits an exploration of how they interact with their clients.

The early Freudians developed the concept of countertransference to emphasize how a therapist can overreact to idiosyncratic personality characteristics of clients. It was theorized that a client's personality might bring up something within the therapist's personality that has yet to be resolved. In other words, for some yet-to-be-determined reason, the therapist does not feel comfortable with the client. The task of the therapist is to analyze his or her countertransference so therapy can resume unimpeded.

During the past few decades we have moved away from a thoughtful examination of the analysis of countertransference. In the era of managed care, we have less time to consult with our colleagues in case conferences. When we do talk to our colleagues, it is much easier to assign a client a diagnosis of a personality disorder than to analyze our own interactions with the client.

Because of our efforts to provide quick and easy access, we have thrown quality and reflection out the window. It is as if we're saying that any counseling is adequate counseling. All we need to do is see more people and put them in "diagnostically appropriate" treatments. There is a great danger that mental health delivery programs will offer no more than a one-size-fits-all approach to people with various psychological problems. In other words, all people who are depressed might be offered just one treatment modality. All people with anxiety-related problems would be offered another modality.

In the mental health field, the LCD has become a manual of diagnostic terms. The handbook, titled the *Diagnostic and Statistical Manual of Mental Disorders*, now in its fourth addition (and referred to as DSM-IV) serves as the catalog of psychological disorders. When the fifth edition of the DSM series is published, some of the terms in the fourth edition will have vanished, as was the case with the previous DSM editions. Certainly, a wide variety of syndromes is common among people, but when clinicians go no further than to refer to a DSM-IV term such as borderline personality, there is a problem in understanding. Use of the DSM-IV does not necessarily result in clinical competence. In other words, clinicians may not ask what factors have contributed to the psychological distress and how their treatment can be tailor-made to best help the person.

Further, many of the disorders described in the DSM catalogs are considered to be actual disease processes amenable only to medication. This is the heart of the medical model. Accordingly, the LCD for mental health providers has been the medical model since the 1980s.

The shift to the medical model was partly facilitated by the development of more efficient psychotropic medications and genetic studies. The great advances in genetic studies led to the belief that all psychological problems can be boiled down to bad genes. The combination of these advances in genetics and the great strides made in psychopharmocology led to a reluctance to look any further for an understanding of psychological problems. There is no question that biophysiological factors are important and affect our mental health, but to play down sociocultural and psychological factors is silly and amounts to gravitation to an LCD under the mask of sophistication and laziness.

Over-simplified one-factor causalities such as the medical model limit our understanding and our effectiveness in treating clients. I have stressed the biopsychosocial approach because human experience cannot be limited to a biophysiological, sociocultural, intrapsychic, or spiritual domain alone.[2] A complete understanding of all these factors and how they are interrelated and coevolve better enables us to explain why people think and behave in any particular manner. One-factor causalities (i.e., disease causalities) leave us boxed into one frame and limit a broader understanding of how a person came to experience psychological distress.

No doubt the increasing sophistication of our understanding of the brain's chemistry and our ability to manufacture medications that target specific brain chemicals, referred to as neurotransmitters, has ushered in a new generation of medications with fewer side effects and more efficiency in ameliorating psychological distress such as depression. A classic example is the drug Prozac. This medication is part of a family of medications referred to as SSRIs or selective serotonin reuptake inhibitors.[3] Generally, SSRIs facilitate more efficient serotonergic processing in the brain, which results in less depression. This is based on the concept that low levels of serotonin cause depression.

The genetic studies also illustrate that some mood disorders, such as bipolar disorder (formally referred to as manic-depression), are more apt to run in families that have had a history of members suffering from this disorder. The treatment of choice for people with bipolar disorder are medications called mood stabilizers (e.g., lithium).

Since the late 1980s, there has been a shift from overdiagnosing schizophrenia to currently overdiagnosing bipolar disorder. Although it is positive that fewer people are inappropriately being diagnosed with schizophrenia, the shift has muddled efforts to understand mood disorders. The bipolar fad has also contributed to thousands if not millions of prescriptions for lithium, a potentially lethal medication if not monitored closely. It is not uncommon to see patients who are addicted to methamphetamines or cocaine being inappropriately diagnosed as having bipolar disorder. This is because methamphetamine use often looks manic when the person is on a run.

Diagnostic fads have also emerged regarding people with cognitive problems. Foremost among these disorders is the now popular attention deficit disorder (ADD). According to a National Institute of Health report, there is a high degree of inconsistency in the diagnosis of ADD. Some diagnosticians either do not use appropriate diagnostic tools and methods of assessments or do not use them at all.[4]

All of these LCD concepts have contributed to a mental health system that has struggled to provide coherent services that are more than just a Band-Aid for those afflicted with psychological problems.

In the past 15 years, managed care has squeezed many private-practice mental health professionals. Meanwhile, mental health treatment in the large HMOs and PPOs has been slimmed down, shortened, and constricted. For this reason we can now refer to managed care therapy as "shrink wrap." Garnished by clinicians who speak in clinicalese, shrink wrap provides the illusion of therapy for half the price.

15

Dumbsizing the Schools

A one-book man is either a slow learner or an ill-equipped
teacher.

Robert William Burke

Americans boast that we live in the richest and most powerful country in the world, yet we have feet of clay. The United States ranks
49th in literacy in the world, and just 18 percent of people responding
to a *Wall Street Journal/NBC News* poll graded the job American
public schools are doing at B or better. Twenty-eight percent graded
schools at D or F.

The Third International Mathematics and Science Study (TIMSS)
revealed that senior high students in the United States ranked 15th
out of 16 countries in math scores and ranked dead last in physics.
The most astounding finding of the TIMSS report was that despite
their dismal performance, seniors in the United States had the highest perception of their performance.[1] In other words, our seniors assume that their abilities are more than adequate for today's complex
world.

According to the National Assessment of Education Progress Survey, reading scores for 4th, 8th, and 12th graders held relatively
constant between 1992 and 1998. Though there was a slight improve-
ment among 8th graders, most students at all levels are still reading
below the levels recommended by the governing body of the testing
program. It was reported that just one-third of 4th and 8th graders
could understand the text and draw inference from it.[2]

Reading scores for students in public schools fared even worse
when compared to reading scores of students in private schools. Not
surprisingly, students who watched more television scored the poor-
est, comprising a fourth of the 12th graders and a third of the 8th
graders. The survey also found a widening gap between good read-

ers and poor readers. Specifically, for the 12th graders between 1992 and 1998, the scores of the top 10 percent rose while scores for the midsection of the bell curve declined.

Pollster Andrew Kohut noted that there has not been an increase in our understanding of sociopolitical knowledge despite the fact that in the 50 years between 1940 and 1990 the percentage of students completing high school rose from 38.1 to 85.7 percent.[3] For example, it is not uncommon that high school graduates have trouble identifying their own country on a world map.

Contributing to the crisis in our school system is the chronic shortage of qualified teachers of science and mathematics. Teachers who have never majored or minored in physics teach about 45 percent of physics classes. During the 2000–2001 year, 163 of New York City's schools did not have a principal. As schools struggle to fill positions with qualified teachers and administrators, they also struggle to maintain funding for buildings and supplies.

THE COMMERCIALIZATION OF OUR SCHOOLS

A crisis in school funding has motivated school administrators to look for money and supplies in any opportunistic location. Corporations have responded with donations but with strings attached. They have contributed in a variety of ways, from donating computers to building gymnasiums.

Interestingly, when companies (such as Apple) donate computers, a maintenance agreement is often not included in the deal. Consequently, when the computers break down—as they invariably do—maintenance costs go up, and the computer companies reap in the profits. Also, as children become familiar with a particular type of computer at school, they convince their parents to buy the same brand for home use.

The influx of computers in the schools serves as a double-edged sword. Sherry Turkle of MIT asks, "Are we using computer technology not because it teaches best but because we have lost the political will to fund education adequately?"[4]

In fact, the 30 years of research related to the impact of educational technology on schools has yielded only one clear finding: that drill and practice programs improve test scores modestly. But these benefits are seen on standardized tests in narrow skill areas. Beyond that, as Barry Cuban of Stanford University notes, "There is no clear commanding body of evidence that students' sustained use of multimedia machines, the Internet, word processing, spreadsheets, and other popular applications has any impact on academic achievement."[5]

The argument that computers in elementary schools help prepare students for their work careers later in life is based on the assumption that technology will stay the same. By the time the child graduates from high school, technology will have changed exponentially. The computer commands we're using now will be as obsolete as mimeograph technology is today.

Corporations have also looked for ways to advertise their products. The now infamous Channel One, which was designed to provide news reports in an entertaining manner, became controversial precisely because it is a commercial enterprise. It has been estimated that approximately 40 percent of 6th to 12th graders watch Channel One at school. Channel One provides a constant bombardment of commercials to which students are a captive audience. They witness as many snappy commercials that address their stylistic cravings as they hear and see news about the world. Levi 501 jeans compete with stories about the quest for Middle East peace. The "educational" stories are packaged for the shortened attention span of the American student population.

School officials argue that because government funding is eroding for education they had to accept a commercialized educational medium. Yet Channel One costs taxpayers $1.8 billion annually.

The *Weekly Reader* is a literary magazine found in numerous primary schools throughout the country. The owner of the *Weekly Reader*, K-III Communications, is the firm of Kohlberg, Kravis, and Roberts. This firm holds a significant interest in RJB Nabisco, the second largest maker of cigarettes. The *Reader* featured an article on "smokers' rights."

General Mills promoted their Box Tops for Education program in the school systems. They give 10 cents for every General Mills box top collected. Campbell Soup did the same thing with their Labels for Education program. They brought Apple Computer into the deal to award schools with a free iMac for every 94,950 labels.

Coca Cola, Dr. Pepper, and Pepsi managed to persuade 240 school districts in 31 states to give them exclusive rights to sell their products on campus. A school district in Colorado Springs has even worked out a deal whereby they receive $8.4 million if they sell 70,000 cans of Coke per year.

Many children sell magazine subscriptions or candies to earn enough money to fund field trips. School officials organize this direct marketing for the companies. Essentially the schools have become marketing entities for the corporations. In some cases, school systems have grown to depend on this support out of an effort to compensate for thin budgets. Like a drug addict who has come to regard the drug as the "only way I can make it in this world," schools are now strung out on the corporate take. Giving up this semblance of support would mean major withdrawal symptoms such as having fewer up-to-date computers available. Teachers know, however, that at the dawning of the next millennium, computer illiteracy will be a disadvantage in the rapidly changing world economy.

As a reflection of the commercialization of education, colleges and universities are beginning to mimic the marketing practices of corporations. In part to compensate for the dramatic drop in federal grants available to students, colleges and universities are offering discounts to certain "customers." The *Wall Street Journal* notes, "Just as airlines offer bargain fares to budget travelers willing to stay over Saturday night, while charging business flyers full fare, the colleges began offering tuition cuts in the form of grants to all but the most affluent who were charged full sticker price."[6] This pricing strategy is known as leveraging. *The New York Times* reported that many colleges and universities are trying to "offer the best deal" to upper- and middle-income students because of recruiting wars.[7] Universities such as Johns Hopkins are hiring consultants to measure "price sensitivity." If the school is convinced that a student will enroll whatever the price, as measured by whether the student initiated the contact early, no incentive is offered.

TRAILER HIGH

As tax phobia swept the country, less money funneled into education. For example, in California in 1978, Proposition 13 (which cut property taxes) set a trend for the rest of the country. Since 1978, the school system in California, once the envy of the nation, has eroded. More recently, Oregon, which offered one of the best educational systems in the West, passed its version of Proposition 13 and the Portland school system laid off 75 teachers in one year alone.

Not only are schools operating with crimping budgets but projected enrollments also continue to rise. Enrollments in both elementary and secondary schools are projected to reach 54.4 million by the year 2006. That is roughly 2.2 million more kids that were in the school system back in 1998.[8]

The already busting-at-the-seams schools will have to accommodate more students because few new monies have been allocated to build needed classrooms. Many school districts have gone to a multi-track format and/or purchased portable classrooms to accommodate the surge in the student population. For example, the exponential growth in enrollment in Broward County, Florida, has resulted in 200,000 more students in the schools. This alarming and unplanned explosion in students has resulted in the massive deployment of portable classrooms and has earned the school system the title "portable capital of the world." This situation is a sad metaphor for how little we value education.

THE NEXT GENERATION OF STUDENTS

The "We" generation of the 1960s gave way to the "Me" generation of the 1970s, which gave way to the "Greed" generation of the 1980s and the "X" generation of the 1990s and early 2000s. The X generation is known for having no coherent belief system. The alienation they are reported to feel from the rest of society reflects how empty our society has become.

Generation Xers are brought up by families considerably different from those in previous generations. The image of Ozzie and Harriet characterized the population metaphor of the typical American family of the 1950s. The reality is that Ozzie and Harriet households are uncommon and—if they existed at all—are phenomena of the past. What is more common is to hear people say, "My family is not like Ozzie and Harriet." In 1970, 40 percent of American families were composed of married couples with children. By 1994 that number shrank to 25.8 percent. By economic necessity, in a large number of households composed of two parents, both parents work. The number of children born to unmarried women has risen dramatically. In 1970, 10.7 percent of all births were by unmarried women, with 5.5 percent by Whites and 37.5 percent by Blacks. By 1996, these numbers rose to 32.4 percent for the entire population, 25.7 for Whites and 69.8 percent for Blacks.[9]

It has been estimated that of the five million pregnancies each year, three million are unintended. With unintended pregnancies, there is a high chance of birth defects. This is partly because a woman who does not know she is pregnant might drink alcohol or use drugs.

The birth rate among more educated women in our society is lower than for women with less education. The less educated women are more inclined to have a child instead of pursuing educational or professional career goals. As a consequence, those with less education are having children when they are comparably young and having more of them. Because these women are less education-oriented than their more educated counterparts, they do not serve as role models for their children by highlighting the importance of learning. Their children see them watching television rather than reading a book. It is also conceivable that they allow their children to watch more television than mothers who have more education.

All children need a sense of belonging, but children from broken families are more susceptible to peer pressure. The prototype of an alienated teen from the inner city feels that "no one out there understands me." This teen is ripe for gang membership that provides a ready-made family and peer culture that gives a sense of belonging. These gangs wear the same color to reinforce group identity. Loyalty to the gang/family drags them down to the gross common denominator in which "gang-banging" is a respected group activity. Gang-banging essentially is hurting people who do not belong to the gang to reinforce group membership.

Instead of building more schools and repairing those badly in need of repair, we are frantically building prisons. One might ask the chicken-and-egg question. Does the diversion of funds away from the schools and toward the prisons mean we are filling a need? Have we also created a need to pump an ever-increasing amount of money into the criminal justice system?

Crime among teenagers not only pumps up the criminal justice system but also exposes the school system to crime. It is not uncommon for teachers to be threatened and assaulted by their students. A high school teacher in Phoenix, Arizona, talked fearfully about the possibility of not being able to get to the security button next to her desk if she was threatened.

Correlated with the trend of violence in the schools has been an increase in drug use. A study performed by the University of Michigan, titled "Monitoring the Future," found that in 1996 the percentage of 8th graders using drugs reached 24 percent—double the percentage in 1991. The most significant increase was with the use of marijuana.[10]

According to another University of Michigan study, drug use among teens is leveling out since the early 1990s. This finding is especially true for marijuana use. However, the use of crack cocaine increased from 1997 to 1998, up .5 percent among 8th graders, .3 percent among 10th graders, and .5 percent among 12th graders.

The most alarming part of this trend is that children are using drugs at younger ages. There was also a substantial increase in the use of cigarettes, which are often considered a bridge to mind-altering drugs. According to a study performed by the Department of Health and Human Services, drug use among children ages 12 to 17 climbed from 9 percent in 1996 to 11.4 percent in 1997. The use of marijuana led the way. Most alarming was an increase in first-time heroin use. In 1995, the number of children who used heroin for the first time was 2.2 million. In 1997, that number jumped to 3.9 million.[11]

Drug use among teens during the past few decades has been one of the many factors contributing to an elongation of the adolescent period of development. Drug use freezes psychological development. The more someone uses drugs, the more that individual feels a sense of alienation. Adolescents who feel alienated, clouded, and less able to modulate their emotions are less motivated to participate in school.

Now, at the beginning of the twenty-first century, the adolescent period extends into the early twenties for many individuals. More and more teenagers live with their parents after graduation from high school. An increasing number of these young people engage in substance abuse and are marginally employed, if employed at all.

With these massive societal changes occurring among our students, schools have in some cases become babysitters or probation officers. The schools consequently have to adjust for higher numbers of acting-out children. Often teachers have to teach to the LCD as well as act as referees, counselors, and surrogate parents.

With increasing student/teacher ratios and continual cuts in funding, teachers are often looking for ways to reach all the children in a classroom. This involves teaching to the LCD, and the children of greater ability lose out. Maintaining heterogeneous classrooms instead of homogeneous classrooms has some philosophical and psychological benefits for students at the bottom, but it is a hindrance for those with higher skills.

Many schools have adopted the strategy of assigning each teacher a wide spectrum of children, from the very bright to those with learning disabilities. It has become socially and politically incorrect to offer classrooms with common abilities.

DISABLED LEARNING

People often cite the increase in computer use over the past 20 years as a sign that our students are becoming more sophisticated and better educated. However, the use of computers and hand-held calculators cannot be regarded as a reflection of what a student can know. The information is stored externally on a computer, not in the students' minds. Calculators help students perform mathematical operations quickly, but they don't necessarily learn how those calculations are performed. Many students might have difficulty with basic mathematical calculations if their computer or calculator breaks down.

A good measure of the type of student in our school system today is exemplified by the percentage of students with learning disabilities. That percentage has steadily risen in the past two decades. While 8.33 percent of students were classified as learning disabled in school year 1976–1977, that percentage jumped to 12.23 percent by school year 1993–1994. [12]

An increasing number of children in the public schools have been labeled dyslexic or as having attention deficit disorder (ADD). Some of the parents of children diagnosed with learning disorders or ADD have been drawn to these labels for an explanation of why their child has not been performing well in school. The media have hyped rationalizations about the causes of learning disorders.

Parents might see a daytime talk show on which guests reveal that they have had terrible problems reading throughout their lives. These guests announce how relieved they were when they "finally discovered that it was dyslexia all along that was to blame." They might themselves have been among the thousands of students who graduated from high school with marginal reading ability. They are now heartened by the news that they no longer have to blame themselves for being lazy during their school years.

Never mind that the individuals rarely attended classes and instead smoked a great deal of marijuana. They can say to themselves, "Now I understand why I was reluctant to attend class." They go tell their friends and often even their employers that they are disabled. Some might argue that people should not expect much from them as a result of their "disability." I have seen individuals who are convinced they have ADD and claim that their employer is violating the Americans with Disabilities Act by holding them to the same standards as other employees. Some even argue that the reason their children are now having difficulty can be explained by the fact that they have dyslexia because of a bad gene. Never mind that they spend no time reading to their children or reading by themselves, home behaviors shown by research to be powerful influences in a child's life. Instead they pass on not a bad gene but bad habits by an LCD rationalization.

The current craze over ADD has swept the country with greater popularity than even dyslexia. Psychologists and psychiatrists receive waves of referrals for assessment and treatment for attention deficit disorder. Over the past few years, these waves often follow exposés on Oprah's TV show. It is not uncommon to see self-diagnosed (would-be) ADD patients who complain of problems maintaining attention and admit to drinking too much alcohol on a regular basis and/or smoking marijuana. Very often their diets are also deplorable. If they eat at all on a regular basis, they might consume large quantities of sugar-laden foods such as candy and/or soft drinks. All these factors can contribute to ADD-type symptoms and poor school performance.

As I noted earlier, ADD is a disorder that has been exacerbated by the LCD mass-media culture. Yet people are more willing to adopt the easiest explanation for their difficulty learning instead of developing the self-discipline necessary to stay focused at school. Disabled learning is the composite result of multiple factors that have contributed to the meltdown in our society.

16
Mall Art

Good artists exist simply in what they make, and consequently are perfectly uninteresting in what they are.

Oscar Wilde

Throughout history, artistic expression has served as a window to the future of a society. Artists worked on the "cutting edge" of creativity in their societies and, therefore, reflected what their society was becoming. However, in recent years, artists and the art they produce have been sold together more for their commercial appeal than as a reflection of ground-breaking creativity. Though art may still reflect what a society is becoming, it serves less as a cutting edge and more as a mirror of a society.

Social critic James Twitchell has observed that prior to the 1960s, popular culture was contrasted with "high" culture on the one hand and folk culture on the other.[1] Folk culture was a collage of noncommercial amateur beliefs and practices that centered on such aspects as how to cook and how to attract the opposite sex. High culture was the province of literature, classical music, and fine art. In other words, creative innovation in art, music, and literature existed outside the popular culture. There was less homogeneity between high culture and popular culture. However, recently we have seen high culture blur with popular culture and gravitate toward LCD aesthetics.

After the Industrial Revolution, a middle class emerged who desired the goods, services, and art not before available. With an explosion of commercialism and mass media in the late twentieth and early twenty-first centuries, popular culture developed around this new stratum of people to blur the boundaries between high culture and popular culture. Popular songs demanded to "roll over Beethoven" and music sprung up that "switched on Bach." The "B" movies became the "A" movies, and the true "A" movies evaporated. Andy Warhol, Robert Rauschenberg, and Jasper Johns produced "pop art." Campbell's soup cans and Day-Glo paintings of Marilyn Monroe became "fine art."

PROMOTIONAL ART

In the LCD society, commercialized art has been sold as the cutting edge. Who the artist is has become more important than the aesthetics of his or her art. In other words, artists who have become successful are those who could be promoted on a large-scale commercial basis. It is difficult for an artist to become successful without the promotion of well-known critics acclaiming the artist's work. Indeed, Tom Wolfe, author of *The Painted Word*, noted that the power of critics is paramount: "The notion that the public accepts or rejects anything in modern art . . . is merely romantic fiction. . . . The game is completed and the trophies distributed long before the public knows what has happened."[2]

Andy Warhol's art represents the success of large-scale promotional image-making and the fusion of popular culture and art. His lithographs of everyday images such as Campbell's soup cans, Day-Glo pictures of Mao Tse-tung and Marilyn Monroe brought the concept of art and history square with popular culture. Equating Mao with Campbell's soup blurred the boundaries between history, consumerism, and art.

Art has always stretched the margins of a society. As Susan Sontag has noted,

Much of modern art is devoted to lowering the threshold of what is terrible. By getting us used to what, formerly, we could not bear to see or hear, because it was too shocking, painful, or embarrassing, art changes morals.[3]

Jeff Koons continued to expand on Warhol's effort to bring art to the largest possible audience. As if to emphasize this consumerism, he said, "I want to communicate to as wide a mass as possible."[4] To celebrate this fusion of art and consumerism, Koons produced a piece with a new vacuum cleaner mounted in Plexiglas. Koons also signed Nike posters and then had them framed to sell for $900 each.

USA Weekend described the art of Thomas Kinkade as defining a "new Americana." Kinkade mass-produces his art, which sells on

QVC at a rate of $10,000 a minute or $15 million a year. In the past several years, he has made $700 million.[5]

Many artists know they need a gimmick to enhance their mystique and get the attention of critics. Some artists, such as Andres Serrano, Damien Hirst, and Robert Mapplethorpe, have resorted to exaggerated shock tactics to become recognized and shown. To stir public controversy, Mapplethorpe created interest in his subject matter featuring sadomasochism and gay eroticism. Serrano threw the spotlight on himself by exhibiting a piece with a crucifix in a beaker of urine. Hirst displayed decaying animal carcasses.

In recent years, the margin-stretching function of modern art has been subordinated by the commercialism of the marketplace. Artists are sold as commodities in themselves. Owning a Mapplethorpe is more important than the aesthetics of the image.

Joseph Epstein has pointed out that successful artists gain their credentials by being "outsiders" or individualists. The further the artist is from the mainstream and the more "victimized" the artist's group affiliation, the greater the artist's standing as a marketable artist.[3] Epstein points out that artists in the outside groups are less likely to receive negative criticism for a variety of reasons. To be critical of them would mean you are critical of the oppressed. No one wants to be called a racist or a bigot.

Native American artists were among the most successful 20 years ago. Native Americans certainly had been one of the most oppressed segments of our society. Many of these artists were later to gain national reputations, while artists with equal talent who were among the majority culture remained obscure.

If Georgia O'Keefe had not married Alfred Stieglitz and spent her summers alone in New Mexico, the promotional value of her work would have been exceedingly low, especially because women at the time were difficult to promote. Fortunately for O'Keefe, a mystique grew around her as a person. She was celebrated by New York art critics as an eccentric and adventurous woman. Few women of her generation would move alone to a remote little village in northern New Mexico. After Stieglitz died and O'Keefe moved to New Mexico permanently in the 1940s, her work sold well in New York. For her day, she had the image of a consummate outsider.[4] As if to punctuate this point, she rarely sold or showed her work in the Santa Fe community. Not only was she able to maintain outside status, but she was also a member of a once oppressed group of artists, women.

THE NEA UNDER SEIGE

In the late 1960s Congress appropriated monies to the National Endowment for the Arts (NEA). The goal of the NEA was to support artists who would not otherwise have the commercial appeal necessary for success in the art world. This government program provided a partial remedy to the flattening of creative expression of art available in the marketplace.

In the industrialized world, the United States ranks very low in federal monies earmarked to support the arts. For example, in Germany, each person's tax contribution for the arts can be broken down to $27 per annum; in France, it is $32. But in the United States, each person contributes roughly 24 cents per year through taxes.

Despite the miniscule government support in the United States, there have been forces in Congress who have threatened the very existence of the NEA. The critics of the NEA claim that the government is promoting pornography. The Republicans in Congress, led by Senator Jesse Helms, have led an attack on funding for the NEA. Helms has used the shock artists—Mapplethorpe in particular—as a reason to cut the funding. Yet only a small minority of the art supported by the NEA is actually of the shock-value type.

Many artists would not receive support for their art without the NEA. If we whittle down the NEA further, art in the United States

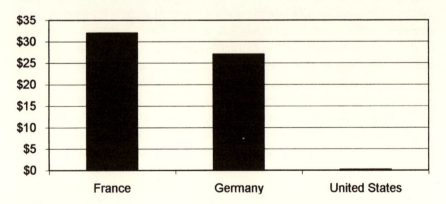

Figure 16.1 Per Annum Contribution to the Arts by Country

Source: J. Epstein. (1996). What to do about the arts. In K. Washburn & J. Thornton (Eds.), *Dumbing down: Essays on the strip-mining of American culture.* New York: Norton.

would be forced to rely solely on the commercialism of the market-place as a lifeline. Under such ironic conditions, the survival of art would be dependent on the very forces that have contributed to the suppression of creative expression and the initial need for the NEA.

PULP PUSHING

Merger mania has moved into the publishing industry and is having a profound effect on what is available to read. These new mega publishing houses include MCA (Putnam), CBS (Henry Holt), Hearst (William Morrow), ITT (Bobbs-Merrill), Pearson (Penguin, Viking, and Dutton), Time-Life (Little, Brown), and Rupert Murdoch (HarperCollins). Then in 1998 the German conglomerate Bertels-mann, which already owned Bantam Doubleday Dell, purchased Random House.

These companies are close to monopolizing the publishing industry. They have mirrored and perpetuated the market dynamics now taking hold in the entertainment industry. What gets published is directly associated with what is considered a potentially big commercial success. Many books that are passed over are considered too specialized to amount to significant sales.

Fewer publishers depend on their editors to contract with authors. And no longer do publishing companies create a market for their goods. Mass public demand determines what is published. Marketing departments assume executive control of most publishing companies. Kent Carroll has pointed out that what is printed and promoted is only what can easily be sold.[5] Publishers have conformed to the demands of the mass market and paid almost exclusive attention to how to reach the largest audience. James Twitchell wrote, "If the three secrets of real estate are location, location, location, then the three secrets of bookselling are distribution, distribution, distribution."[6]

Publishers have promoted only a handful of best-selling authors. To ensure that these authors will remain best-sellers, publishers announce large advance sums for their books as a promotional tactic. They are essentially suggesting that they expect the book to be a huge success.

Profits and potential losses are now prime concerns. Publishing houses have opted to narrow their goals to the profit margin by initiating a new strategy. They have gone from publishing a wide range of subjects with a short run of actual printed copies of a book to a narrow range of subjects and a long run (high number) of printed copies. Whereas the wide-range/short-run books were relatively expensive, the new narrow-range/long-run books are relatively cheap. Indeed, as Twitchell wrote, "The economic equation between price and print run has been resolved: long print runs + low unit prices = maximum profit."[10]

Publishing Houses are also increasingly looking to the large retail bookstore chains to determine what books could be huge commercial recesses. Massive chains such as Barnes and Noble, Walden, and Borders sell more than half the books sold in the United States. As if to illustrate this, Walden Books is a subsidiary of Kmart. Because these large chains are high-volume retailers, they gear themselves to stock books that sell big. Publishers look to the retailers for what they are willing to stock. Therefore, the publishers are less inclined to publish books that the retailers are not willing to stock.

To conform to market pressures, publishers are increasingly producing books with flashy and sensationalistic covers. The trashy romance novels often feature lurid scenes with partially clothed lovers. The techno-thrillers feature bombs blasting and horrified people fleeing.

From the 1980s on, the three most successful authors in terms of overall number of times on the bestsellers list were Danielle Steele, Tom Clancy, and Stephen King. Each of these authors continues in the early 2000s to dominate a de-elevating niche. Danielle Steele produces simplistic, stereotypic, and sensationalistic romances about the rich and privileged, Tom Clancy pumps out techno-thrillers, and Stephen King remains the king of the horror genre. These three have written the same book over and over again with little more than cosmetic changes in characters and scenes. Their mass-produced paperbacks are now available at supermarket and drugstore check stands. There is little wonder that these books are referred to as "pulp fiction."

Publishing companies have perpetuated the gravitation to the LCD of antisocial themes. The National Conference on Television Violence found a 61-percent increase in antisocial and pro-violence themes in fiction between 1966 and 1988. When compared to the first half of the century, the decade of the 1980s saw a 300-percent increase in violent themes. Before 1949, 41 percent of the best-sellers had pro-social themes. The percentage dropped to 27 percent by 1965 and to 18 percent by the early 1990s.[11]

Hollywood is also infiltrating what is being printed. In fact, producers in Hollywood are looking to journalism and the publishing world for "true-life stories." They have been hunting for sensationalistic stories from journalists to remake into feature films. For example, Miramax has even developed a magazine and publishing company to develop stories. This effort illustrates the increasingly seamless interface between publishing and the LCD screenplays coming out of Hollywood.

As if to emphasize how literature had become fused with entertainment and how high brow became low brow, authors began to promote products based on their books. Elizabeth Wurtzel, author of *Prozac Nation*, came out with a CD, as have Joyce Maynard, author of *Where Love Goes*, and James Redfield, author of *The Celestine Prophesy*.

All these changes have factored into dragging what is being printed down to the tastes of the increasingly illiterate LCD society. The public is offered little opportunity to explore new ideas and perspectives. Under these conditions, literacy takes on a new meaning.

RAPPING UP THE GRUNGE

Like the publishing industry, the music industry is controlled by a small, select group of mega-corporations. This powerful group includes Sony, CBS Records, Poly Gram, Matsushita's MCA Records, Thorn Capitol-EMI Records, N.V. Philips Poly Gram, Bertelsmann AG's BMG init, and Time-Warner Records. Many of these mega-corporations are also involved in the production and distribution of other forms of media, making them powerful sources of LCD "culture."

These mega-companies have dominated popular music. Some have argued that there has been a lack of creativity in music over the past 30 years. It is no wonder that "oldies stations" have become so popular.

With the advent of MTV, many musical groups pushed their creative expression into the visual medium. Just as in the visual arts, musicians have resorted to shock tactics to get the attention of critics and fans. Even Michael Jackson, who was extremely popular among latency-aged children, is shown on his MTV video grabbing his crotch and zipping up his fly.

Some of the new music is popularly referred to as "raunch," "heavy metal," or "rap." These like-minded extremes carry adolescent rebellion beyond defiance to advocate for social strife among people and pushes adolescence into adulthood. Because one of the challenges of adolescence is to develop a sense of identity and learn to live in a cooperative adult society. This music cultivates shock and "in your face" social interaction. Indeed, as music historian Martha Bayles has noted:

Something has gone seriously wrong, both with the sound of popular music and with the sensibility it expresses. It is possible to find the tough, affirmative spirit of the blues in contemporary forms. But increasingly, that spirit is rejected in favor of antimusical, antisocial antics that would be laughable if they weren't so offensive.[12]

When one assumes there are no lower depths to which music can fall, new depravity emerges to shock listeners into believing they can rebel more grotesquely than any previous rebels have dared. Marilyn Manson not only dresses as if to appear dead, but he also promotes the glamour of death in his songs. Even Manson noted:

We applaud the creation of a bomb whose sole purpose is to destroy all mankind, and we grow up watching our President's brains splattered all over Texas. . . . Disgusting vultures looking for corpses, exploiting, fucking, filming, and serving it up for hungry appetites in a gluttonous display of endless stupidity.[13]

Regressive fads such as the so-called "hard-edged" or "alternative music" sweep the adolescent world. Many of the musicians in this genre have sung glowingly about death. They tout the image of the "white butterfly" and sing that suicide is an option worthy of consideration.

"Goths" are fascinated with death, nihilism, and a love of the morbid. The songs of Morticia Adams, Manson, Sisters of Mercy, and Death in June all rant about the meaninglessness of life. Gothic music fans often dress in black, wear their hair unkempt, cover their faces with pancake make-up, and wear red inside of black lipstick to depict blood. Boys sometimes wear fingernail polish to add a gender-bending touch.

Parents of teenagers who listen to this music often do not realize the extent to which their teenaged son or daughter might be at risk for follow-through with these frighteningly regressive images and actually suicide. Teen suicide is alarmingly high. The suicide rate for people age 15 to 24 has tripled since 1950. Suicide is the second leading cause of death among teenagers 15 to 19.[14]

Harris and Klebold, the Littleton Colorado High School assassins, were particularly attracted to the German Industrial Rock group called KMFDM (for Kein Mileid fur die Mehrheit, meaning "no pity for the majority"). The actual sound of the music utilizes factory clanging and industrial noise. The lyrics of many of KMFDM's songs also rant about the meaninglessness of life, self-loathing, and pro-motion of violence.

In the spring of 2002, 19-year-old Robert Steinhauser shot 17 peo-ple, most of them teachers at his school in Erfurt, Germany. One of the heavily played CDs found at his house was titled "School Wars" and contained lyrics such as "shoot down your naughty teachers with a pump gun."

Beginning some 20 years ago with the emergence of punk rock, fans and performers touted skinheads and safety pins in their cheeks. Punk performers made good on their promise to degrade adolescence angst. The names of the punk groups reveal but a hint of their emphasis on cruelty. With groups such as Carcass, Morbid Angel, Napalm Death, and Godflesh, the horrors of savagery were blasted into the ears of rebellious teenagers.

Elements of punk filtered into a new musical expression dubbed "grunge." Much of this genre emerged in Seattle and was led by a group with the misleading name "Nirvana." In the mid 1990s, Nir-vana featured an album titled "In Utero," with lyrics about rape and cannibalism. Listeners are asked to imagine eating a cancerous tumor.

In her book *Hole in Our Soul*, Martha Bayles argues that in the "perverse postmodernism," much of what has been considered pop music has deteriorated into baseness, anti-art, and rage. She wrote:

Today the punk legacy persists whenever noise, shock, and ugliness are cultivated for their own sake, and whenever the fires of adolescent anger and aggression are stoked in ways that are almost totally destructive. It is no accident that Rick Rubin, one of the driving forces behind "gangsta" rap, got his start in a New York punk band called the Pricks.[15]

Indeed, punk rock in many ways set the stage for the development of rap. Whereas one of the hallmarks of punk was anger, shock, and a kind of antimusic music, rap provided inner-city African American youth with a means to express their angst by rapping words of hate and aggression.

Rap star Ice-T personifies the brutal inner-city rage. He has sung about "hos" and "bitches" who get raped by "gangs of niggers" with their extraordinarily large sex organs or "evil dicks." But Ice-T did not stop there. He rapped about a preacher's daughter who "takes a broomstick up her butt" by an "N.W.A."

Many rappers expressed their rage by wrapping themselves in the image of a "gangsta." Gangstas routinely engaged in gang banging, including drug-dealing and drive-by shootings of rival gang members. One of Ice-T's albums was titled "Body Count" and featured the notorious single "Cop Killer."

During the 1992 Presidential Election, Bill Clinton made headlines when he angered Jesse Jackson by objecting to rapper Sister Souljah's comment following the Los Angeles riots. She said, "If Black people kill Black people every day, why not have a week and kill White people."[16]

More recently, a style of music referred to as rock'n'rap has emerged in the white adolescent population. Essentially, rock'n'rap is rap or hip-hop. In a concert in Albuquerque, New Mexico, 16,000 teenage boys in baggy jeans and KILLED KENNY tee shirts moshed and body-surfed as they heard Limp Bizkit "sing" songs with lyrics such as "God gave ya, fakin' al the flava. . . . You're sick of yourself/ Well I'm sick of you too, fake!"[17]

The point is that these forms of music do not by themselves cause teen suicide or deadly massacres in our schools. They are part of a de-evolving LCD society that also includes gratuitous violence in the entertainment industry and graphic computer games and the denigration of social linkages that support a sense of belonging and social responsibility. Music is but one aspect of this experience.

Like other forms of art, music defines who we are becoming. The cutting edge of creativity is a mutually agreed-on definition of aesthetics—what is pleasing and attractive. If that creative expression becomes a celebration of depravity, we ourselves become depraved and spiritually bankrupt. Indeed, it is to the spiritual domain that we turn next.

17
The Spiritual Supermarket

The New Age? It's just old age stuck in a microwave oven for over fifteen seconds.

James Randi

The marketplace has dramatically infiltrated and changed what we regard as a spiritual or religious experience. Within many shopping centers are stores that offer crystals and pyramids to the "spiritually" inclined. Television evangelists litter our airwaves, preaching a theology of self-righteousness while asking for contributions for their theme parks. The fastest-growing churches in the United States are large, nondenominational, theater-type congregations, and theater is what they offer.

Millions of people are experiencing an ever-increasing sense of alienation from the world around them. They want to feel that their relationship to the world around them has meaning. Simple, ready-made answers have rushed in to fill the void. Religious fundamentalism and New Age fads provide the ready-made and commercially available answers to nagging existential questions. Larger numbers of people than ever before have gravitated toward ready-made explanations for the meaning of life.

Because of the pervasive power of the emerging LCD society, many people have found themselves feeling empty and spiritually bankrupt. New Age or fundamentalist perspectives compensate for that empty feeling that life has lost its meaning.

In this chapter we will explore how New Age fads and religious fundamentalism appear on the surface to be opposite poles, yet both represent gravitation toward the LCD of antiquated concepts. They are sold in the spiritual marketplace as methods of renewal called New Age or as a "revival" for those who want to be born again.

NEW AGE OR GLOSSY OLD AGE?

In the past three decades there has been an increase in the desire for a deeper understanding of life; however, many people have gravitated to shallow and highly commercialized beliefs. Many of the fads associated with this trend have been marketed as New Age. The term "New Age" represents an attempt to break from a materialistic society, but many of the so-called New Age beliefs are in many ways not new. What has become immediately popular is not new but from the "Old Age."

It is certainly not the case that spiritualism is regressive; quite the contrary. But commercialization and the tendency to flock around New Age fads promote nothing but regression. True spiritualism (the subtle experience of a connection with the world) is perhaps the most profound experience someone can have.[1] But the commercialization of old concepts such as reincarnation, channeling, and astrology complicate a full appreciation of the profound sense of connectivity that forms the basis of spirituality. Essentially, these antiquated ideas are tacked onto the garb of New Ageism and, like junk food, do not satiate our hunger for meaning.

A useful analogy of the emptiness inherent in the New Age fads was written long ago in Matthew:

But no one puts a patch of unshrunk cloth on an old garment; for the patch pulls away from the garment, now a worse tear results.

Nor do men put new wine into old wineskins, otherwise the wineskins burst, and the wine pours out, and the wineskins are ruined; but they put new wine into new wineskins, and both are preserved.[2]

Fifteen years ago Buddhist author Chogyam Trungpa wrote in his book *Spiritual Materialism* that Westerners cannot find true spiritualism by simply looking to Eastern religion. He argued that Westerners who simply try on an Eastern philosophy are being spiritually materialistic.[3] They wear the clothes of Eastern mystics but do not follow the essence of the philosophy.

There has been an increase in the commercial value of ready-made routes to enlightenment. This can be regarded as more than just a symptom of the emptiness people feel as they look for meaning in a world they are experiencing as increasingly meaningless. In a society in which immediate gratification and commercialism are paramount, "meaning" is subordinated by spiritually materialistic fads.

The spiritual supermarket is perhaps the best example of how we as a culture have gravitated to the LCD of meaning for our lives. Spirituality requires subtle contemplation and sustained practice, but recipes for spiritual enlightenment are sold at our local mall. Many people buy the latest fad, not for its wisdom but for its popular appeal.

Sugar-coated and bite-size spiritual truths are offered as tapes from people who "channel" other spirits and as books on angels, UFO contacts, reincarnation, and astrology. Each of these fads has tremendous commercial value. People do not have to sit and contemplate their meaning. They are ready-made, almost as if appropriate for a drive-through shop. As we drive through, we can ask the proprietor to "give me two channeler tapes, three crystals, and that new book on reincarnation by AKA Cleopatra."

Because immediate gratification is regarded as healthy in the emerging LCD society, the wisdom of spiritual traditions is considered obtainable as a quick fix. But achieving spiritual insight requires us to maintain discipline over a period of time. Selling enlightenment in ready-made packages is therefore a contradiction in terms. Enlightenment and commercialism do not mix.

Commercial spirituality has made unnatural what should be thought of as a natural aspect of living in the world. New Age writers pay little attention to the major paradigm shifts occurring in the natural sciences.[4] Instead of integrating an understanding of how the natural world functions, New Age concepts such as reincarnation, astrology, and channeling adhere to antiquated models of the natural world.

These old models are based on a deterministic perspective. Determinism implies that a mechanistic and rigid lock-step process occurs in the universe. This mechanistic paradigm is consistent with the Newtonian world view, which does not explain evolution. Because the evolution of life is a dynamic and multidimensional process, a deterministic model is not helpful to our efforts to understand and appreciate spirituality. True spirituality should reflect a reverence for nature and unity with the natural world.

Astrology is an example of a deterministic perspective. This Babylonian "science," invented almost 4000 years ago, models the universe as a giant clock. Astrologers believe that the rotations of the planets predict what we experience. Fortunately for us, human beings are not mechanical devices determined by the rotations of the planets.

Astrology proponents would argue that these planetary rotations influence human beings but do not require changes in our lives. They believe that humans still have free will and can choose to respond to these planetary influences with some degree of freedom. Despite this rationalization, no one has been able to put forth a coherent explanation as to how or why the movements of the planets can determine or even influence the lives of human beings. Life is far more complex than can be modeled by archaic, deterministic models of reality. Human beings and the universe itself are complex evolving systems—not machines or giant clocks.

Another old-age concept is reincarnation. This philosophically narcissistic concept suggests that we travel through space/time and change bodies almost like we change clothes. If there is a fundamental unity in the universe, as most theologies suggest, the concept of reincarnation runs contrary to this belief. But most believers in reincarnation also profess to believe there is unity in the universe. Reincarnation suggests that we can be sealed off from being absorbed by this unity, as if we are in some kind of spiritual bubble. All the research related to reincarnation has yet to prove any validity.[5]

"Channeling" is another New Age concept. Before channeling went by the wayside in the spiritual supermarket, some people made millions of dollars convincing others that they channel a special connection with an extraterrestrial being who imparts wisdom to them. More recently, angels have become very popular. There are even television shows, such as *Touched by an Angel*, that emphasize the power of angels.

Both channeling and believing in angels have in common the belief that we should find some paranormal being outside ourselves to achieve wisdom. These antiquated beliefs represent a throwback to the mind-set of our ancestors a few thousand years ago, again not New Age but *very* "old age."

When members of the LCD society believe in the necessity of channeled extraterrestrial beings or angels as indispensable supernatural forces that help them navigate through the world, they also accept the concept of dualism. Dualism suggests that there are two worlds, ours and the "other world"—two levels of reality, the spiritual level and the level of mere mortals.

Despite the fact that these old-age beliefs are based on the anti-quated concepts of determinism and dualism, astrology, reincarnation, and angels are increasing in popularity. Some have argued that, because people have believed in these concepts for thousands of years, there is some truth to them.

These beliefs were popular because our ancestors knew little else about the nature of the universe and the world they inhabited. Unfortunately, now at the beginning of the third millennium, millions of people have gravitated toward these LCD "answers" to questions about human existence as if they had just visited the local mall.

FUNDAMENTAL REGRESSION

Just as we can witness an outbreak of old-age concepts masquerading as New Age concepts, so have we seen old interpretations of the major theologies explode in popularity. These old views have been referred to as fundamentalist because they are erroneously assumed to be fundamental derivations of original theology. Not only do we see fundamentalism in its Christian form, but similar trends are seen in Islam and Judaism.

A study titled *All in the Family: Religious Mobility in America* found wholesale flight from the mainstream denominations such as the Congregational, Methodist, and Presbyterian churches with a simultaneous expansion in membership of conservative churches such as the Southern Baptists and Assemblies of God. In the Jewish faith, Orthodox synagogues have expanded, while the Reform and Conservative (not really conservative) synagogues have lost membership.[6]

In the United States, Christian fundamentalism turned the essence of Christian philosophy upside down. True Christian philosophy is so admirable that it's hard to find fault with concepts of loving thy neighbor and turning the other cheek. Yet Christian fundamentalists have thrown out these concepts and embraced judgmentalism. Fundamentalists seemed to be driven by fear and prejudices. Although claiming piety, they seem to have forgotten the Christian concepts of tolerance, charity, and compassion.

Fundamentalists periodically complain about those who are overly concerned about disadvantaged people. They call their Christian brethren "secular humanists" and regard them as misguided.

Apparently, fundamentalists are so closed off from compassion that they have rejected one of Christianity's fundamental tenets.

Fundamentalists also preach that we should read the Bible for its literal meaning. They reject science if it conflicts with a literal interpretation of the Bible. Many fundamentalists argue that creationism must be taught alongside evolutionary science in the public schools. In their own schools, they drop the evolutionary science altogether and teach only creationism. Fundamentalist forces have gained so much political power in Kansas that it is now illegal to teach evolutionary theory in public schools.

Christian missionaries embark on their proselytizing journeys in countries that are already Christian. The diversity of Christian denominations is being challenged. Evangelical and Mormon missionaries have attempted to convince other Christians that their brand of Christianity is closer to God. For example, it is very common to see Mormons all over Catholic South America. With the new surge of evangelicals, many missionaries are embarking on fishing expeditions in Christian countries such as Great Britain and Romania.

Many fundamentalists profess themselves to be the sole followers of the true path to God. The fundamentalist Christians, for example, argue that other Christian denominations are not actually Christian because they "lead their misguided flocks away from Christ."

It is not as if this trend is new. Throughout history, one culture has attempted to impose its theology on another culture. However, particularly noteworthy now are the sheer numbers of people embracing this regressive fundamentalism.

Evangelicals began as practitioners of spiritual theatrics. They provided entertainment featuring preachers who wave their arms and people who speak in tongues. In recent years these American strands have transformed into commercialized ventures. The popularity of these beliefs in the United States has been partly fueled by television. Within the spiritual marketplace, we have seen television evangelists preaching damnation and salvation for a humble donation.

The 1980s ushered in an epidemic of TV evangelists including Jimmy Swaggart, Jerry Falwell, Jim and Tammy Bakker, and Pat Robertson. These television evangelists were all over the airwaves, raising money and preaching their brand of judgmentalism and self-righteousness.

Jimmy Swaggart went on to tearfully confess that he had been caught during a rendezvous with a prostitute. After he was able to come back on the air, he was caught for a second time. He went again to his congregation for a televised and tearful request for their forgiveness. Jim Bakker went to jail for inappropriate use of money he raised from his television audience/parishioners.

Pat Robertson took his piety into the Presidential Campaign of 1988. Years later, on his *700 Club*, he accused President Clinton of having Vincent Foster murdered. Pat Robertson also came out in support of the soon-to-be-overthrown dictator of Zaire, Mobutu. Robertson was reported to have said, "You don't have to worry about the political situation. . . . Because God loves your country you only have to care about the kingdom of God. . . . Mobutu is a good man. He got his power from God."[7] It just so happened that Robertson held considerable interests in the African Development Company that controlled diamond and gold mines in the country that Mobutu ruled over with an iron fist.

Jerry Falwell was reported to have called Bishop and later Prime Minister Desmond Tutu of South Africa "a phony." Falwell argued that former Philippine dictator Ferdinand Marcos should be supported by the United States.[8] After the September 11, 2001, terrorist attacks, Falwell argued that God was punishing the United States for its tolerance of homosexuality.

Falwell, Robertson, and their brethren can be regarded as the true American Taliban. They express an almost psychotic anti-Christianity and try to impose those distorted views into the political system.

Despite the fact that leaders of Christian fundamentalism behaved in arguably anti-Christian ways, they were able to tap their viewing parishioners for continued donations. They also led parishioners into the Right Wing of the Republican Party. The "Christian Right" bargained with gun-control opponents and death-sentence proponents to share their proposal to reintroduce prayer into the classroom. The result was that members of the Christian Right became pro-death (death penalty) and pro-life (anti-abortion). The cognitive dissonance resulting from their opposing views is lost in the blur of the LCD society.

During the same period when we have seen a massive growth of religious fundamentalism, we have witnessed a proliferation of cults. Some of these cults have been based on extreme versions of fundamentalism combined with a large dose of paranoia. Cults such as the infamous Waco group built a belief system around paranoia about the government. They stockpiled weapons to defend themselves and then made their worst fears come true. Other cults, such as the Stargate Cult in San Diego, have built their belief systems around a fascination with extraterrestrials.

In January of 1999, members of a "Christian" cult from Denver were caught in Israel before an attempt to incite violence. Reportedly they had planned to create such violent mayhem in Jerusalem on New Years Eve 2000 that Jesus would reappear to save the world.

The people who are the most vulnerable to cult membership are alienated from a social support system and feel jilted in relationships. These people can find a ready-made and exclusive social support network in the cult. The loneliness they felt can be overwhelmingly satiated by the intensity of the group support. People in cults are told to avoid individualistic ideas.

Cults and fundamentalists share a tendency toward a group-think social structure that seals them off from outside influence. Many of these groups argue that inside the church or cult there is life, while outside there is death or evil. These groups affect their members the way drugs affect drug addicts. People become addicted and go through withdrawals when outside the cult. Consequently, many in the mental health treatment community have specialized in "deprogramming."

Fundamentalism and the prominence of cults can be seen as symptomatic of the emptiness and social alienation of the emerging LCD society. People want to believe in something. Fundamentalism and cults provide a means for those with little capacity for insight to feel special and pious.

The cheapened concept of God has filtered into the entertainment domain. Even sports figures profess to have God on their side. One of the sports heroes from the 1997 World Series said, during a postgame interview, "Our faith in God made the difference." Moises Alou apparently thought that God cares what team wins a game. In today's era, in which sports, entertainment, and religion have been fused in the LCD society, no one flinched at hearing that God would take sides in a World Series game. Because we have increasingly experienced our lives vicariously through entertainment, we have infused the meaning of life with our trivialization of the concept of God.

18

Rebuilding the Future

The accelerating meltdown in American culture today will be difficult to slow down. The forces at play have infiltrated every aspect of
our social fabric and consciousness. Virtually everyone has been
steeped in the bland homogeneity of the corporate- and media-
driven LCD society.

But together we can build break walls and jetties and stake out
beachheads of sanity in the mass media, in the political arena, in
education, and in health care. We must develop sociopolitical solutions through which we can rescue ourselves from the encroaching
tide. In this chapter I describe a spectrum of possible solutions for
our dilemma.

REAL DEMOCRACY

Several political principles and initiatives need to be embraced to
ensure the health of our society. Broad-based political change requires addressing the basic principles of a healthy society, including
compassion, tolerance, and flexibility.

Compassion for people who are disadvantaged has always been
more easily talked about than demonstrated. Political compassion is
not a simple matter of ensuring that the "haves" share with the
"have-nots." Neither is it a matter of combining the term "compassion" with another term as in "compassionate conservatism."

People on the margins of society, including mentally ill and
homeless people, need a coherent route into our society. Aiding
these disadvantaged people must involve the development of a com-

prehensive means through which they can eventually take care of themselves. Encouraging people dependent on welfare to work is only an initial step in building a viable infrastructure of society. Monetary investments need to be made to ensure that disadvantaged people can find their way into full participation in our economy. Outreach, child care, and adequate job training programs must be part of the political agenda.

If we work with mentally disabled citizens to provide a means through which they can learn to be independent and self-efficient, they might not become homeless or migrate into the criminal justice system. A full spectrum of psychosocial rehabilitation programs, including residential treatment, day treatment, and vocational rehabilitation, have not only been shown to reduce hospitalization but also to stem the tide of homelessness and increase people's chances for independent living. In the long run, such programs would be cheaper and government would actually become smaller and more efficient.

We need to think beyond an LCD mind-set that supposes that "government is bad." Although there are countless examples of inefficiency, government is not inherently evil. The social services and mental health systems that are part of local governments administer programs that serve disadvantaged clients while simultaneously trying to survive state and federal budget cuts.

Government should be structured to serve people, not corporate interests. To this end, we should embark on a thorough examination of who influences our political leaders. Federal and state agencies that oversee corporate activity must protect the citizens, not the corporations. For example, the Environmental Protection Agency (EPA) must ensure that corporate interests do not outweigh environmental interests. Similarly, the Food and Drug Administration (FDA) and the Federal Communication Commission (FCC) must act in the best interests of the public instead of protecting the interests of corporations. Efforts such as those made by David Kessler, formerly of the FDA, against the tobacco industry have unfortunately been too rare.

Antitrust laws must be observed to protect consumers from megamergers. Corporations such as Exxon should not be allowed to merge with other violators of the public trust. The merger between Exxon and Mobil is but one example of an antitrust case that should have been pursued. Those who have been responsible for major pollution violations, such as Exxon, should be held responsible for paying a disproportionate amount of tax dollars, which could fund the EPA.

Public interest groups such as Common Cause and Ralph Nader's Washington Action must be brought to the forefront to help the public weed out corporate exploitation of our government. These groups should be made eligible for a wide range of federal grants.

Campaign finance reform will remain a hot political issue for years to come until those benefiting from the current system are no longer in office. Here are a number of constructive steps we can take to avoid the LCD of retail politics:

1) We should prohibit soft money and gifts.

2) We should prohibit money contributed by corporations to political candidates to ensure that all citizens have a voice and a part to play in their own government.

3) Because the networks essentially have been given the airwaves by the government, they should be required a public-service stipulation as part of that gift. Each network should be required to air a specific amount of time to all political candidates running for office in the general election.

4) Paid-for ads should be banned from television and radio.

5) Tax deductions awarded corporations for advertisement should be eliminated. In place of these deductions, corporations could be awarded tax breaks for the creation of environmentally responsible products such as automobiles with low emissions and high gas mileage.

6) Tax breaks for hiring welfare recipients should be expanded.

7) Corporate welfare given to companies such as those that support selling burgers in China should be abolished.

The above changes will induce corporations to channel less money toward commercials in the multi-media and more into socially responsible endeavors. Simultaneously our citizens would enjoy a cleaner environment and those less fortunate can have an opportunity to participate in the economy.

DIVERSITY AND SOCIETAL EVOLUTION

According to systems theory, open systems evolve as they feed on "new energy" or "information." In contrast, societies that are closed feed on themselves and stagnate. Therefore, if we wish to promote an evolving society, we must appreciate the vast diversity of human experience. We cannot limit and restrict those elements that homogenize and flatten the expression of new ideas.

Recent demographic changes present us with an opportunity to evolve as a society. For example, it has been projected that ethnic and race diversity in the United States will increase in the next few decades. The most dramatic increase will be in the Asian and Hispanic populations. Although Hispanics comprise 10 percent of the population of the United States, by the year 2050, Hispanics are projected to be the second largest ethnic group in the United States, with an estimate at 24.5 percent. California is already more than 50 percent non-White. Each of these non-White cultures offers a wealth of different perspectives that can help jar our society out of its LCD homogeneity.

True diversity depends to some degree on cultural relativism—the concept that any one culture does not have a hold on the "truth." Each culture offers truths through culturally relative and context-dependent perspectives of its own. According to this view, there is no real objectivity.

However, if relativism is taken to the extreme, a neo-deconstructivism develops that results in nihilism, whereby no objective truth is possible. People operating with this perspective may ask, "Why take part in a socially constructed truth?" This kind of logic is reckless because societies are based on socially constructed truths and need common beliefs to ensure cooperation among members of society.

A healthy society necessitates flexibility, tolerance, compassion, and a thoughtful investment in the future health of the society. Flexibility provides "shock absorbers" that allow a society to get through a crisis. Germany of the 1930s illustrated an example of an inflexible society. To deal with the economic and political crisis, the German government devolved into Nazism and became inflexible and intolerant. The Netherlands illustrates an example of a generally flexible society. People in the Netherlands have enjoyed a relatively open and low-conflict society, except of course during those few years when the Nazis occupied the country. Tolerance is one of the basic tenets of true Christianity. It enables a society to absorb diverse viewpoints and cultural expressions without insisting on conformity. By promoting tolerance, we can condition ourselves for the challenges of the twenty-first century.

"Cultural elasticity" would allow our society both tolerance and flexibility. Elasticity will ensure that a cooperative atmosphere prevails, whereby members of society tolerate one another and flexibility considers diverse viewpoints. Without elasticity, we impair our ability to come together during times of crisis.

CHANGING COURSES

Over 60 years ago, Benjamin Whorf and Edward Sapir proposed the theory that each language creates a unique structure for thought. Though the extreme of this view is not viable, a modified Whorf-Sapir theory is reasonable. Language does affect how we think. Therefore, by preserving the diversity of languages spoken by members of our society, we preserve a diversity of perspectives.

As the English language spreads across the globe as the international language, so do the concepts and syntax that English facilitates. Though we need to ensure that our children can use English with sophistication, we also need to preserve the variety of language skills still spoken in this country. To this end, language courses should be offered in schools, beginning at the elementary school level.

We need to set goals that will enable us to participate completely in the world economy. The wave of the future will involve high technologies such as bioengineering, medical research, and the computer industries. Currently the educational system in the United States has major limitations in these areas, resulting in a less than competent workforce. The technical training required to meet this challenge necessitates that we restructure the curriculum in the educational system to prepare students for the technical demands of the twenty-first century.

Nobody likes to sit for exams or tests, yet it is one way we can be assured that our children are learning what they need to learn before being passed on to the next grade. Academic tests combined with reports from teachers will ensure that the students who graduate from our high schools have learned what is expected for graduation. Students who do not pass the appropriate tests should not advance to the next grade or graduate. Governor Gray Davis of California signed a bill in mid 1999 abolishing advancement to the next grade and establishing a high school graduation exam. This should spread through the nation.

In addition to ensuring that minimum standards are met, we need to ensure that schools do not provide LCD cookie-cutter classrooms. Schools should devote at least as many resources to gifted students as they do to learning disabled students. All students should be allowed to reach their full range of learning potentials.

If classroom assignments were based on the skill level of the child, teachers could more easily tailor the curriculum to reach a higher common denominator. Teachers could, therefore, focus on maximizing children's specific and individual skills.

Our schools should instill a hunger for creative thought and lifelong learning. Schools should teach students to learn and to think creatively. To this end, an excellent and underrated method of stimulating learning skills is to teach the arts. Music and the visual arts stimulate more than an appreciation for the arts.

Though art programs have been decimated in schools, evidence has been accumulating that they do, in fact, enhance the overall academic development of children. For example, Shirley Brice Heath of Stanford University found that children who participate in after school arts programs were 1) four times more likely to win an academic award, 2) eight times more likely to receive a community services award, 3) three times more likely to win a school attendance award, and 4) four times more likely to participate in a science or math fair.[1]

Participation in arts programs also results in tangible college-ready skills. For example, a study of college admission scores found that students who studied the arts for more than four years scored 59 points higher on the verbal section of the SAT and 44 points higher on the math section than did children who did not participate in the arts.[2]

We must also ensure that our institutions of higher learning are instilled with vigorous and stimulating programs. The trend toward fragmentation and compartmentalization need not continue. The educational system would better serve its students by transforming into multidimensional learning environments that emphasize the interrelationships between subjects. That is, those scholastic efforts that bridge the gaps between subjects hitherto thought divergent can stimulate actual "higher education." Interdisciplinary programs can teach college students how to learn, can encourage curiosity, and can inspire a love for life-long learning.

An excellent example of such a program is the Hutchins School at Sonoma State University in Northern California. The Hutchins School offers its students an opportunity to explore the interrelationships between the natural sciences (biology, botany, geography, geology, physics), the social sciences (anthropology, sociology, psychology, economics), and the humanities (art history, philosophy, theology). The Hutchins School and those with a similar curriculum provide a dynamic foundation from which to build careers in a wide variety of fields.

Our professors need a means through which they can broaden their appreciation of interdisciplinary studies. The Santa Fe Institute has provided such a resource. Established by three Nobel Laureates, the Santa Fe Institute has been a haven for scholars who crave to break out of the sterility of their compartmentalized subject areas. Since the Institute's inception in the late 1980s, economists, computer scientists, neurophysiologists, anthropologists, physicists, philosophers, and mathematicians have attended its seminars, which explore the highest common denominators between their respective subject areas.

The field of complexity theory has emerged from this interdisciplinary effort. Complexity theory attempts to not only explain how divergent fields have commonality but, more important, how the dynamics of "complex systems" such as a society, an organism, or an economy can "self-organize" at "the edge of chaos."[3]

RESPONSIBLE ENTERTAINMENT

A poll done by TV-Free America found that 79 percent of the respondents believe that violence on television promotes more violence in communities.[4] This is a hopeful sign because it represents receptivity to non-LCD programming. We can capitalize on this trend by expanding public financing of PBS.

Despite the cuts in funding and the need to acquire underwriting, PBS has enriched its viewers with responsible entertainment. Numerous educational programs on PBS stations, such as *Bill Nye The Science Guy*, offer an entertaining way to learn about science, the arts, history, and a wide range of other subjects.

Television is one of the many means through which educational or health information can be transmitted to isolated people. For example, the CableQuit program offered a six-week, community-based, smoking-cessation program, with 13 live 30-minute sessions that were followed by 30-minute phone call-in support segments. Follow-up data was gathered through the mail, involving nicotine analysis of saliva samples. Those who managed to quit were found to have lower levels of depression and greater levels of self-efficacy than smokers.[5]

However, most television has little substance at best. Through selective viewing, television can enrich rather than detract from our leisure time. Children, too, can benefit by selective viewing habits. Parents need to accept responsibility for limiting access to television. Parents might say to their child that they can have only a specific number of hours each week to watch television. Parents must set an example by rationing their own television viewing. They can model selective television watching and show their children that reading and other learning activities are worthy ways to spend time. Children learn by watching what their parents do, more than by what they say.

The explosion of technology related to the Internet provides an excellent opportunity for people to have access to a wealth of information but a click away. Using the Internet for educational purposes can teach students to be motivated learners. In contrast to the dominant entertainment source—television—the Internet is an active process. Viewers sit passively in front of a TV and are programmed by commercial interests, but the Internet requires users to read and direct a search by exploring their own research interests.

Commercial television promotes homogenization, but the Internet promotes intellectual diversification. The Internet offers a means through which its users can link across cultures while resisting the meltdown into programming at the LCD. Websites do not need a viewing audience of millions to be available.

Censorship on television or the Internet drives us close to trashing the constitution. But a completely laissez-faire attitude about censorship is not tenable. Dissemination of child pornography and information about how to build bombs undermines the very society that the Constitution was designed to protect. Similarly, television and movies that contain gratuitous violence should be regarded as pornography.

REAL NEWS

The news media underestimates the public's tastes and gravitates more toward sensationalism than toward in-depth reporting. *U.S. News and World Report* ran a story noting a survey in which 71 percent of the respondents believe the media gets in the way of solving problems.[6]

Beverly Kees and Brian Phillips produced a report titled *Politicians and the News Media.* This survey detailed how far the public has come to distrust the news media.[7] Though we depend on the news media for information, we find that the information is not objective and too easily manipulated by special interests.

The Public Broadcasting Service (PBS) needs an infusion of funding to expand its news programs. It also needs to be assured of the flexibility to broadcast thoughtful investigative news programs even if a particular political party might object.

Both PBS and network news programs need to be free from commercial accountability. News vendors must disseminate the news outside of commercial obligations. The Federal Communication Commission (FCC) should be fully empowered to do its job to ensure that corporate interests do not subjugate the democratic process.

Public television should foster and support production companies such as Globalvision. Unfortunately, PBS shifted its support away from the program *Rights and Wrongs,* produced by Globalvision, because it did not meet the shift toward noncontroversial themes.[8] *Rights and Wrongs* is a series on human rights issues and should not offend anyone professing to support the ideals of the Constitution. Public television should cover issues that are, in fact, controversial.

Some journalists are now advocating for a major change in the production of news called "public journalism." Public journalism emphasizes sharing of information between journalists and less competition to produce breaking new stories. Such a collaborative effort will enhance the depth of stories while dampening the tendency to produce sensationalistic headlines.

We need more journalism such as *Utne* magazine, which attempts to synthesize and make contextual sense of numerous stories on the same general subject. *Utne* is a bimonthly newsletter whose editors correctly refer to it as the "best of the alternative media."

Danny Schechter has advocated for a "Media Channel" that would feature "edu-mercials" in place of commercials. It could offer "Edu-tainment Tonight" instead of *Entertainment Tonight*. Schechter proposes that the Media Channel could offer "self-censorship minutes, quick takes in which prominent journalists offer sound-bites on the stories where they pulled their punches and why."⁹

Groups such as the Rocky Mountain Media Watch will continue to be helpful in tracking local TV content. Their pamphlet called "Let the World Know: Make Your Cause News" is a recipe book on how to train staff and organize seminars to monitor the news. Such groups should be given greater opportunity to apply for federal grants.

THE AIR WE BREATHE

In recent years there have been signs that the age-old concept of manifest destiny has been reemerging. The current form of manifest destiny suggests that if land is going to waste, we must make use of it for the sake of the economy. Large corporations, including those in the timber and oil industries, propose that harvesting trees or drilling for oil is critical to the maintenance of economic prosperity for all and jobs for the underemployed. But now at the beginning of the twenty-first century, we need public acknowledgement of the interdependence between our species and the earth. But we are altering the global climate as we cut down the forests. As we over-fish the oceans, the fish population plummets and the livelihood of fishermen becomes squeezed. Their cry to dismantle fishing restrictions for the sake of their jobs should be met by the implementation of retraining programs.

The true meaning of the term "conservative" is to conserve. The irony is that many people who profess to be conservative are typically anti-environmentalist. We need to be true conservatives when it comes to the environment. Teddy Roosevelt urged us to conserve the environment and treat it as a national treasure.

By necessity we can agree on the higher common denominator of environmentalism. Truly becoming an environmentalist society will require vigorous government oversight and intervention. Yet, in the corporate world today, conditions do not exist to ensure that companies will be responsible to the environment. Companies will manufacture what will make profits, despite adverse environmental consequences. The government must make it economically advantageous for companies to act with environmental responsibility. Tax breaks and incentives directed toward environmental cleanup and preservation will be critical. Stiff and real fines should be set up to put a company out of business for major pollution violations.

It is our job as a society to vote and support a government that ensures the longevity of our shared living environment. Candidates who joke about the spotted owl do not act in the national interests. Candidates who share the national interests as their own are environmentalists. But it is not enough to give lip service to environmental issues. True environmentalists are those who can participate in a thoughtful analysis of each issue impacting the environment.

DISARMAMENT

Far too often, governmental bodies are reactive rather than proactive when it comes to ensuring that our citizens are safe from senseless gun violence. Only after Buford Furrow walked into the North Valley Jewish Community Center in the Los Angeles suburb of Granada Hills and opened fire with his automatic weapons, injuring two women and three small boys, did local politicians respond legislatively. The Los Angeles County Board of Supervisors voted 3 to 2 to bar gun shows from government land, which had included the nation's largest, the Great Western Gun Show.

Despite claims to the contrary, gun control efforts do suppress crime. For example, gun murders in Richmond, Virginia, fell by 41 percent after federal prosecutors initiated an effort to put in prison for five years any felon caught carrying a gun. The local police referred cases to federal court, and a publicity campaign was mounted to inform the public of the new policy.[10]

Gun control laws, however, can defeat themselves if not thought out well. For example, Missouri has become a lightning rod for critics of gun control because the state's gun control law was too inclusive, preventing off-duty police officers from carrying a concealed weapon. Large numbers of police officers and police fraternal organizations objected because they feared that criminals either arrested or testified against by an officer might act out in revenge. Police officers are usually for gun control, but they joined with gun control opponents to argue that the Missouri law was faulty.

If we limit background checks to only those who have been convicted of crimes, we will fail to scrutinize those who have yet to be arrested. Many people who are active drug addicts, end-stage alcoholics, or spousal abusers are not yet identified by the background checks. Most studies have indicated that 30 percent of the adult population have used drugs. Under the current law, all these people are eligible to buy guns.

Approximately 1.4 million persons a year are convicted of drinking and driving. Over the years, the criminal justice system has come to acknowledge that drinking and driving amounts to possession of a deadly weapon; thus many repeat DUI offenders lose their license to drive. Guns are obviously deadly weapons. Why not deal with guns the way we deal with the right to drive a car? We license people to drive, so why not license people to own and operate a rifle? The licensure process for owning rifles should include a gun safety test. We should also ensure that gun owners are legally responsible to keep weapons away from children.

It is necessary to clearly define the term "weapon." Hunting rifles and assault weapons should be differentiated, but the NRA has fought to bundle the two together. They have therefore been successful in convincing the general public that outlawing assault weapons takes away the rights of hunters.

Automatic weapons and handguns are designed with one primary purpose: to kill people. They should therefore be banned for all people except military and law enforcement personnel. Both buying and selling weapons of mass destruction should be considered a felony offense.

HEALTH CARE AND PREVENTION

With far more contact between people taking place throughout the world, new strains of viruses and bacterial infections threaten us all. Denying immunization shots to the children of undocumented aliens serves to undercut everyone's health. We need to ensure that immunization and access to quality health care are available to all citizens and residing non-citizens alike. We will spend far more money trying to fight epidemics later if we do not make a preventive effort now. Free health care is not only critical but a necessity for the third millennium.

Health care must be regarded as one of the main priorities of our federal, state, and local governments. All the countries that generally rank above us in standard of living and quality of life have health care readily available either free of charge or for a nominal cost. We can do no less for our citizens if we care to provide a quality of life representative of a democratic society. If we do not make these investments, we will perpetuate a neo-oligarchy in which the "haves" do have access to health care at any level but the "have-nots" are screened out. Those on the far right would say, "Well, that's socialism, isn't it?" When conservatives use buzzwords that scare potential voters at the LCD levels of thought, progressives must not retreat.

We must penetrate the artificial and organizational obstacles to integrated and comprehensive treatment. One of the positive steps being taken to break down artificial barriers in some health care systems is to integrate mental health care and primary medical care treatment. This need is underscored by the fact that 60 percent of all psychotropic medications are prescribed by primary care physicians. Many physicians in a primary care setting estimate that as many as 60 percent of the patients they see in an average day might be suffering from psychological problems that complicate and/or exacerbate their medical conditions or they are simply somaticizing.

The solution is to deploy psychologists in the primary care environment. According to a retrospective study of patients in the primary care environment 30 years ago, those who were seen by a psychologist subsequently visited a primary care physician 67.5 percent fewer times.[11] This category of psychological work is referred to as behavioral medicine. In the Kaiser Permanente Medical System, we are redesigning primary care in a broad initiative referred to as Adult Primary Care Redesign (APC). One of the core members on the APC team is the Behavioral Medicine Specialist. This psychologist can take immediate referrals within the primary care departments and even see patients in the examining room. This is one-stop shopping. There are fewer chances for patients to fall through the cracks in the fully integrated primary care environment. This coordinated effort shows patients that providers know that how people feel physically has a lot to do with how people feel emotionally.

Even if a coherent health care system were available to us, we need to own the responsibility for our own health. Though Americans often boast of being the richest country in the world, we rank 18th in life expectancy. In fact, we are becoming a fatter and lazier society. Despite all the marketing hype about calories, fat, and cholesterol, people are eating more and exercising less. Americans who are now considered overweight amount to one-half of the population. In the period between 1976–1980, 26 percent of women and 24 percent of men in the United States were overweight. By 1988–1994, 35 percent of women and 33.7 percent of men were overweight. It is no wonder that heart disease—a disease never even heard of in 1900—is the leading cause of death in the United States. Only 14 percent of Americans say they exercise regularly, and 30 percent say they never exercise.

We want others, such as our doctors, to be responsible for our health. Most people expect a physician or a psychologist to know all about them within the first few minutes after their initial meeting. They expect someone to give a comprehensive diagnosis simply by looking at them. People believe that doctors know all.

But patients have better longevity who are willing to invest the time and effort to take care of their own health by exercising, dieting, and staying up with the latest literature regarding important lifestyle enhancements to health.

The best patients are those who come in for a health care appointment with a list of symptoms and questions clearly outlined, not necessarily expecting a "quick-fix." After a treatment is applied, patients who take the time to read about their illness and its treatment will have the best results. The best patients are those who are informed.

Therapeutic integration of the two domains, mind and body, provides the most comprehensive health care. Indeed, one of the most exciting areas of medicine and psychology to develop in half a century is the emerging field of psychoneuroimmunology. This field synthesizes psychology, neurology, and immunology and finds the link between the body and the mind by describing in detail the interdependence of thoughts, emotions, the brain, and the immune system.

Since the late 1960s, researchers have demonstrated that what someone believes and feels has a direct effect on the integrity of their immune system. For example, widowers have depressed immune systems for at least a few months after their spouse dies. A popular illustration of the positive aspects of this interdependence is the so-called "placebo effect." In such a situation, a patient swallows a capsule, not knowing there is a harmless substance within it but thinking instead that it is a medicinal compound. The patient then recovers from the ailment being "treated." This is not a simple matter of mind over matter. Rather, the field of psychoneuroimmunology has made clear that there is a complex bidirectional interaction between our belief system, our emotional and physical condition, and our current thoughts.

WAKING UP

Any effort to escape the omnipresent forces contributing to the meltdown must involve more than an awareness of the LCD society. We must understand ourselves first if we are to understand how we can transcend the meltdown. Such transcendence requires an understanding of our interdependence with the world around us.

In this book we have not dealt with the biological aspects of consciousness. Those evolutionary and neurological issues have not led the way into the meltdown. However, before we disregard the role of the brain, it is important to note that the LCD society actually does adversely affect the brain. This might sound like a giant stretch, but consider that research has shown that a stimulating environment during infancy and intellectual activity during adulthood promote an increase in the development of nerve connections (dendrites) between neurons. In other words, though we do not actually grow new neurons after early childhood, we can influence the development of our brains by intellectual stimulation. Conversely, if someone becomes intellectually lazy and watches an inordinate amount of television, we can say there is a pruning of connections between neurons because of a lack of use. Essentially, if you do not use it, you will lose it. The LCD society promotes losing. People who put their brains through the pruning process become less able to deal with the complexity in their lives. Then they deal with complex situations with stereotypical responses, such as a bigot expressing prejudices. We are the most socially adaptive species in the world. Not only can we invent ingenious means through which we can thrive in complex and continually evolving circumstances but we also create the conditions to which we must adapt.

Anthropological and sociological studies of various cultures and subcultures have demonstrated an immense array of cultures. The degree of complexity of a social system has a direct bearing on the degree of complexity of thought of the average member of that society.

Seventy years ago Alexander Luria surveyed the transition of cultures in Soviet Central Asia, where people were taken from a feudalistic culture with 98-percent illiteracy to a communal culture with 90-percent literacy. To his astonishment, he found that the people in the medieval hamlets had little ability to use abstract and conceptual reasoning. After they were taught to read and were exposed to a greater diversity of views, Luria found that their ability to use abstract and conceptual reasoning had increased in sophistication tenfold.[12]

At this point in our evolutionary history, cultural factors have become exceedingly complex. Contemporary cultures in the industrialized world are imbued with multiple layers of complexity. But as noted in the first chapter, we are deluged with stimulation and many people suffer from an associated numbness. In part because of the deluge of information, people are now receptive to the emerging LCD dynamics.

There appears to be a de-complexification occurring in American society. As the LCD society gains steam, oversimplified images and homogenized consumer habits shroud ideas that were once complex. As noted in chapter 8, assault cruisers (ACs) have widespread appeal across the United States. These ACs have become a way for consumers to pretend they are interested in healthy living and the environment. The power of conformity not only has a bearing on what people buy but also leads them to believe they are something they are not. Apparently most people want to appear as though they are interested in the outdoors, so they find it hard to resist the temptation to buy their own AC. These ACs promote neither environmentalism nor healthy living. Because they have been classified as trucks, they have escaped the emission control standards of automobiles. They also consume twice the gasoline and are deadly for everyone in a collision. Thus the concept of environmentalism has come to be represented by a contradictory image—a symbol of anti-environmentalism.

To transcend the pull into the LCD, each of us must seriously consider every purchase we make and not act as if we are on automatic pilot. Transcending the consumer culture will necessitate that we purchase products that reflect our interdependence with the world we inhabit.

Transcending the LCD society will also require us to be aware of ourselves as individuals. In his book *The Saturated Self,* Kenneth Gergen notes that the demands of modern society require us to constantly shift roles and undergo a kind of "population of the self" whereby we develop a "pastiche" personality.[13] We are but a result of our relationships, and those relationships are fluid; therefore, our sense of self is fluid.

Robert Jay Lifton has proposed that because modern society has created so many social uncertainties, we are losing our "psychological moorings." But he proposes that the new sense of self in American society is flexible and adaptive.[14] Despite constant role-shifting and fragmentation of the self, we are able to maintain resiliency. However, the LCD society has far-reaching consequences for our consciousness and sense of self. What we adapt to may not be so healthy for our sense of self. The point is that we have to adapt by changing the psychologically destructive aspects of our society.

Changing the LCD society requires a change in attitude. Martin Seligman of the University of Pennsylvania points out that we should avoid the attitude underlying the concept of "learned helplessness" and cultivate "learned optimism." A person who has experienced learned helplessness early in life becomes depressed, but the self-generated experience of learned optimism results in feelings of satisfaction and the motivation to make constructive changes in oneself and the environment.[15] Learned helplessness results from repeated unsuccessful experiences in which, no matter what a person does, the effort is useless. A battered wife might experience learned helplessness because nothing improves while she remains in a home with domestic violence "to try to work it out." A mother who argues with her family that the television need not be on constantly finally gives up and watches it herself.

Learned optimism, in contrast, results from learning how to find and follow through on the most productive course of action to take. That same woman might leave and devote her energies to developing a thorough sense of independence. Or the man whose family watches television endlessly puts his foot down and shuts it off. Because of this energized feeling of independence, he feels more optimism about his future. A schoolteacher relishes the challenge of teaching hard-to-reach children and finds pleasure in seeing those children learn to enjoy learning.

We are creatures of habit. Much of our daily lives is patterned conditional responses that we perform without reflection. Many of these responses and habits are culturally conditioned and rarely include our conscious participation in the process.[16]

We need to invest more time and energy in appreciating the natural environment in which we live. To do so will necessitate that we minimize the bombardment of advertisements. Just as Santa Fe, New Mexico, the entire state of Vermont, and many countries in Europe have restricted the use of billboards, we should make similar restrictions across the nation. People must be allowed to drive down the highway without being assaulted by distracting billboards that clutter the mind with useless information.

It is difficult to drive down the same road each day and notice the novelty of something new or appreciate the same sights from a fresh perspective. When not exposed to novelty, we often sink back into our petty worries and daydreams. Making a concerted effort to notice new and subtle aspects of our surroundings or appreciate the same repetitive experiences requires an attitude adjustment.

Early last century the Armenian/Greek philosopher Gurdjieff developed a methodology to stimulate "waking up." These techniques are derived from the Sufi tradition and are not unlike those found in Zen Buddhism to achieve an experience of satori. Though there are some methodological and philosophical differences between these schools of thought, the common goal is to become awake. In fact, when the Buddha was asked if he was a god, he responded by saying, "No, I'm just awake."

Appreciating the complexity of life requires work and good frustration tolerance. Fighting the propensity to conform to the LCD society will necessitate resisting the temptation to react automatically. Many human automatic reactions carry with them the results of cultural conditioning.

Waking up requires a sense of wonder. Just as Zen shines a lens on our senses and our cravings, we need to stay awake so the consumer culture does not ignite cravings by attempting to blur our senses. We must resist the power of the LCD society to blur our senses. Waking up requires us to tap into the cultural resources we already have available before they blur together into the meltdown.

We are influenced to a greater degree by social dynamics. Social changes condition us to think and behave in ways that differ from culture to culture. What may be thought pleasurable or attractive in one culture may be considered intolerable or ugly in another. For example, in some cultures, such as the Masi in Kenya, ritualistic scarring is thought to enhance one's attractiveness, while in Western cultures plastic surgeons are employed to blend out scarring. The experience of pleasure varies among people. In Southeast Asia a fruit called a "durian" is considered a delicacy. For the Western palate, the taste of durians is often described as nauseating.

Though time is running out, we have the opportunity to try to appreciate how beauty and tastes vary across cultures. Not everyone must taste a durian or travel to Kenya, but we must make an effort to resist the homogenizing trend. In so doing, we can expand our own aesthetic appreciation for the diversity of human experience.

By preventing ourselves from being pulled into the conceptual LCD dictated by the commercialization and expansion of the mass media, we can promote the ability to appreciate the true richness in life. This effort can result in a widening of perception and a temperament more durable over the course of time. Embarking on this effort to stay awake results in the foundation of better mental health and enjoyment in life. To do otherwise promotes internal conflict and the feeling that life is a struggle.

SPIRITUAL DIVERSITY

We have a valuable opportunity to benefit by the cross-fertilization of theological ideas and perspectives. To do so will require us to resist the pull of the spiritual marketplace. Many of the theological perspectives now accessible require only quiet observance and subtle reflection. Twenty years ago, while in Peru, I attended an Easter service in a small Andean village. The clothing worn and the rituals practiced during the service radiated with post-Incan culture. On Good Friday, the Christian crucifixion and the Incan belief in the God of the Earthquakes were jointly celebrated. A large procession followed three men carrying a cross through a sea of the descendents of Incas assembled in the large square in Cusco. Their job was to present the cross at the main cathedral to ensure that the God of the Earthquakes would spare the region during the following year of cataclysmic disasters.

In Northern New Mexico, the Pueblo cultures celebrate Easter. Crosses are not evident, but dancers wear deerskin and eagle feathers and carry corn in reverence of a particular aspect of nature.

Someone might say, "Well, sure, these tribes danced on Easter and observed certain saints so the Spanish colonialists would be fooled and they could observe their own religion." Certainly part of that was true in the eighteenth century, but consider that today in pueblos such as Taos, 80 percent of the population identify themselves as Christian. There is no compulsory attendance at church. Simultaneously, there is a great resurgence in Native American rituals and pride in their own culture. The magic of these rituals is that the dances meld many cultures.

Theological systems are a synthesis of many once-foreign beliefs and rituals. Each continually evolving theological system is practiced through rituals that soak up the imagery of the society as it transforms.

I have applied a similar perspective to an analysis of all major theologies.[17] Throughout the history of the world's religions, cultural factors have had a great deal of influence on the language used to describe a spiritual experience. We experience God in a manner related to the way we have been taught to envision God.

We interpret our lives through the lenses we have learned to look through. The vast literature of anthropological studies has shown us that people all over the world have constructed a wide variety of cultural/theological systems through which they interpret their lives. Culture essentially prescribes the lenses we use to interpret our experience in the world. Our experience is set in the context of our cultural system.

Just as a society has members within it that practice a religion that in essence is a synthesis of many theologies, so the society itself is a synthesis of many cultures. We can stem the tide of the LCD society by ensuring that we allow a rich synthesis of ideas and perspectives to percolate up through members of our society.

At the dawning of the new millenium, the future of our society need not melt down into the blandness of commercial homogeneity. Resisting the meltdown starts with you, the individual, and requires that you stay more than awake. A healthy future requires you to participate with others in constructing a society of clarity as we usher in the new millennium.

Notes

CHAPTER ONE

1. Putman, R. (2002). *Bowling alone: The collapse and revival of American community.* New York: Simon & Schuster.

2. For data on leisure time, see: *The Pew Charitable Trust: News Room* www.pewtrusts.org/ne . . .t_item_id = 9487page = nr3. Accessed May 1, 2002.

3. Kubey, R., & Csikszentmihalyi, M. (1990). *Television and the quality of life: How viewing shapes everyday experience.* Hillsdale, NJ: Erlbaum.

4. Stephens, M. (1998). *The rise of the image, the fall of the word.* New York: Oxford University Press.

5. Robinson, J. (1990). About time: Thanks for reading this. *American Demographics,* (May).

6. Cohen, S., & Wills, T. (1985). Stress, social support, and the buffering hypothesis. *Psychological Bulletin, 98,* 310–357.

7. Gomery, D. (1993). As the dial turns. *Wilson Quarterly,* (autumn).

8. Stephens, p. 107.

9. *Wall Street Journal Almanac.* (1999). *Living in America.* p. 469. New York: Ballintine Books.

10. Dershowitz, Alan M. (1998). *Sexual McCarthyism.* New York: Basic Books.

11. Orwell, G. (1949). *1984* (p. 7). New York: Harcourt & Brace.

12. Huxley, A. (1946). *Brave new world* (p. 56). New York: Bantam Books.

13. Postman, N. (1986). *Amusing ourselves to death: Public discourse in the age of show business.* New York: Viking.

14. Twitchell, J. (1992). *Carnival culture.* New York: Columbia University Press.

15. Ibid.

16. Myers, D. (2000). The funds, friends, and faith of happy people. *American Psychologist,* 55 (1), 56–67.

17. Ibid.

18. Bertmand, S. (1998). *HyperCulture: The human cost of speed* (p. 67). Westport, CT: Praeger.

19. Meyers, p. 56–67.

20. Bertmand, p. 112.

21. Milgram, S. (1970, March 13). The experience of living in cities. *Science,* 1461–1468.

22. Shenk, D. (1997). *Data smog: Surviving the information glut.* San Francisco: HarperCollins.

23. Murray, Bridget. (1998). Data smog: newest culprit in brain drain. *American Psychological Association Monitor,* vol. 29, no. 3, 1461–1468.

24. Rosen, L., & Weil, M. (1997), *TechnoStress.* New York: John Wiley & Sons. Also Toffer, A. (1970) in his book *Future Shock,* New York: Random House warned that people in the American society are beginning to experience "massive adaptive breakdown." As technological and social changes occur increasingly fast people become confused, disoriented, and more easily manipulated by advertising interests.

CHAPTER TWO

1. *U.S. News and World Report,* May 3, 1999.

2. Greg Gittrich, Do video games teach killing? *Denver Post Online.* http://uss.002.infi.net/denver/post/news/shot0427d.htm. Accessed April 27, 1999.

3. Video games increase aggression. *Journal of Personality and Social Psychology.* Reuters online, accessed April 24, 2000, http://dailynews.yahoo.com/h/nm/20000424/h1/games_1.html.

4. *Wall Street Journal.* (1998). *Wall Street Journal Almanac 1998* (p. 896). New York: Ballantine Books.

5. Turkle, S. (1995). *Life on the screen: Identity in the age of the internet.* New York: Touchtone.

6. Ibid. (p. 30)

7. Turkle, S. (1980). *The second self: Computers and the human spirit.* New York: Simon & Schuster.

8. Turkle, S. (1995) p. 83.

9. Kraut, R., Patterson, M., Lundmark, V., Kiesler, S., Mukopadhyay, T., & Scheklis, W. (1998). Internet paradox: A social technology that reduces social involvement and psychological well-being? *American Psychologist,* (September), 1017–1031.

10. Ibid.

11. Sleek, Scott. (1998, September). Isolation increases with internet use. *American Psychological Association Monitor,* 29 (9): 1, 30–31.

12. Kraut et. al., p. 1030.

13. Kraut et. al., p. 1028.

14. Quoted in S. Turkel, p. 115. Get in the Mood. (1994, November 7). *Newsweek.*

15. Sleek, S. (1998, September). New cyber toast: Here's MUD in your psyche. *American Psychological Association Monitor,* p. 30.

16. Turkle, S. (1995) p. 182.

17. Turkle, (1995) p. 189.

18. Arden, J. B. (1996). *Consciousness, dreams, and self: A transdisciplinary approach.* Madison, CT: Psychosocial Press.

19. Turkle, S. (1995) p. 222.

20. Turkle, S. (1995) p. 230.

CHAPTER THREE

1. *Detroit News,* quoted in Wayne Kilpatrick, Are you an addict? http://www.newtestamentchurch.org/OPA/Articles/1987/10/are%20an%20addict.htm. Accessed February 8, 2003.

2. *Wall Street Journal Almanac.* (1998). *Wall Street Journal Almanac 1998.* New York: Ballintine Books.

3. Kaiser Family Foundation. (1999). *Kids and media at the new millennium.* Menlo Park, CA.

4. National television violence study, vol. 3. (1998). Santa Barbara, CA: Center for Communications and Social Policy, University of California.

5. *The New York Times.* (1999). *1998 New York Times Almanac.* p. 397, New York: Penguin Reference.

6. Ibid., p. 397.

7. Schickel, R. (1985). *Infinite strangers: The culture of celebrity.* Garden City, NY: Doubleday.

8. Gabler, N. (1999). *Life: The movie: How entertainment conquered reality.* New York: Alfred Knoff.

9. Verri, A., Vertiche, V., Vallero, E., Bellone, S., & Nespolip, L. (1997). Television and eating disorders, a study of adolescent eating behavior. *Minerva Pediatr,* 49 (6), 235–243.

10. Tiggeman, M., & Pickering, A. (1996). Role of television in adolescent women's body dissatisfaction and drive for thinness. *International Journal of Eating Disorders,* 20 (2), 199–203.

11. Quoted in Twitchell, p. 195.

12. *The New York Times.* (1998). *1998 New York Times Almanac.* New York: Penguin Reference.

13. Twitchell, p. 143.

14. Bagdikian, B. (1997). *Media monopoly* (5th ed.). Boston: Beacon Press.

15. Max Frankel, Media madness. *The Gatto Report on Journalism and Society.* www.bollier.org/pdf/mediamad.pdf. Accessed February 12, 2003.

16. Lopate, P. (1996). The last taboo. In K. Washburn & J. Thornton (Eds.). *Dumbing down: Essays on the strip-mining of American culture.* New York: Norton.

17. Ibid.

18. Schechter, D. (1996). *The more you watch the less you know.* New York: Seven Stories Press.

19. Ibid.

20. Weiss, H. (1996). Viewing of horror and violence by adolescents: A study of speech samples of video consumers with the Gottschalk-Gleser speech content analysis. *Prax Kinpsychol Kinderpsychiatr,* 45 (5), 179–185.

21. Hough, K., & Erwin, P. (1997). Children's attitude toward violence on television. *Journal of Psychology,* 131 (4), 411–415.

22. Scheungrab, M. (1990). Representation of relations between television watching and delinquency within the scope causal analysis models. *Archives of Psychology* (Frankf), 142 (4), 295–322.

23. Steamshovel Press Office of Illumination by Url Dowenko. www.umsl.edu/˜skthoma/offline6.htm. Accessed February 8, 2003.

24. Greg Gittrich. (April 27, 1999). Do video games kill? *Denver Post.*

25. Greg Gittrich (April 27, 1999). Do video games teach killing? *The Denver Post Online—Columbine Tragedy,* http://uss001.infi.net/denver/post/news/shot0427d.htm. Accessed February 21, 2003.

26. Rodriquez, S., Esteban, J., Takenchi, M., Clausen, T., & Scott, R. (1995). Television violence: A Japanese, Spanish, and American comparison. *Psychological Reports,* 77 (3 pt 1), 995–1000.

27. Ibid.

28. Bushman, B. J., & Anderson, C. A. (2001). "Media violence and the American public: Scientific fact versus media misinformation. *American Psychologist,* 56 (6/7), 447–489.

29. Charlton, T., Coles, D., & Lovemore, T. (1997). Teacher's nursery class children's behavior before and after availability of television by satellite. *Psychological Reports,* 81 (1), 96–98.

30. Brody, G. (1990, April). Effects of television viewing on family interaction: An observational study. *Family Relations,* 29, 216–220.

31. Sidney, S., Sternfeld, B., Haskell, W., Jacobs, D., Chesney, M., & Halley, S. (1998). Television viewing and cardiovascular risk factors in young adults: The CARDIA study. *Annals of Epidemiology,* 6 (2), 154–159.

32. Anderson, R., Crespo, C., Bartlett, S., Cheskin, C., & Pratt, M. (1998). Relationship of physical activity and television watching with body weight and level of fitness. *Journal of the American Medical Association,* 279, 938–942.

33. Kubey, R., & Csikszentmihalyi, M. (1990). *Television and the quality of life: How viewing shapes everyday experience.* Hillsdale, NJ: Erlbaum.

34. Canary, D., & Spitzberg, B. (1993). Loneliness and media gratification. Communications of the ACM, 39 (12), 68–74.

35. Twitchell, J. (1992). *Carnival culture.* New York: Columbia University Press.

36. Stephens, M. (1998). *The rise of the image, the fall of the word* (p. 135). New York: Oxford University Press.

37. Kigus, M., & Pamariega, A. (1994). Experimental manipulation of cocaine craving by videotaped environmental cues. *Southern Medical Journal,* 87 (11), 1138–1140.

38. Sobell, L., Sobell, M., Toneaatto, T., & Leo, G. (1993). Severely dependent alcohol abusers may be vulnerable to alcohol cues in television programs. *Journal of the Study of Alcoholism,* 54 (1), 85–91.

39. Grube, J., & Wallack, L. (1994). Television beer advertisement and drinking knowledge beliefs, and intentions among school children. *American Journal of Public Health,* 84 (2), 254–259.

CHAPTER FOUR

1. Bagdikian, B. (1997). *Media monopoly* (5th ed.). Boston: Beacon Press.

2. Ibid. p.x.

3. Schechter, D. (1996). *The more you watch the less you know.* New York: Seven Stories Press.

4. Ibid., p. 400.

5. Bagdikian, p. xxiii.

6. Ibid.

7. Ibid., p. xx.

8. Ibid., p.xviv.

9. Barber, B. (1995). *Jihad vs. McWorld.* New York: Times Books.

10. Bagdikian, p. 3–9.

11. Quoted in Schechter, p. 53.

12. Ibid. p. 48.

13. Ibid. p. 170.

14. Ibid. p. 160.

15. Jamie McKenzie. Teaching Media Literacy in the Age of Entertainment. www.newlibrary.org/n17.html. Accessed February 14, 2003.

16. Quoted in Schecter, p. 193.

17. Ibid., p. 57.

18. Quoted in Schechter, p. 53.

19. Stephens, M. (1998). *The rise of the image, the fall of the word.* New York: Oxford University Press.

20. Bagdikian, p. 195–199.

21. Schechter, p. 407–408.

22. Ibid., p. 191.

23. Ibid., p. 199.

24. Quoted in Schecter, p. 418.

25. Schechter, p. 35.

26. Quoted in Ibid., p. 208.

27. Ibid., p. 380; Editorial, *The New York Times,* June 20, 1995, p. 16.

28. Ibid.

29. Quoted in Schechter, p. 237.

CHAPTER FIVE

1. Contributions prior to 1996 Telecommunication Act reported by the Center for Responsible Politics.

2. Jaspen, Bruce. (1999, January 31). AMA denies political motivation in the firing of editor. *San Francisco Chronicle,* p. A5.

3. The doctor is out. http://slate.msn.com/id/33630/. Accessed February 21. 2003.

4. Philip-Morris contributions source: Common Cause and Campaign for Tobacco Free Kids.

5. Adatto, A. (1990, June). *Sound-bite democracy: Network evening news presidential campaign coverage 1968 and 1988* (Research Paper R-2). Cambridge, MA: Harvard University, The Joan Shorenstein Barone Center.

6. Shorr, D. (Reporter). *All Things Considered.* Washington, D.C.: National Public Radio.

7. Schechter, D. (1996). *The more you watch the less you know.* New York: Seven Stories Press.

8. *$1 billion for ideas: Conservative think tanks in the 1990s.* Special report from the National Committee for Responsive Philanthropy, March 12, 1999. http://www.ncrp.org/psr/pressreleases/thinktanks.htm. Accessed February 21, 2003.

9. Cannon, L. (1991). *President Reagan: The role of a lifetime.* New York: Simon & Schuster.

10. Brainy quote. www.brainyquote.com/quotes/quoteslm/q135596.html. Accessed February 21, 2003.

11. Quoted in the Corporate Welfare Information Page. www.corporations.org/welfare. Accessed February 7, 2003.

12. How smart do you have to be to be president? (1999, July 12). *U.S. News and World Report.*

CHAPTER SIX

1. The costs of gunfire. (1999, August 9). *Washington Post.*

2. Lazarus, David. Gun sales in California up 30 percent over last year. (1999, August 28). *San Francisco Chronicle,* p. A1, A8.

3. Quoted in Mahoney, The American Gun, *Crime Magazine*, www. crimemagazine.com/guns/htm. Accessed February 21, 2003.

4. Lazarus, p. A1, A8.

5. Mahoney, p. 13.

6. Whitcomb, Dan. (1999). Los Angeles bans gun sales on county property. *Reuters*, http://dailynews.yahoo.com/h/nm/19990824/p1/jewishcenter_ban_2.html. Accessed August 24, 1999.

7. Psychiatrist legally amasses huge gun arsenal. (1999, August 14). *Reuters*. www.yahoo.com/h/nm/19990814/ts/guns_arsenal_1.html. Accessed August 16, 1999.

8. Quoted in, Gun play: How the NRA and gun manufacturers are targeting your children. (1999, July 29–August 4). *Sonoma County Independent*, p. 6–7.

9. Ibid.

10. Ibid.

11. Quoted in Ibid.

12. Quoted in Ibid.

13. Ibid.

14. Ibid.

15. Ibid.

16. Kleck, G. (1991). *Point blank: Guns and violence in America*. New York: Aldine de Gruyter.

17. Mahoney, p. 1–16.

18. Young, Cathy. (1999, June 21). Stop over-simplifying the gun debate. *Jewish World Review*, www.jewishworldreview.com. Accessed May 1, 2002.

19. Quoted in Mahoney, p. 1–16.

20. *Washington Post*, August 9, 1999, p. A14.

21. Tapper, Jake. (1999, August 12). The NRA's big guns. *Salon*. www.salon.com/news/feature/1999/08/12/nra. Accessed February 21, 2003.

22. Ibid.

23. Mahoney, J. J. (1999, June 21). The American gun. *Crime Magazine*. www.crimemagazine.com/guns/htm. Accessed February 21, 2003.

24. Ibid.

25. *Newsweek*, (1999, August 23).

26. Detained and confused. (1999, August 16). *Time Magazine* , 154 (7).

27. Leland, John, and Brown, Corie. (1999, August 23). A lower body count. *Newsweek*, p. 46–48.

28. Quoted in Betsy Streisand. (1997, June 14). Lawyers, guns, money: Hollywood, under new probe, may have a lot to hide. *U.S. News and World Report*, p. 56–57.

29. Ibid.

30. Lifton, R. J. (1999, August 23). Guns in America: What must be done. *Newsweek*, p. 23–24.

31. 75% of guns used by children come from home. (2000, May 9). *Reuters.* www.yahoo/news/topstories/guns/children/htm. Accessed August 13, 1999.

CHAPTER SEVEN

1. Oklahoma bombing victims to sue government agencies. (1997, March 19). *CNN Online.* www.cnn.com/us/9703/19/okcbomb/. Accessed February 21, 2003.
2. Limbaugh, R. (1993). *The way things ought to be.* New York: Pocket Books.
3. *The New York Times.* (1999). *1999 New York Times Almanac*, (p. 382). New York: Penguin Reference.

CHAPTER EIGHT

1. Gregory Zuckerman. (2000, July 5). U.S. debt reaches a record. The *Wall Street Journal Europe*, p. 8, 11.
2. Ibid.
3. Myers. D. (2000). The funds, friends, and faith of happy people. *American Psychologist*, 55 (1), 56–67.
4. *Wall Street Journal.* (1999). *1999 Wall Street Journal Almanac.* New York: Ballantine Books.
5. *Wall Street Journal.* (1999). *1999 Wall Street Journal Almanac.* New York: Ballantine Books.
6. Packard, V. (1957). *The hidden persuaders.* New York: MaKay.
7. Packard, V. (1960). *The strategy of desire.* Garden City, NJ: Doubleday.
8. Cheskin, L. (1950). *Color of profit.* New York: Liverlight.
9. Larsen. (1992). *The naked consumer: How our private lives become public commodities.* New York: Henry Holt.
10. Bertmand, S. (1998). *HyperCulture: The human cost of speed.* Westport, CT: Praeger.
11. Ibid., p. 73.
12. Postman, N. (1986). *Amusing ourselves to death: Public discourse in the age of show business* (p. 128). New York: Viking.
13. *Detroit News Auto Insider* (2002, January 11).
14. *U.S. News and World Report.* (1999, May 24).
15. Ibid.
16. Wolf, N. (1991). *The beautiful myth: How images of beauty are used against women.* New York: Morrow.
17. Bardo, S. (1993). *Unbearable weight: Feminism, Western culture, and the body.* Los Angeles and Berkeley, CA: University of California Press.

18. Csikszentmihalyi, M. (1998, August). Are we happy enough? Paper presented at the annual convention of the American Psychological Association, San Francisco.

CHAPTER NINE

1. Roberts, R. (1993). *Who we are: A portrait of America based on the latest U.S. census.* New York: Random House.
2. See Bertmand (1998) for a good review.
3. In fact, there are some hunter-gatherer societies still in existence today. In such societies women communicated verbally more with one another and with children than did men.
4. Maccoby, E., & Jacklin, C. (1974). *The psychology of sex differences.* Stanford, CA: Stanford University Press.
5. Hyde, J. (1991). *Half of the human experience: The psychology of women* (4th ed.). Lexington, MA: Heath.
6. Eagly, A. (1995). The science and politics of comparing women and men. *American Psychologist,* 50 (3), 145–158.
7. Eagly, A., & Wood, W. (1999). The origins of sex differences: Evolved differences versus social roles. *American Psychologist,* 1, 408–423.
8. Bass, D. (1995). Psychological sex differences. *American Psychologist,* 50 (3), 164–168.
9. Eagly & Wood, p. 408–423.
10. Bass, D. (1990). International preferences in selecting mates: A study of 37 cultures. *Journal of Cross-Cultural Psychology.* 21, 5–47.

CHAPTER TEN

1. Quirk, J., & Fort, R. (1999). *Hard ball: The abuse of power in pro team sports.* Princeton, NJ: Princeton University Press.
2. *Financial World,* quoted in Quirk & Fort.
3. Quirk & Fort.
4. Baade, R. (1987). *Is there an economic rationale for subsidizing sports stadiums?* Chicago: Heartland Institute.
5. Wall Street Journal. (1998). *1998 Wall Street Journal Almanac.* New York: Ballantine Books.
6. Quoted in the 1998 *Wall Street Journal Almanac,* p. 258.
7. 1998 *Wall Street Journal Almanac,* p. 259.
8. Inside-out olympics. Letter from Atlanta by David Rehnnick. (1996, August 5). *The New Yorker,* vol. 72, p. 26.
9. Dover, J., & Mayocchi, L. Life after winning gold. (1998, June). *The Sport Psychologist,* 12 (2), p. 119.

CHAPTER ELEVEN

1. O'Brien, T. (1998) *Bad bet: The inside story of the glamour, glitz, and danger of America's gambling industry.* New York: Times Business Random House.

2. 1996 United States Gross Annual Wager. (1997, August). *International Gaming & Wagering Business*, p. 14.

3. Meatto, Keith. (1997). The gambling dished out. *Mother Jones.* July/August, p. 35.

4. O'Brien, T. (1998). p. 41.

5. 1996 United States Gross Annual Wager, p. 60.

6. Quoted in O'Brien, T. (1998). The personal bankruptcy crisis. (1997), SMR Research Corp.

7. O'Brien, T. (1998). Las Vegas has grown to be by far the highest population center in the state of Nevada. Between 1980 and 1996, the population went from 465,000 to 1.6 million.

8. Ibid.

9. Ibid.

10. According to federal studies in 1980, only 60 percent of people who identify themselves as Native American were full blooded. That percentage is expected to drop to 34 percent by the year 2000.

11. O'Brien, T. (1998). p. 135–138.

12. 1996 United States Gross Annual Wager. Quoted in O'Brien, p. 138.

13. Littman, Jonathan. (1991, September 4). *San Francisco Chronicle.* Quoted in O'Brien, p. 137.

14. *The New York Times.* (1958, March 25). Quoted in O'Brien, p. 162–163.

15. 1996 United States Gross Annual Wager, p. 59–60.

16. O'Brien, T. (1998), p. 171.

17. Ibid.

18. A 1995 study of New York. (1995, December 4). *Newsday.* Quoted in O'Brien, p. 179.

19. Jones, T., & Amalfitano, J. (1994). "Lottery revenues do not help schools. In W. Eadington & J. Cornelius, (Eds.), *Gambling: Public policies and the social sciences* (p. 568). Reno, NV: Institute for the Study of Gambling and Commercial Gaming.

20. O'Brien, T. (1998). p. 155–180.

21. Ibid.

22. Ibid.

23. Lesieur, Henry (1984). *The chase: Career of the compulsive gambler.* Cambridge, MA: Schenkman Publishing Company.

24. Harvard Medical School. (1997, December 10). *Estimating the prevalence of disordered gambling.* Cambridge, MA: Harvard Medical School, Division on Addictions.

25. Quoted in O'Brien, p. 245.

26. Eadington, W. & Cornelius, J. (Eds.). 1997. *Gambling: Public polices and the social sciences* (pp. 477, 482). Reno, NV: Institute for the Study of Gambling and Commercial Gaming.

27. Quoted in O'Brien, p. 247.

28. Based on an interview reported by O'Brien, p. 115.

29. Dobbin, Tim. U.S. state regulators slam day trading firms. (1999, August 10). *Reuters*. www.yahoo/topstories/daytrading/htm. Accessed August 10, 1999.

30. Kadlec, Daniel. Day trading: It's a brutal world. (1999, August). *Time* magazine, p. 26.

CHAPTER TWELVE

1. Schor, J. (1991). *The over-worked American: The unexpected decline of leisure*. New York: Basic Books.

2. McGuire, P. (1999). Worker stress, health reaching critical point. *American Psychological Association Monitor*, vol. 30, no. 5, p.1.

3. Ibid.

4. Ibid.

5. Arden, J. (2002). *Surviving job stress*. Frankin Lakes, NJ: Career Press.

6. Ibid.

CHAPTER THIRTEEN

1. *The New York Times*. (1999). *1999 New York Times Almanac* (p. 371). New York: Penguin Reference.

2. *Wall Street Journal*. (1999). *1999 Wall Street Journal Almanac* (p. 554). New York: Ballantine Books.

3. Ibid.

4. It is undeniable that the wide spectrum of medications now available has been dramatically helpful in medicine. Certain vaccines have had a powerful ameliorating effect on various diseases such as polio. Antibiotic medications have been extremely effective for treating infections.

5. *The New York Times*. (1999). *1999 New York Times Almanac*. (p. 368). New York: Ballantine Books.

6. *Journal of Personality and Social Psychology* (2000) 78: 772–790. From Reuters, http://dailynews.yahoo.com/h/nm/20000103/h1/psa_26.html. Accessed January 6, 2000.

7. In consultation with Dr. Walter Maach at Healdsburg Community Hospital California regarding the use of the drug +PA. April 29, 2002.

8. Petersen, Melody. Suit says company promoted drug in exam. (2002, May 15). *The New York Times*. www.nytimes.com. Accessed May 15, 2002.

9. Farberman, Rhea. (February 1999). As managed care grows, public unhappiness rises. *American Psychological Association Monitor,* 30 (2), p. 14.
10. Ibid.
11. Blander, R., Leitman, R., Morris, I., & Donlan, K. (1990). Satisfaction in ten nations. *Health Affairs,* 9 (summer), 185–192.

CHAPTER FOURTEEN

1. Thurber, J. (1992). *Carnival culture.* New York: Columbia University Press.
2. Arden, J. B. 1996. *Consciousness, dreams, and self: A transdisciplinary approach.* Madison, CT: Psychosocial Press.
3. SSRIs actually block the reuptake of serotonin so that it remains longer in the synaptic gap, thereby further potentiating its absorption in the post-synaptic membrane.
4. Azar, B. Some clinicians misusing ADHD diagnosis tools, report says. (1999, February). *The American Psychological Association Monitor,* 30 (2), p. 8.

CHAPTER FIFTEEN

1. TIMSS Study Third International Math and Science Study. (1999). Department of Education. http://nces.ed.gov/times. Accessed February 15, 2003.
2. National assessment of education. (1999, February 8). *The San Francisco Chronicle,* p. A1, A17.
3. Quoted in Scheuter, p. 246.
4. *Fools gold: Executive summary.* 2003. Report for the Alliance for Childhood. Retrieved February 11, 2003 from www.allianceforchildhood . . .r/computers_reports_fools_goldexec.htm.
5. Ibid.
6. *Wall Street Journal.* (1999). *The Wall Street Journal Almanac.* New York: Ballantine Books.
7. *The New York Times* (1998, June 21).
8. Enrollments in school. U.S. Department of Education, National Center for Education Statistics. Retrieved February 12, 2003 from www.nce.ed.gov/pubs2002/digest2001/.
9. *The Wall Street Journal Almanac,* p. 298.
10. National Institute of Drug Addiction. Vol. 14, No. 1. (April 1999). Retrieved February 13, 2003 from www.drugabuse.gov/NDIA_notes/NNV.1241/teenagers.html.
11. Ibid.

12. Azar, B. (1999, February). Some clinicians misusing ADHD diagnosis tools, report says. *The American Psychological Association Monitor.* p. 8.

CHAPTER SIXTEEN

1. Twitchell, J. (1992).*Carnival culture.* New York: Columbia University Press.

2. Wolf, T. (1976). *The painted word.* New York: Bantam.

3. Sontag, S. (1982). *The Susan Sontag reader.* New York: Rarra & Giroux.

4. Taylor, Paul. (1996, October 27). The hot four. *New York Magazine,* sec. 4, p. 4.

5. Guttman, M. (2000, February 4–6). Thomas Kincade's artistic values. *USA Weekend,* p. 15–16.

6. Epstein, J. (1996). What to do about the arts. In K. Washburn & J. Thornton (Eds.), *Dumbing down: Essays on the strip-mining of American culture.* New York: Norton.

7. One does not have to look far to find artists such as Dorothea Lange and Imogene Cunningham. The point is that O'Keefe was more easily promoted because of her mystique of being an outsider and an individualist.

8. Caroll, K. (1996). The facts of fiction. In Washburn & Thornton.

9. Twitchell, J. (1992), p. 99.

10. Ibid., p. 68.

11. Quoted in Ibid., p. 126.

12. Bayles, M. (1994). *Hole in Our Soul: The loss of beauty and meaning in American popular music* (p. 3). Chicago: University of Chicago Press.

13. Manson, M. (1999). Columbine: Whose fault is it? Rolling Stone.com. Accessed May 1, 1999.

14. Reuters. (2000, May 9). Guns in the home increase the risk for teen suicide. *Suicide stats for adolescents.* http://dailynews.yahoo.com/h/nm/20000509/h1/gun_suicide_1.htm. Accessed May 9, 2000.

15. Bayles, M. (1994), p. 13.

16. Mills, David. (1992, May 13) "Sister Souljah's call to arms. *Washington Post,* p. B1.

17. Rock n' rap. (1999, July 19). *Newsweek.*

CHAPTER SEVENTEEN

1. Interest in spiritualism has always been the foundation for all major religions.

2. Matthew, 9: 16–17.

3. Trungpa, Chogyam. (1987). *Cutting through spiritual materialism.* Boston: Shambhala.

4. Arden, J. B. (1998). *Science, theology, and consciousness: The search for unity.* Westport, CT: Praeger. I have made an effort to integrate the major paradigm shifts occurring in the natural sciences with the salient concepts from the major theologies.

5. All we have are anecdotal reports to date. The research that involves using hypnosis to investigate reincarnation has shown no validity.

6. Quoted in Klinghoffer, D. (1994). Kitsch religion. In K. Washburn & J. Thornton (Eds.), *Dumbing down: Essays on the strip-mining of American culture* (pp. 250-260). New York: Norton.

7. Skeptic Tank. (2003). One of Pat Robertson's latest frauds. www.skeptictank.org/robem2.htm. Accessed February 10, 2003.

8. History News Network. (2003). Comment about mummed [sic] was a terrorist. www.hnn.us/comments/3565.html. Accessed February 10, 2003.

CHAPTER EIGHTEEN

1. Highlights of Arts Education Research. Americans for the Arts. www.artusa.org/publicawareness/facts. Accessed February 11, 2003.

2. Ibid.

3. Wolport, G. (1993). *Complexity: The emerging science at the edge of order and chaos.* New York: Touchtone.

4. Labalme, Henry (Executive Director of TV-Free America). (1999, May 30). Testimony before the U.S. Senate Committee on Health, Education, Labor, and Pensions.

5. Valois, R. F., Adams, K. G., & Kammerman, S. K. (1996, October). One year evaluation results from CableQuit: A community cable television smoking-cessation pilot program. *Journal of Behavioral Medicine*, 19 (5), 479–499.

6. *U.S. News and World Report.* Quote in Schecter, D. (1996). *The more you watch the less you know* (p. 75), New York: Seven Stories Press.

7. Kees, B., & Phillips, B. *Politicians and the news media.* Quoted in Schecter, D., p. 75.

8. Schecter, D. (1996). *The more you watch the less you know.* New York: Seven Stories Press.

9. Ibid.

10. Mahoney, J. J. (1999). The American gun. *Crime Magazine,* Retrieved February 12, 2003 from www.crimemagazine.com//guns.htm.

11. Cummings, N. (1998, August). Psychologists in primary care. Paper presented at the annual convention of the American Psychological Association, San Francisco, CA.

12. Vocate, D. (1987). *The theory of A. R. Luria: Function of spoken language in the development of higher mental process.* Hillsdale, NJ: Erlbaum.

13. Gergen, K. (1991). *The saturated self: Dilemmas of identity in contemporary life.* New York: Basic Books.

14. Lifton, R. J. (1993). *The protean self: Human reliance in the age of fragmentation.* New York: Basic Books.

15. Seligman, M., & Csikszentmihalyi, M. (2000). Positive psychology: An introduction. *American Psychologist, 55,* 5–14.

16. All species have a tendency to react to their environments with automatic behaviors. In those species that have much smaller brains, behavior is more the result of instinctual automatic responses. Reptiles, for example, do not have a cortex. Their behavior is instinctual and repetitive. Humans have the most complex brain and the most complex social system of all species.

17. Arden, J. B. (1998). *Science, theology, and consciousness: The search for unity.* Westport, CT: Praeger.

Further Reading

Arden, J. B. (1996). *Consciousness, dreams, and self: A transdisciplinary approach*. Madison, CT: Psychosocial Press.

Arden, J. B. (1998). *Science, theology, and consciousness: The search for unity*. Westport, CT: Praeger.

Bagdikian, B. (1997). *Media monopoly*, (5th ed.). Boston: Beacon Press.

Barber, B. (1995). *Jihad vs. McWorld*. New York: Times Books.

Bardo, S. (1993). *Unbearable weight: Feminism, Western culture, and the body*. Los Angeles & Berkeley, CA: University of California Press.

Bayles, M. (1994). *Hole in Our Soul: The loss of beauty and meaning in American popular music*. Chicago: University of Chicago Press.

Bertmand, S. (1998). *HyperCulture: The human cost of speed*. Westport, CT: Praeger.

Eadington, W., & Cornelius, J. (Eds.). (1977). *Gambling and commercial gaming: Essays in business, economics, philosophy, and science*. Reno, NV: Institute for the Study of Gambling and Commercial Gaming.

Hyde, J. (1991). *Half of the human experience: The psychology of women* (4th ed.). Lexington, MA: Heath.

Kubey, R., & Csikszentmihalyi, M. (1990). *Television and the quality of life: How viewing shapes everyday experience*. Hillsdale, NJ: Erlbaum.

Lesieur, H. (1984). *The chase: Career of the compulsive gambler*. Cambridge, MA: Schenkman Publishing Company.

O'Brien, T. (1998). *Bad bet: The inside story of the glamour, glitz, and danger of America's gambling industry*. New York: Times Business Random House.

Postman, N. (1986). *Amusing ourselves to death: Public discourse in the age of show business*. New York: Viking.

Rosen, L., & Weil, M. (1997). *TechnoStress*, New York: John Wiley & Sons.

Schechter, D. (1997). *The more you watch the less you know.* New York: Seven Stories Press.

Schor, J. (1991). *The over-worked American: The unexpected decline of leisure.* New York: Basic Books.

Shenk, D. (1997). *Data smog: Surviving the information glut.* San Francisco: HarperCollins.

Stephens, M. (1998). *The rise of the image, the fall of the word.* New York: Oxford University Press.

Trungpa, C. (1987). *Cutting through spiritual materialism.* Boston: Shambhala.

Turkle, S. (1980). *The second self: Computers and the human spirit.* New York: Simon & Schuster.

Turkle, S. (1995). *Life on the screen: Identity in the age of the internet* (p. 20). New York: Touchtone.

Twitchell, J. (1992). *Carnival culture.* New York: Columbia University Press.

Valois, R. F., Adams, K. G., & Kammerman, S. K. (1996, October). One year evaluation results from CableQuit: A community cable television smoking cessation pilot program. *Journal of Behavioral Medicine,* 19 (5): 479–499.

Washburn, K., and Thornton, J. (Eds.). (1996). *Dumbing down: Essays on the strip mining of American culture.* New York: Norton.

Wolf, N. (1991). *The beautiful myth: How images of beauty are used against women.* New York: Morrow.

Wolf, T. (1976). *The painted word.* New York: Bantam.

Wolport, G. (1993). *Complexity: The emerging science at the edge of order and chaos.* New York: Touchtone.

Index

About the Author

JOHN BOGHOSIAN ARDEN is Director of Training in the Department of Psychiatry at Kaiser Permanente Medical Center, Vallejo, California. Among his earlier publications are *Consciousness, Dreams, and Self* and *Science, Theology, and Consciousness* (Praeger, 1998).